America's Jews

America's Jews

MARSHALL SKLARE

Brandeis University

To My Children
DANIEL, JUDY, and JOSHUA

◎ Foreword

"Nation of nations" or "Herrenvolk democracy"? Melting pot or seething caldron? How does one describe the ethnic character of the United States?

The conventional wisdom, reflected in traditional texts on American history and society, tells of the odyssey of one group of newcomers after another who came to these shores: some of their own free will and others in the chains of bondage; some to escape religious persecution, others fleeing from political oppression, and many seeking their fortunes. "Rich and poor," goes the story, "mighty and meek, white and black, Jew and Gentile, Protestant and Catholic, Irishman and Italian and Pole . . . a motley array who, together, make up the Great American Nation."

Although many a school child can recite the litany, even they know that it has a rather hollow ring. For most people there are at least three kinds of Americans: whatever one happens to be, the members of the dominant group (viewed differently depending where one stands in the status hierarchy), and everybody else. And, if one happens to see himself as a member of the dominant group, the number of alternatives may be reduced to two: they and we.

For a variety of reasons writers of textbooks and teachers of American history have tended to overlook or underplay this essential fact of American life. While acknowledging the pluralistic character of the social structure and celebrating the extent to which "our differences make us strong," they rarely convey the true meaning of membership in an ethnic group. And none know this better than those whose life experiences belie the notion of tolerance for all. Recently, a common plea has arisen from various quarters: "Give us equal time."

In response to such demands there have been attempts to alter the rather lop-sided image of American history and of the American people. Historians and social scientists have begun to respond to the call for a more accurate and meaningful view of race and ethnicity in America. Many have sought to "redress the balance," as they say, by upgrading the status of one group or another and rewriting their history to parallel that of the dominant group. One finds new volumes that appear to make the same strategic errors as those they wish to complement, i.e., placing emphasis on great events and prominent figures while avoiding in-depth description of patterns of social organization, cultural traditions, and everyday activities.

Fortunately, there have been some other approaches tried recently, most notably studies seeking to reassess the entire ethnic experience not by playing the mirroring game (we have a hero, you have a hero; we have a holiday, you have a holiday; everybody has . . .) but by getting to the core of the social and economic and political realities of existence for the various people who came (or were brought) and stayed. The work of the latter scholars is far more important and, by its very nature, far more difficult. It involves new ways of looking, new perspectives. It encourages the examination of history and biography, of episode and event as before. But it also requires careful study of culture and community and character, the examination of everyday life.

Those who have and use such an imagination (C. Wright Mills called it "the sociological imagination") must possess a willingness to challenge the old homilies, to get away from stereotypes and deal with real people, and to relate that which is revealed with both detachment and compassion.

This volume is one of an original series written to provide student-readers with the sort of background material and sociological evaluation just mentioned. Like the others in this series, Ethnic Groups in Comparative Perspective, it offers information about the origins and experiences, the cultural patterns and social relationships of various groups of Americans. Taken together, the volumes in the series should provide a new and different look at the ethnic experience in the United States.

In planning the series it was decided that all books should follow a relatively common format which would include chapters on social history, descriptions of social organization of the various communities and their differing cultural characteristics, relations with others and with the wider society, and a conclusion to tie the early chapters together.

The very best qualified historians and social scientists would be invited to join in the venture, those not only informed but committed to the approach sketched earlier. Each author would be given the freedom to work within the framework in his own way and in his own literary style so that each volume would be a unique contribution to the overall project—and each could stand alone.

Most of what is written about American Jews comes from the pens of Jewish specialists—novelists and playwrights, journalists and yiddishists, many outside the formal academic community (some within) whose primary concern is to contribute to continuing deliberations with fellow Jews about themselves and their problems. Too frequently it appears that the *sine qua non* for understanding interpretations of Jewish history, the nuances of religious practice, or even contemporary problems is that the reader already be *au courant*. ("If you don't know what I'm thinking about, you will never be able to understand.") Little wonder the general public remains in the dark and that the non-Jew learns so little. And, one should not be too surprised that so much of what is assumed about Jews has to come from the distorted premises of those who have little to guide them save for the stereotypes of fellow "ignorants."

There are exceptions and they are worth noting. Some social scientists have made an effort to put the American Jewish experience in a context by which it can be understood by most Americans. Notable among this small body are sociologists such as Seymour Martin Lipset, Nathan Glazer, Sidney Goldstein, Seymour Leventman, and, especially Marshall Sklare, who has devoted his entire scholarly life to the sociology of the American Jewish community.

Educated at the University of Chicago and at Columbia where he received a Ph.D. in sociology, and now Professor of American Jewish Studies at Brandeis University, Sklare has long recognized the necessity of getting beyond description of the history and character of the Jewish community and considering the role of its constituents in an ever changing but still primarily Gentile world. As one who spent many years as Director of the Division of Scientific Research of the American Jewish Committee, he is sensitive both to the uniqueness of his people and to their concern (or, perhaps, persistent anxiety) about how others will interpret Jewish pride in this uniqueness—and Jewish clannishness.

His many interests are already evident in the various books he has published, all of which have been widely used as classroom texts or guides. The first, *Conservative Judaism: An American Religious Movement,* is a study of the new syncretist religious form that emerged as traditional (and often Orthodox) Jews underwent acculturation in America and took their place in the "triple melting pot."

The story of America's Jews may be marked by signal words and phrases (some esoteric, some mundane, some homely, some—as the Jews might say—*haimish*): pogrom, steerage, Ellis Esland and Hester Street, sweatshop, seltzer, *shul,* City College, downtown, uptown, and suburbia. The last named might not have been the promised land but it meant arrival. Sklare's *Jewish Identity on the Suburban Frontier* is about people in a place code-named *Lakeville,* and deals with what happens to the acculturated Jews in their new environment.

In addition to these studies, and many others which have been reported in his articles and essays, Sklare edited *The Jews: Social Patterns of an American Group,* in which he pulled together many studies published in the 1940s and 1950s.

This book updates much of what was discussed in the previous volumes. It does more as well. Here, in keeping with the original mandate, Professor Sklare has attempted to set the Jews in the broader context of their society and to compare their situation with others who are frequently if erroneously measured by and against Jewish norms.

I am confident that this book, like his others, will help those who are not Jewish to understand the Jews and those who are to better understand themselves.

PETER I. ROSE
General Editor

Northampton, Massachusetts

◎ Preface

Of the making of books on Jews there is no end—the "People of the Book" have given rise to a huge literature. The bulk of this literature has been the creation of Jews themselves, though Gentiles too have been fascinated by the subject. Whether Jewish or Gentile, writers have discussed the subject with varying competence and objectivity—some have idealized the Jews while others have vilified them. But in any case the literature on Jewish life is centered on the study of the Jewish past.

America's Jews seeks to make a contribution to what is in many ways the most underdeveloped area of Jewish scholarship: contemporary Jewish studies. The question of why contemporary Jewish studies have lagged behind other areas of Jewish learning may be left for another time. Suffice it to say that there are many more investigators digging at ancient sites of Jewish civilization than are engaged in unearthing the story of contemporary Jewry.

My objective in writing *America's Jews*, however, goes beyond that of contributing to a very young field of Jewish scholarship. I have also sought to provide an alternative to other treatments of American-Jewish life. With the exception of some notable studies from a historical or demographic perspective, many widely read books on American-Jewish life have serious limitations. They are based more on feeling than on reflection, more on quick observation than on sustained study. Seeking to take advantage of the widespread curiosity of Jews about themselves, and of Gentiles about Jews, many such treatments are written from a highly dramatic, even sensational perspective. Consequently they seek to expose rather than to analyze. These authors also fail to locate their subject in the context of Jewish history and culture. Finally, they do not integrate their subject matter into the mainstream of sociological thinking.

The reader must decide for himself whether I have succeeded in avoiding such hazards. Even if I be adjudged successful by the reader, he must be cautioned that *America's
Jews* is only a beginning; it was necessary to be ruthlessly
selective in deciding what topics were essential for an understanding of American Jewry.

It is a pleasant task to acknowledge the debts that I have
accumulated in writing this volume. Ben Halpern read the
manuscript and gave me the benefit of his insight and scholarship. Sidney Goldstein did the same for one section of the
manuscript. Harry Alderman and his staff at the Blaustein
Library of The American Jewish Committee extended help in
the same friendly spirit that they have manifested on many
previous occasions. Carol Liebman and Stuart Schoffman
served as my research assistants at Yeshiva University and
rendered exemplary service. Alvin Chenkin, Joseph Edelman,
Jack J. Diamond, Myron Schoen, Theodore Solotaroff, and Ray
Goodman were kind enough to answer my inquiries. Esther
Corcia and Anne Falkof rendered devoted secretarial help. A
grant-in-aid from the Memorial Foundation for Jewish Culture
was helpful in preparing some of the background material
for the book.

Editors are obliged to divide their attention among many
books, but Peter Rose manifested an interest in this volume
beyond the call of duty. I hope that I have achieved his objective of writing a book that should be accessible to a wide circle
of readers.

My wife Rose has shared the birth-pangs of authorship with
patience and humor.

MARSHALL SKLARE

Waltham, Massachusetts

◎ Contents

America's Jews

◎◎◎◎

Chapter 1 ◉ American Jewry: Social History and Group Identity

In 1654 the first Jews, some twenty-three refugees from Brazil, arrived on American soil. Three centuries later the Jewish population of the United States totaled an estimated 5,800,000. While modest in size as a group, the impact of Jews on American life has been out of all proportion to their number and percentage of the population at large.

The significance of America's Jews must also be understood in a wider perspective. (In our usage "America" and "American" means the United States.) Here is the largest Jewish community on earth, indeed, the largest in the millennial history of the Jewish people. About 42 percent of the world's Jews live in the United States.

The importance of the United States as a center for Jews and Jewish life has been greatly increased by the impact of Nazi genocide against the Jewish people. Nazism reduced European Jewish communities to a shadow of their former importance. Only Great Britain and France survive as important centers, the latter largely because of the recent settlement of North African Jews. The importance of the United States has also been magnified by the cultural persecution of communist regimes, particularly by the government of Soviet Russia. About 2,568,000 Jews live in Soviet Russia, constituting the second largest Jewish settlement in the world. But this community exists under severe repression. For the past several decades opportunities for the expression and transmission of Jewish identity have been proscribed, fraught with grave penalties, or made difficult in other ways. While Jewish life of a sort goes on in the Soviet Union and expressions of Jewish identity make surprising appearances, this community is not to be compared to those of the free world.

The only other country with more than a million Jews is Israel. Its Jewish population of 2,365,000 (as of 1967) is even more recently arrived than that of the United States. But while only 17 percent of the world's Jews live in Israel, its significance as a center for Jews and Jewish life is little affected by its size. Israel and the United States, then, constitute the two great centers of contemporary Jewish life.[1]

While American Jewry plays a crucial role in contemporary Jewish life, it has a significance beyond the Jewish situation. In studying America's Jews, we are able to clarify the problem of the ethnic minority in modern society. While ethnic conflict in the United States centers on black–white confrontation rather than on Christian–Jewish tensions, the Jews still best exemplify the condition of being a minority group. They do so because their religion is non-Christian, and it remains so in spite of the modifications of traditional Judaism made by those Jews who have adopted prevalent cultural modes. Second, no matter how harmonious the relationship between Judaism and Christianity may appear, it is inherently a stressful relationship—the religions are closely related and historic rivals. Third, despite the current stress on pluralism, Judaism is the only significant non-Christian religion encountered in American society.

The position of the Jews as the quintessential ethnic minority is reinforced by the presence of anti-Jewish prejudice and discrimination. As prejudice and discrimination are difficult to measure, differences of opinion about their extent are inevitable. Whatever the actual situation, however, present levels are sufficiently high as to imprint on Jews a feeling of minority status. Furthermore, virulent anti-Semitism is more than an ancestral memory—it is a phenomenon of the contemporary era as well as of the ancient and medieval world.

All of these factors are not sufficient to make the Jews an "ideal type": in the final analysis it is their *goal* as an ethnic minority that makes them such. Most Jews are retentivist in orientation—that is, they reject the idea that assimilation is the end toward which they should strive. Being retentivist, Jews attempt to pass their identity on to their children. Jewish efforts to retain an ethnic identity tend to be more strenuous than those of other groups and the structure of the Jewish community is consequently more elaborate. Paradoxically, because of this retentivism the Jew must separate himself from the general society while he simultaneously seeks to integrate himself into it. Since he is racially one with the dominant group and increasingly has opportunities for a dignified (in contrast to a demeaning) assimilation, his separatism—whatever its nature and extent—is an act of crucial sociological significance.

Jewish Immigration Until World War I: Germans and East Europeans

To understand the rise of an American Jewish community we must realize that the eighteenth and nineteenth centuries were times of rapid population growth in Europe. That growth was shared by Jews. Population growth, in combination with poverty, persecution, and the changing attitudes of Jews themselves resulted in vast movements of people. Some of these movements took place within the same land, as for example the population flow from Bavarian villages to Munich or Berlin, or from Polish villages to Warsaw or Lodz. Some of it took place across frontiers. But some of it spanned continents and resulted in the establishment of new Jewish communities in Australia, Argentina, South Africa, and the United States. Immigration was to have unique meaning for Jews. With the exception of some parts of the Soviet Union, the bulk of the families remaining in traditional places of Jewish settlement on the European continent were later to be exterminated by the Nazis; only those who resettled themselves in distant places survived.

Since the immigration of Jews to America extends over three centuries, we would expect it to include diverse strands. But among Jews such diversity has been even sharper than with most other groups, for Jews originated in different countries, frequently with contrasting traditions. Conventional historical wisdom has it that there have been three waves of Jewish migration to America: the Spanish–Portuguese, the German, and the East European.[2] During the latter part of the nineteenth century, and for several decades thereafter, some felt that differences between Jews were so sharp and immutable that the American-Jewish community would be permanently bifurcated—that it would be composed of an underclass consisting of a large and shiftless *lumpenproletariat* and an upper middle class led by a small group of aristocratic families. If this idea strikes us today as ludicrous, equally invalid is the notion that generational and place of origin differences have entirely eroded away. Differentiation traceable to the separate waves of immigration is still present despite an ever-increasing convergence with respect to class attainment, educational levels, and style of life. But such differentiation does not mean that American Jewry presently consists of two or more subcommunities, or even that it betrays the present structure of Israeli Jewry where Oriental and Western Jews are readily distinguishable, and where certain group characteristics involve deep and abiding social problems.

American Jewry traces its origin to Sephardic Jews whose families came from the Iberian Peninsula and who lived in one or another European country (or their colonies) before journeying to America. While these seventeenth and eighteenth century Spanish-Portuguese settlers numbered only a few hundred—indeed they were no longer a majority in the American Jewish community as early as 1720—their social status and leadership role in Jewish communal affairs, together with the fact of their early arrival, has magnified their importance. Thus the synagogue that they established in Newport, Rhode Island is a national shrine. Another one of their institutions, the Spanish and Portuguese Synagogue Shearith Israel, was the first synagogue in New York City.

Ashkenazic Jews, those originating in western and eastern Europe, began coming to America in the eighteenth century. Some of the early Ashkenazim were assimilated by the Sephardim. However, by the early nineteenth century their numerical superiority had gained a cultural and institutional predominance. Until the 1880s the immigration of Ashkenazic Jews was primarily composed of individuals originating in Germany or in adjoining areas dominated by German culture. Even though the East European immigration that came afterwards exceeded the German immigration many times over, the settlement of German Jews in the nineteenth century is of more than historical and antiquarian interest—the German influence in the Jewish community is still discernible in contemporary life.

One explanation for the German-Jewish influence is their settlement throughout the length and breadth of the land: German Jews established themselves in all large- and medium-size cities and in hundreds of smaller communities as well. Their spread was facilitated by their concentration in the merchandising trade. Many began by carrying a pack, then graduated to a horse and wagon; they became full-fledged merchants when they were able to set themselves up in a shop. Some expanded a small shop into a large shop, or a shop into a chain of shops, or into a department store. To be sure, while German Jews were widely spread across the nation the spread was never perfectly even. They had their favorite communities, as for example Cincinnati, which came to be known as the "Jerusalem of the West."

Geographical spread, while necessary to establish the predominance of the German Jews, would not have been sufficient. It was the spectacular rise of the German Jews into the upper reaches of the middle class, and particularly into the upper class, that brought them into positions of authority. Not only did they penetrate these class levels, but there arose in the last half of the nineteenth century a group of families whose great wealth was comparable to that of some of the richest Gentiles of the nation. These families were concentrated in New York City.[3] While they had marital and financial connections with rich merchandising families in the country at large their wealth was derived from a different source: merchant (or what we now call "investment") banking. Thus Jewish-dominated financial houses were powerful at a time when merchant banking played a crucial role in the economy.[4] However, while such banking was the cornerstone of many of the greatest German-Jewish fortunes, it was fated to decline in significance. Commercial banking, controlled almost entirely by Gentiles, grew apace and overall the banking function lost a good deal of its old significance. But by that time the position of the German Jews—as dramatized by the success of the Seligman, Loeb, Lehman, Schiff, Sachs, and Goldman families, as well as by others—had been secured both within the Jewish community as well as outside of it.

It was inevitable that the German Jews became Jewish high society. Some, like Jacob Schiff and Felix Warburg, were scions of important Frankfurt or Hamburg families and would have become members of the club in any case. But it was the social position of the thousands who came from obscure villages that was transformed by their economic success. Of course there were those whose financial rise was not very spectacular (such families tend to be overlooked by scholarly and popular writers alike), but even they could improve their social position by borrowing status from their more successful compatriots. In any case the new German Jews overwhelmed the ever-thinning ranks of the Sephardic (and Sephardized Ashkenazic) families who had constituted Jewish society.

The mass of America's Jews was yet to arrive. Coming between the 1880s and the World War I period, their settlement transformed the Jewish community. No longer would it be composed of a bourgeoisie that rapidly was acculturating, even if still attached to a widely admired German *Kultur*. No longer could it be confidently predicted that the group would disappear without incident into the great melting pot. In 1877 Jews were only .52 percent of the population; by 1917 they were 3.28 percent. In fact the new immigrants swamped the older element. The 400,000 Jews in the United States in 1888 were joined by 334,338 more by 1896. Thus the ratio of net migration to initial population after a mere decade was an astonishing 83 percent.

The new immigrants were East European Jews originating from Russia, Poland, Lithuania, Hungary, Rumania, and adjacent territories. They came without capital or a knowledge of the English language. Frequently they had little or no training in the occupations most common in the United States at the time. They were too numerous to spread themselves in the way the German Jews had done, and they arrived after the frontier had been settled. But in any case they lacked the desire to distribute themselves evenly. They settled in a relatively few of the largest cities, locating in conspicuously ethnic neighborhoods.

These new immigrants gave the American Jewish community a future. Their numbers made it viable demographically even as their Jewish culture did so spiritually. Nevertheless, important segments of the German-Jewish leadership viewed the new immigration as a threat to American Jewish life. It was feared that the immigrants would imperil Jewish status, create anti-Semitism, and ultimately wreck all that had been created by the older immigrants. The solution was clear: stop, or at least reduce, the flood of immigrants. There is still some dispute as to the extent to which efforts were made in this direction, either by controlling immigration at the European source or by encouraging officials to refuse admittance to those who landed at American ports. But there is no question that at the same time the older element assisted those who settled in the United States. Much of this help was geared to speeding adjustment to the new environment. Such assistance was not always accepted in a manner that its donors deemed appropriate.

If the East European immigrants introduced a Jewish lower class to the United States and populated the first American-Jewish slums, they were nothing like the *lumpenproletariat* that the German middle and upper classes had conjured up. Although the Lower East Side of New York did have a small complement of Jewish racketeers, its streets were safe at night. Although a few Jewish husbands did not meet their family responsibilities (leading to the establishment of a social agency, the National Desertion Bureau), the Jewish family remained intact. Although relief had to be extended in some exceptional cases, the "ghettos" of the nation had a very low rate of indigence. In sum, aside from the crowded and noisome environment none of the sociological conditions associated with slum life were present in these immigrant districts.

If the East European found himself initially confined to the slum, he did not reside in tenements for very long. Moving rapidly from one newer neighborhood to another, by the 1950s the trend toward suburbia was unmistakable. And in the better suburbs Germans and East Europeans encountered each other once more. The social mobility of the East Europeans, which made this rendezvous possible, never seemed as spectacular as that of the Germans. It was not associated with the mystique of merchant banking and thus it lacked a "House of Rothschild" image. Rather, it was based on a steady rise, although sometimes temporarily halted by economic depression. The East European story is that of a group which remains in the working class for only a brief time (although long enough to make the experience of the sweatshop part of the American-Jewish saga). The majority leaves this class by the route of establishing small businesses, some of which grow into substantial enterprises in the course of time. During the past several decades East European mobility has broadened to include the practice of professional occupations as well. At present the descendants of the pre-World War I East European group are found in all segments of the middle class, as well as in the upper class.

While the social mobility of the East European Jew lacks the glamour and dizzy heights associated with the rise of the German Jew, it may be in fact a more spectacular achievement, having been accomplished against greater odds. The East European Jews could not base their success on distributing manufactured goods in a developing nineteenth century economy, because they entered the economy at a more mature phase. Also, East Europeans were too numerous to achieve success by fulfilling a single economic function. Finally, they were concentrated in a few places, rather than being widely separated and serving as a national middle class. Thus they were forced to compete against each other. As the history of the garment trades reminds us, such competition could be murderous indeed.

Do the terms "German" and "East European" have any relevance today? Some feel that distinctions between the groups have eroded away. They believe that those who claim that distinctions still exist are attempting to revive an era now blessedly past. Certainly German and East European Jews no longer constitute two distinct groups in the sense that they did barely a half-century ago. Restrictions against the admittance of East Europeans to German clubs and organizations are uncommon today. Marriage between the two groups is no longer an unusual occurrence. Germans and East Europeans now meet as peers in a variety of endeavors both in the Jewish and in the general community.

Yet differences and antagonisms persist and can be readily observed even when Germans and East Europeans are no longer separated by wide class and cultural gulfs. We may take the example of Lakeville, an upper status Midwestern suburb in which both groups are represented. Despite the fact that East Europeans in Lakeville are highly successful and very prosperous, their income is noticeably smaller than that of residents of German descent.[5] Another aspect of the cleavage is in levels of education. In this case it is the East Europeans who exceed the Germans. Thus some 37 percent of East Europeans have studied for an advanced degree in contrast to only 9 percent of the Germans.[6] Given their superior educational attainment, East Europeans are impelled to claim equal status with Germans despite their fiscal inferiority.

Demographic differences have their counterpart in the religious life of the community. The old German-East European cleavage is readily observable in the history and in the present composition of the four Reform congregations which serve Lakeville.[7] Furthermore, certain attitudes with which we are already familiar crop up again, although in contemporary form. Oldtimers (predominantly Germans) are highly critical of newcomers (predominantly East Europeans). Instead of being overjoyed that East Europeans, whom they had once thought would be long-term paupers and thus a constant drain on their resources, are now so successful that they can afford to move to the best suburbs, many Germans in Lakeville are unhappy. A number of the most bitter decided to take action when a Conservative synagogue was formed; they sought to bar the congregation from the property it had purchased.[8]

As was true in nineteenth century America, oldtimers in Lakeville feel that their work of establishing good relations with Gentiles is being undermined by Jewish newcomers.[9] The new Jews, who are responsible for this sabotage, are characterized as *"nouveau riche,* ostentatious, materialistic, and overly Jewish" by a long-time resident whose response is fairly typical.[10] For their part, newcomers have a feeling of being unappreciated and unwanted by oldtimers. In fact, more of them know about discrimination practiced against Jews by other Jews than about such practices perpetrated against Jews by Gentiles.[11]

Of course some assimilation has taken place from the Jewish to the general community. This process has affected the German group more than the East European, if only because of its greater acculturation and more advanced generational position. However, up to the present time the German who retains his Jewish identity does not necessarily fuse into the overwhelmingly larger East European group. Or to put it somewhat differently, in spite of his numerical superiority the East European has not been able to assimilate the German.

A reconnaissance of Lakeville suggests that Germans still retain a sense of their special identity although increasingly expressing it in a private rather than a public context. While the Reform congregation that has had the strongest German influence is now cooperating in an adult education program with a neighboring synagogue that is overwhelmingly East European, cleavages persist.[12] One Lakeville resident, who comes from a socially mobile East European family and grew up in a German neighborhood in Lake City, feels that Germans manage to retain a sense of identity in spite of the fact that Lakeville becomes more heavily East European with each passing year:

> The German Jews have attempted to bring the psychology of "our crowd" with them from Lake City. They stay very much to themselves and they marry and remarry within the group. German Jews and East European Jews may associate during childhood and adolescence but this diminishes very much during adulthood. The German Jewish youngster is more controlled by his parents than

our East European children. Germans continue with their
own crowd. The German Jews remain within their own
world. They don't want new homes, new furniture.
Rather they take the good furniture from their parents'
and grandparents' homes and bring it with them to Lakeville. Perhaps this associates them with their past. They
have a feeling of closeness with the old. Maybe this is
their tie with stability. Whatever it is they are happy with
their associations in the Einhorn Temple and in the Wild-
acres Country Club.[13]

If "status panic," the internalization of anti-Jewish stereo-
typy, minority status, and strong feelings of cultural superiority made the initial differences between Germans and East
Europeans appear so threatening, little if any attention was
paid to the fact that both groups were Ashkenazim and hence
shared a common heritage. It was also overlooked that both
German and East European Jews were Western men—that
whatever the differences between the environments from which
they came these environments bore some relationship to each
other. In reality, the Jews of western and eastern Europe had
always been in communication; for centuries these Jewries
were interdependent entities.

Thus far we have not commented upon the immigration of
Oriental Jews to the United States. Neither do they constitute
a major segment of the community nor do they have historical
importance like the early Sephardic immigrants who were of
European origin.[14] Nevertheless, Oriental Sephardim in the
United States provide us with an instructive example of the
possibility of enduring social differences within the minority
community. The Syrian Jews are perhaps the best example.
They are subject to the pulls of the general culture that all
Jews experience, as well as to the Ashkenazic domination of
the American Jewish community. However, when they are
concentrated (as occurs in areas of Brooklyn), and when they
retain links with their past (as occurs with religious traditionalists), an Oriental component in their culture becomes
apparent. One small-scale study of Jewish children in Brooklyn
illustrates this connection. The study population was selected
from children applying for admittance into the first grade

classes of two Jewish all-day schools in Brooklyn, one catering to Ashkenazim (East Europeans) and the other to Sephardim (Syrians). Parents' income, place of residence, use of English as the language of the home, and nativity were matched. According to the investigator:

> Here were two Jewish middle-class groups and, yet, marked differences in school readiness were apparent. Indeed, the differences resemble those uncovered in Negro-white studies in the United States . . . all aspects studied indicated a superiority on the part of the Ashkenazim and consistent inferior academic preparation in the case of the Sephardim. . . . It is clear from this study that Jews do not constitute a monolithic structure in regard to early academic preparedness or attitudes toward education.[15]

Whether or not Oriental Jews eventually merge into the Ashkenazic mass (and it would be the East European group into which they would merge) their present distinctiveness highlights the fact that however stressful the relationship between the German and East European strands of American Jewry, both share the same Western culture. Additionally, both Germans and East Europeans share a common Ashkenazic past, even though they have responded differently to the challenge of modernism. In sum, both belong to one community that—as we shall see—is a kind of *gemeinschaft* writ large.

While Germans and East Europeans can still be distinguished from each other, the descendants of East European Jews who came to the United States before World War I can no longer be distinguished by their places of origin. Their ancestors came from a variety of places and felt a sense of uniqueness about their origins. Although the lodges, societies, and synagogues of the first generation were frequently organized by place of origin (whether on the basis of the same city, province, territory, or country), by the second generation the feeling of being a Russian, Polish, Lithuanian, Hungarian, Galician, or Rumanian Jew was on the wane. Negative stereotypes that these groups held about each other diminished as they came to mean less and less to the younger generation.

The use of English instead of Yiddish aided the process; place of origin, as evidenced by variations in Yiddish pronunciation and vocabulary, was not very apparent when English was spoken. While differences in the pronunciation of Hebrew persisted for a time, there emerged a more or less standard Ashkenazic pronunciation in the Jewish school and later in the synagogue.

However, the main factor promoting fusion has been that the subgroups that composed the East European immigration lacked a distinctive sense of their own mission. Differences between them were a matter of localisms, folklore, and sentiment; rarely did they possess strong ideological superstructures. As a consequence the differences soon became irrelevant in the American environment. Furthermore, East Europeans who were the most traditionalistic and localistic in outlook (as, for example, Hungarian Hasidim), did not come to the United States in the period before World War I. Also, those who were most assimilationist, in the sense of being closely attached to the nationalism and emerging culture of the surrounding people (as were, for example, some Hungarian as well as Polish Jews), generally remained in eastern Europe. Finally, home countries did not attempt to retain the loyalties of overseas Jews. When Queen Marie of Rumania established contact with American Jews from her country during a tour of the United States in 1926, the gesture was exceptional.

The effect of these factors made marriage possible between the children of immigrant families who came from different East European countries or territories, and indeed even between the immigrants themselves. Such intermarriage is both symptomatic of changing social relationships between groups as well as of factors that influence these relationships. Such intermarriages helped, of course, to diminish the force of remaining distinctions. But whether or not they are offspring of intermarried families, present-day third and fourth generation Jews of East European descent know little about their ancestors' places of origin. Many members of the third generation have difficulty pinpointing where their grandparents came from. And if geographical knowledge is limited, there is total ignorance of the subcultural distinctions that once characterized the Jewries of eastern Europe. In fact the process of fusion has been so thoroughgoing that when American Jews desire to learn their ethnic heritage, they express no interest in the subcultural distinctions that loomed so significant in eastern Europe. The reception accorded the well-known study *Life Is With People* is a case in point. The book had a very wide appeal to acculturated Jews of East European descent who sought to acquaint themselves with the world of their ancestors. The fact that it made no distinctions among the Jewries of eastern Europe went unnoticed by its readers.[16]

The Characteristics of the Immigrants and the Impact of America

The immigrants who arrived before 1917 established the basic forms of American Jewish life. It is therefore essential that we inquire who these immigrants were, together with the impact that America had on them.

With all of the adversities of life and the anti-Semitic restrictions that pressed upon him, the immigration of the European Jew was basically elective rather than enforced.[17] As a consequence those who came did not constitute a cross section of the Jewish population. On the crucial matter of religiosity, for example, relatively few of the most learned and the most observant came to America.

The pious had in fact been forewarned. A constant theme in the reports of American correspondents who wrote for the German or Yiddish newspapers and periodicals was that whatever other virtues were esteemed in America, piety was not one of them. Letters from American immigrants to their European relatives emphasized the same theme. Examples are found as early as the eighteenth century. Writing to his family overseas in 1783, no less a patriot than Haym Salomon stated "the nature of this country [is] *wenig yiddishkeit*" [little Jewishness].[18] Not only were the faithful alerted by letters and newspaper reports but rabbinical leaders such as the famed Hofetz Hayim spread the word. One notable authority told American Jews to their faces that they had sinned by coming to America. In 1900, Jacob David Wilowsky, the Slutsker Rav, on a visit to the United States, told an audience in New York City that they had acted improperly by migrating, that Judaism had no chance on American soil, and that they should rectify their mistake by returning to eastern Europe: "It was not only home that the Jews left behind in Europe, . . . it was their Torah, their Talmud, their *yeshivot* [schools for advanced Talmudic learning]—in a word their *Yiddishkeit*, their entire Jewish way of life."[19]

Ironically, American Jews now talk about the piety of the immigrant generation, projecting onto their ancestors all manner of fancied religious virtues. In the popular view, New York's Lower East Side or Chicago's Maxwell Street district were great centers of religiosity. There is little recognition of the fact that a significant group of the post-1905 immigrants had moved away from Jewish culture; while in eastern Europe they had been deeply influenced by newer currents in Russian culture. Accordingly, the record indicates that immigrant districts were centers for Socialist meetings, areas in which Yiddish newspapers of the freethinking variety were published, and places where adult night-school classes were held in subjects quite different from those studied by pious Jews.[20] A recent authoritative study even questions whether many of the traditionally inclined immigrants can be described as anything more than nominally Orthodox:

> According to [the popular] notion, the masses of East and Central European Jews who came to the United States between 1870 and 1924 were overwhelmingly Orthodox. . . . There is reason to challenge this notion. . . . That the new immigrants founded countless small synagogues almost immediately upon arrival was not in itself evidence of religiosity. . . . If the immigrants were indeed religiously motivated, the practical exigencies of strict ritual requirements would demand a *mikvah*, the lustration bath, before a synagogue. . . . There is at least anecdotal evidence that *mikvaot* were scarce and inaccessible outside New York City, and sometimes even within it.[21]

If the piety of the East European immigrant group has been inflated so has its social status and class position. While conceding that their families had to start from scratch when they arrived here, many present-day American Jews look upon their immigrant ancestors as having been solid and esteemed householders in the communities from which they came. In point of fact, well-established and well-regarded middle class families, not to speak of the upper classes, generally remained where they were. If they changed their place of residence they generally settled in a large city nearby. Few of those with above-average *yichus* (family reputation—by extension, social status) were motivated to make the move to the United States. Perhaps they were dimly aware of an admonition contained in Haym Salomon's letter quoted previously: "Your *yichus* is worth very little here."[22]

Selective migration allowed American Jewry to develop without the shackles of the old system of stratification. New grounds for esteem were developed; deference could now be given where one thought deference was due. As a consequence, people of distinguished *yichus* who did come to America found that they would receive social honor only if they were successful according to the new value system. Even an august personage like Jacob Schiff, for example, made his way through his accomplishments and leadership qualities rather than on the basis of his singular *yichus*. Those who could not compete in the status marketplace were passed by.[23]

The absence of traditional constraints, the erosion of the old status structure, and the overrepresentation of the nominally Orthodox provide the backdrop for what was to be a revolutionary experience for Jews. So revolutionary was that experience—and so agreeable when measured against life in eastern Europe—that few Jews who experienced it returned home or moved to other countries. While for certain ethnic minorities return and resettlement in the motherland was a common phenomenon, for Jews emigration was exceptional.[24]

What, then, was so revolutionary about America? For the first time the fact of Jewishness became irrelevant in the public sphere. The millennial Jewish experience had been quite the opposite. Jews not only occupied a special status, but the position of the individual in the social structure was entirely determined by his Jewishness. Even when the status accorded the Jew conferred privileges as well as disabilities, it implied subordination. We should remember that no other American immigrant group, including those whose homelands were under the domination of a foreign power, had a history of subordination comparable with that of the Jews. Although they might suffer subordination if they were ruled by outsiders, other peoples lived as majorities. Their culture was the prevailing one. They possessed historical memories of their former independence. They had faith in their ability to achieve independence once again.

America was the first new nation. It did not have to make the transition from medieval society, with its corporate structure and ascribed statuses, to modern society with its concept of individual freedom and equality. Thus there was no group in American society that had a distinctive stake in redefining the position of the Jew. And since the Jew did not have to be emancipated, there was no segment of the population seeking to restore the Jew to a *status quo ante*.[25] In sum the Jew was free, free at last. And his history meant that freedom had a special meaning for him which it did not hold for the Italian, the Pole, or the Irishman.

The meaning of freedom for the Jew can be analyzed in one way by his response to the duties of citizenship. These duties were eagerly shouldered, as for example the obligation to vote. As a leading authority has noted: "The [Lower] East Side Jews registered and voted in greater proportion than any other immigrant group, except perhaps the Irish, and they treated the franchise with greater seriousness than any other group, especially the Irish."[26] The Irish could of course afford to be relaxed—they never expected to be discriminated against at the polls. Though their power as a group depended on their getting out the vote, voting itself never became a sacred rite for them in the way it did for the Jews.

If the Jew was intoxicated with the freedom of the ballot his newly found position as a citizen was manifested in an even more significant area. This was in the area of education. For the East European Jew in particular the idea that Jewishness was irrelevant to one's admittance to an elementary school, to a high school, or to a municipal college or state university (and also irrelevant to how one was treated there) was astonishing. The notion that such institutions were supposed to be neutral in the area of religion was also unheard of. Accordingly, the Jewish response to public education was similar to their response to the ballot. Jews not only sent their children to school but they also made the principle of public education an article of faith. In fact loyalty to the cause of public education was so overwhelming that as late as 1917 only five small Jewish day (that is, parochial) schools had been established in the entire country.[27] Jews were simultaneously attracted to public education and suspicious of private education—they feared that the establishment of day schools would constitute disloyalty to America. Their fears were not allayed by the example of their Irish Catholic neighbors, who never doubted for a moment that they had the right to establish their own schools.

If voting was not an act that committed the Jew in any ultimate sense, his attachment to public education had more significant implications. It signified that he was prepared to render unto America that which belonged to America, and that he felt that he must reserve his Jewishness for his remaining life space. It meant that he would not be a sectarian, insisting on special rights and privileges and asking that the public order accommodate itself to his demands. It meant that he would refrain from educating his children to be sectarians. Rather, when he educated his children Jewishly he would do so on a supplementary basis so as not to interfere with public education. It meant that he would not signify his uniqueness by his manner of dress. He would don a skullcap only in the privacy of home or synagogue and thus not invade the public domain. America offered the Jew freedom; the Jew offered America accommodation in return.

We are justified in asking whether or not America actually required accommodation as the price of freedom. Or did the Jew offer accommodation out of gratitude for his newly found status as citizen? Whichever alternative is correct not all American Jews are prepared to abide by the "social contract" established by the German and East European Jews who settled in America before World War I. Some of the immigrants who arrived later felt that the contract placed Jews at a disadvantage. And some descendants of the earlier immigrants—much more sure of themselves as Americans than were their progenitors—have come to feel that their ancestors misunderstood America, or had been too eager to please. They believe that a new contract must be negotiated—one which will show greater fairness to Jews without doing violence to essential American doctrine.

Jewish Immigration to the Present

After 1921, and especially after 1924, the number of Jews arriving in the United States, particularly from eastern Europe, was severely limited by immigration restrictions. Before then, all of those who wanted to come were able, in effect, to do so. The post-World War I East European immigration was directly related to the social changes which the war brought in its wake. Some of the new immigrants had been well-established but lost everything when their communities were ravaged. But even if the old life continued intact it was no longer what it had been before the war. The small town, or *shtetl*, stagnated after World War I, losing whatever significance it had enjoyed as an economic and administrative center. Furthermore, in newly independent Poland, Jews were subject to laws and practices which were meant to displace them from middle class occupations.

One of the decisive factors motivating emigration from eastern Europe was the triumph of communism in Russia. As with other segments of the bourgeoisie, the revolution displaced the Jewish middle and upper class and fragmented the traditional status system. Equally significant, the triumph of communism meant that those who were not prepared to conform to the new ideology either had to leave or to suffer grave penalties. Jewish counterrevolutionary elements included religionists, Zionists, and Hebraists. Finally, those Jews who had no strong Jewish identity but whose political views deviated from the then-current version of communist ideology had every good reason to leave the Soviet Union.

All of these strands were represented among the post-World War I immigrants. Those who were Russified had little impact on American Jewish life. But this was not the case with regard to those who had a strong Jewish identity. Their influence was felt because the Jewish standards to which they were accustomed were more advanced than those that prevailed in the United States. This became evident in the field of Yiddish journalism and literature, in Hebraist circles, and in the world of Orthodoxy. But whatever their ideology, the reduced circumstances in which these new immigrants found themselves made their situation that much more poignant: they were confronted by former townsmen from the lower depths of society who had managed to raise themselves into the solid middle class or even beyond.

The most widely known of the groups that arrived between the wars were not the East Europeans, however, but those immigrants who came from Germany and Austria after 1933. This wave of immigration gave currency to the term "refugee," although some of those coming from Russia and Poland could have been similarly described. The term refugee implied that the immigrant was not moving but fleeing, that he was escaping impending catastrophe, and that under normal conditions he would never have come to America. The refugee immigration also meant that unlike their predecessors the new arrivals were drawn from a variety of class and status levels. It also meant that in contrast to the unmarried young men who had come from Germany a century earlier, entire families arrived.

There is a stereotype that the German Jews who came to the United States after 1933 did not realize that they were Jewish until Hitler reminded them of it. This notion, which apparently emanates from East Europeans, is more a reflection of the intragroup hostilities discussed earlier than an accurate description of the social situation. In fact one segment of the German immigration was comprised of East Europeans who had settled in Germany in the recent past. Furthermore the new German immigration included individuals with very strong Jewish commitments. For example, sectarian German-Jewish Orthodoxy—hardly known in the United States—made the transition from Frankfurt to the Washington Heights section of Manhattan.[28] Additionally, Orthodox Jews who did not follow sectarian ways were also in evidence.

We would expect that those German Jews who were Orthodox—admittedly a minor segment of the group—would find little in common with their American cousins, who were mainly Reform Jews. But whatever his viewpoint on Jewish identity the new German Jew rarely integrated himself into the social world of the old German Jew. Frequently, class differences made such integration difficult. But even in cases where these differences were minimal or of little consequence and where both new and old German Jews were equally distant from traditional Jewish patterns, they found that they were separated by a cultural gulf. Generally, new German Jews of liberal conviction were devoted to German culture—or more specifically to a German-Jewish variant thereof.[29] This variant was unknown to the descendants of old German Jews. It had been relatively unfamiliar even to their immigrant ancestors, who had originated in villages and had come to America without the benefit of a university education, and in many cases without being exposed to the full curriculum of the *gymnasium* as well. In sum, even when there was no ideological difference between old and new German Jews, the immigrants found themselves alienated from American counterparts who lacked their humanistic learning and cultural sophistication. The Jewishly committed, on the other hand, were in a less-ambiguous situation. American pluralism sanctioned the formation of sectarian associations, from which an attempt could be made to preserve the heritage of German Jewry. Or the Jewishly committed had the option of integrating themselves into East European dominated institutions where standards essentially conformed with those they had known before.

Throughout this period the immigration of East Europeans continued, some arriving even after the start of World War II. But immediately after the war such immigration became particularly noticeable. Some of the immigrants were concentration camp survivors. If the only uniqueness that they shared was their tragic life experience, they generally found whatever niche they could and attempted to reconstruct at least the semblance of a normal existence. But some of these new immigrants brought more with them: they had very strong convictions about their Jewishness. Two groups can be discerned—the Yiddishists-Bundists and the Orthodox, particularly the Orthodox sectarians.[30] The Orthodox sectarians' impact has been the most noticeable, and their example has created controversy within the minority community.

Instead of acculturating to prevailing Orthodox standards the sectarians proceeded to challenge them. They wished to preserve their form of dress, their beards and earlocks. Appearing on the streets and subways of New York, they produced highly ambivalent reactions among East European Jews whose immediate forebearers had been of similar appearance.[31] In sum, the sectarians refused to abide by the social contract. Frequently they considered themselves to be brands plucked from the fire, miraculously saved so that the way of life hallowed by tradition might be preserved. They were loath to expose their children to any substantial amount of secular education, much less to enroll them in public institutions. They proceeded to establish a network of *yeshivot,* they stimulated day school education, and they profoundly influenced the Orthodoxy of the older East European group.

Through Hasidic Jews represent only one segment of this immigration they have preempted the popular imagination. While some of the earlier East European immigrants had come from families with a Hasidic tradition, Hasidic life was never established on American shores. The courts of the *rebbaim* (plural of *rebbe,* Hasidic leader) remained in eastern Europe; immigrants of Hasidic background had only dimming memories of their special traditions. The emergence of Hasidism during World War II and shortly thereafter was made possible by the arrival of a number of *rebbaim,* together with small circles of their followers. Some refugee intellectuals were also active in creating an interest in the neo-Hasidism of Martin Buber.

Bringing the story of immigration up to date, we find that Latin America, rather than eastern or western Europe, is currently the largest source of Jewish immigration to the United States. True many such immigrants, or their parents, were born in Europe. For some their arrival in America means coming to the country that was their first choice when they or their families left eastern or western Europe, but to which they could not gain entry at the time. For others it means moving to a nation that has greater political stability than the country in which they are resident, or improved educational opportunities, or more abundant possibilities for leading a Jewish life.

All of the Jewish newcomers we have been describing, whatever the time of their immigration and the circumstances under which they came, did not need to justify their arrival either to themselves or to others. The freedom offered by America was justification enough. Whatever liberties were enjoyed (or promised) in the old society, and whatever prejudices and discriminations might be present in the new, the consensus was that America offered the Jew greater freedom and a deeper sense of belonging than he could ever possess in his homeland.

None of this holds true for immigrants who come from Israel. In recent years some 2,000 to 3,000 such persons have been admitted to the United States annually. The Hebrew term for such emigrants, *yordim* (literally, "those who descend"), provides a clue regarding their special position. Israelis are the first newcomers who must justify their immigration to themselves and to their fellow Jews. They have uprooted themselves from the Holy Land to return to the *Galut* (literally, the lands of the exile). Leaving a country where Jews constitute the majority they have resumed the age-old pattern of Jews occupying a minority group status. In a sense they have moved from a position of greater freedom to one of lesser freedom.

The freedom motif has served the Jew as his justification for coming to the United States. The significance of this motif endures, regardless of the fact that economic advancement was an important motivating factor in the immigration of some Jews, as it was with many other Americans. But the motif of freedom does not justify the immigration of the

Israeli. His reason for coming is consequently subject to scrutiny. Even if the *yored* is European-born and reared, as he is likely to be, rather than a *sabra* (a native-born Israeli), he may be subject to invidious evaluation. The ambiguous situation of the *yordim* is exemplified by their failure to establish any formal associations—whether of a religious, fraternal, or philanthropic nature—as has invariably been the case with their predecessors who arrived from western or eastern Europe or from other areas.

Group Membership and Identity

If the foregoing constitutes some of the essential social history of American Jewry we must next inquire how individuals who think of themselves as Jewish assume this particular definition of their group membership.

According to *halachah* (Jewish law) the essential requirement for being Jewish is to be born of Jewish parentage, more particularly to be the offspring of a Jewish mother. Being Jewish involves two complementary aspects: membership in the ethnic group and membership in the religious community. The extent to which the individual exercises his prerogatives by participating in ethnic group affairs, and particularly in the life of the religious community, is a matter of choice. But no matter to what extent the prerogatives of birth are exercised, all Jews are essentially equal members of the ethnic group and of the religious community.

Aside from the special case of male circumcision, there is no ceremony of induction into the group or of confirmation of identity. Interestingly enough, as Jews have acculturated, and as the problem of group identity has become more complex, they have sought such ceremonial confirmation. Thus the rites of Confirmation for boys and girls and of Bat Mitzvah for girls have been developed. Furthermore, the traditional Bar Mitzvah ceremony has assumed an entirely new importance. So deep is the need to confirm identity that there are cases on record of men not having had a Bar Mitzvah at age thirteen who underwent the ceremony in adulthood. From the traditional point of view their action was superfluous, for upon attaining the age of thirteen they had automatically become fully adult members of the group.

If psychological needs make certain individuals overconform, Jewish law tends in the direction of considering that not only are all born Jews considered Jewish but that they always remain so. A question then occurs about the individual who converts to another religion. Jewish law—surprisingly enough—tends to claim him as Jewish. Jewish public opinion, on the other hand, generally does not, as became evident when the Supreme Court of Israel adjudicated the case of Brother Daniel, a Carmelite Monk who described himself as a Jew of the Catholic religion. The Court decided that Brother Daniel was not a Jew and therefore that he be denied an immigrant's certificate under the Law of the Return as well as the right to register as a Jew under the registration law. In sum, Jewish public opinion generally reserves group membership for those born of Jewish parents who either practice Judaism or who are religiously inactive in the sense that they have not converted to another faith. A religiously inactive person is thus identified as Jewish by the following rule of thumb: the religion that he does not practice is Judaism rather than Christianity.

Thus whatever the strength of the identity, one important aspect of being Jewish is the individual's resistance to accepting membership in a competing group. The bulk of American Jewry is thus the offspring of Jewish parents whose identity they have assumed. From some points of view it may seem remarkable that in an age of rapid social change so many accept their parents' identity. But actually the surprising thing about the American Jewish community is that so high a proportion of parents want their children to accept the parents' identity. Of course such a desire flows from the most profound psychological mechanisms, but also important is the fact that the life chances of children will not be severely or irretrievably modified by their taking on Jewish identity. There is clear evidence that parents have acted differently under other circumstances. Some Jewish parents in early nineteenth century Germany insisted on giving their children an identity different from their own. To be sure, their motives had patho-logical implications but these parents were engaged—as they saw it—in creating a better future for their children. Most American Jewish parents, on the other hand, feel that they are acting in their children's best interest when they seek to instill in them a Jewish identity. However enduring the identity on a long-range basis, only in a disordered parent-child relationship will it be rejected by the child out of hand.

All that we have said is based upon the assumption that Jewish group membership in the United States is a matter of private sentiment rather than of public commitment or legal definition. Thus the transmission of identity becomes a problem inasmuch as the state does not decide who is a Jew—persons do. This places a heavy burden upon the indi-vidual, because he must make the decision about his group identity. In theory at least, the state is not prepared to offer him any guidance. In fact, the individual is not even asked by the state to define himself for statistical purposes, as for example in connection with the decennial census.[32]

Individual decision is crucial in assuming the role of Jew. Yet these decisions are influenced by, and are dependent upon, larger entities: definitions by both the minority group and the majority. It is not enough that an individual considers himself Jewish: he must be so considered by other Jews as well as by Gentiles. In most cases all three parties are in tandem. Thus the great majority of born Jews consider them-selves Jewish, are so considered by their fellow Jews, and are regarded as Jewish by Gentiles. To be sure, on occasion there are instances where discrepancies exist. For example, while many Jews would not consider members of the Hebrew Chris-tian group to be Jewish, Hebrew Christians assert the con-tinuing legitimacy of their former group affiliation.[33]

For every minority-group member the possibility of non-identification—that is, of assimilation—exists as either a present or remote possibility. Such assimilation may be dis-tinguished by the degree to which it is purposive, and indi-viduals who are assimilating could thus be arranged along a continuum of passive-active assimilators. Assimilation may be said to be complete when the individual no longer considers himself a Jew, when he is thought of as a Gentile by Jews, and when he is regarded as a Gentile by Gentiles. Of course both minority and majority are composed of diverse strands of opinion and hence may not present a unified front. A given individual might be considered Jewish by one segment of the minority or majority, while another might think of him as Gentile.

We must remember, in examining Jews as they adjust to the conditions of life in a comparatively open society such as America, that individuals move both toward the minority group as well as away from it. The process of joining the Jewish group is intriguing because students of ethnic groups generally think of movement as being in the opposite direction: from membership in the minority to membership in the majority.

As we have emphasized the dominant way of joining the group is by birth. Such Jews are immediately members of an ethnic group and of a religious community. Other modes of affiliation present some ambiguities, for example those who join the group by way of conversion. Because of Judaism's minority status and its position through the centuries as a persecuted religion, its stance with respect to conversion has gone through various stages. But in the United States converts are regularly received and number several thousand each year. Such converts share the essential obligations and prerogatives of born Jews—they are religiously Jewish in the fullest sense. Because they are not born Jews, however, some Jews may consider converts to be ethnically Gentile or of indeterminate position, and may have varying degrees of self-consciousness in their relationships with them.[34] In any case when the convert changes his primary group from Gentile to Jewish he is well on the way toward assimilation into the Jewish group.

In addition to birth and conversion there is a third way of joining the group: through marriage to a Jew. While such a marriage does not make one religiously a Jew, it does mean that ethnically the person is placed in a new, and indeterminate position. If the marriage occasions severing bonds with Gentiles and joining an all-Jewish primary group, assimilation into the Jewish group is in process.

The majority of cases of conversion are in fact connected with marriage to a Jew. Some religionists in the Jewish community feel that not only should such conversions be encouraged but that Judaism should become a missionary religion (or, more correctly, recapture the missionary stance which it had once had). They argue that such a position would normalize Judaism in a pluralistic America and have a salutary effect upon Jewish life—the example of converts would energize born Jews who are apathetic to their Jewish religious heritage. However, no major Jewish group has made an unambiguous declaration on the matter or has sponsored any large-scale missionary activity. The ethnic aspect of Jewish identity remains strong—converts are only a relatively small group in comparison with the total Jewish population and the majority of them are married to Jews or are preparing for marriage.

The fourth and final way of joining the Jewish group involves integrating oneself into a Jewish primary group. This, in effect, means changing one's ethnic loyalties. Such cases are highly exceptional and generally are encountered only in the largest cities. Frequently Gentiles of this type work in occupations that are strongly Jewish in composition. But this fourth way of joining the Jewish group is not to be compared to the previous three. Because there is no religious commitment, and because there is no ethnic commitment comparable to that of marriage to a Jew, neither Jew nor Gentile are impelled to regard it seriously.

Our tacit assumption thus far has been that the person assimilating into the Jewish community is white. What then of the comparative handful of black Jews? Their situation has unique aspects but it also highlights the general problems encountered in the assimilation process. In the case of black Jews physical appearance raises questions as to the origin of Jewishness. The Jewish identification of some black Jews stems from family tradition, or from the usual routes of conversion and intermarriage. A more vocal, unified group claims distant descent from the *Falashas* (Ethiopian Jews), at times extending their claims of Jewishness to all American Negroes.

Until recently, identification as a Jew appeared more attractive to most black Jews than identification as a Negro. Now, however, there is pressure to identify as a Negro. Of course such pressure has always been present if only because of the existence of anti-Negro prejudice. But feelings of black pride have compounded the problem; they have created new pressures to identify as a Negro as well as to perpetuate what was to have been only a transitional arrangement: a separate black Jewish community. Finally, there is the problem of anti-Semitism. The white who is assimilating into the Jewish group is either shielded from anti-Semitism or experiences it at second or thirdhand. But the situation of the black Jew is different: he is exposed firsthand to a very direct kind of anti-Semitism in the Negro community and hence is forced to confront the problem of his own identity in a traumatic context. If he defends the Jew what kind of black is he?[35]

Conversion, marriage, and a shift in the primary group all have their counterparts when the process moves in the opposite direction: when the individual is leaving the minority rather than joining it. Statistics on such assimilation remain elusive for several reasons. Assimilation occurs across generations rather than at a given point in time. Furthermore, the assimilated are not conscious of their state—only assimilationists are. Finally, assimilation is not widely esteemed and assimilationists tend to be conflicted about changing their group identity. Thus they are under pressure to portray themselves as different from what they are.

Whatever the numbers involved, assimilation has not been widespread enough to disorganize the American Jewish community, contrary to the expectations of an earlier generation of sociologists who saw Jews as progressing steadily from self-segregation to acculturation to assimilation. True, this movement was not viewed as a straight-line trend: the theory anticipated that the process might be interrupted temporarily by prejudice and discrimination. As a consequence, one of the final chapters of Louis Wirth's classic study *The Ghetto* is entitled "The Return to the Ghetto." Wirth felt that efforts to strengthen Jewish identification were a result of what he called at the time ". . . the revival of anti-Semitism on a world-wide scale."[36] He went on to say: "Apparently there is no limit to the extent to which pressure from the outside is able to solidify a group."[37] In his view, "Prejudice from without has revived the ghetto wall, less visible, perhaps, than before, but not less real."[38] This prejudice and discrimination, Wirth felt, was in large measure a Gentile response to overly hasty Jewish assimilation. The Jews, in their desire to leave the ghetto, had overloaded the circuits and the system had consequently suffered a temporary breakdown: "As the Jew emerges from the ghetto and takes on the character of humanity in the outside world, the ghetto declines. But as this freedom is restricted, generally as a result of too massed or hasty an advance, distances between Jews and non-Jews arise; and the retreat to the ghetto sets in."[39]

Just as prejudice and discrimination can no longer be viewed in the context of an overly hasty Jewish assimilation, so contemporary sociologists have had to grapple with the reality that Jewish identity is clearly more than a response to Gentile dislike. The efforts of both individual parents and of communal bodies to transmit Jewish identity cannot be reasonably interpreted as a "return to the ghetto." One current sociological perspective that attempts to explain the unexpected pervasiveness of ethnic identity takes the view that it results from modern man's need to protect himself from the impersonality and alienation of contemporary life. In seeking to protect himself he clings to familiar forms of social organization which go back to a more primitive stage of human culture. The critical attitudes of the analyst toward ethnic loyalties are manifest in the following statement:

. . . the sense of ethnicity has proven to be hardy. As though with a wily cunning of its own, as though there were some essential element in man's nature that demanded it—something that compelled him to merge his lonely individual identity in some ancestral group of fellows smaller by far than the whole human race, smaller often than the nation—the sense of ethnic belonging has survived. It has survived in various forms and with various names, but it has not perished, and twentieth-century urban man is closer to his stone-age ancestors than he knows.[40]

Whether ethnic loyalties are any more characteristic of modern man's primitive past than other allegiances remains to be seen; it is doubtful that we have as yet a satisfactory theory to explain group membership and belonging. The starting point for such a theory, it would seem, could best be located in a psychological rather than a sociological framework. But whatever the reason for the Jewish community's desire to persist, we should bear in mind that its dominant thrust is survivalist. As we shall see, however, the forces working to subvert group membership and belonging are manifold in number and strong in influence.

Notes

[1] For the figures see Leon Shapiro, "World Jewish Population," *American Jewish Year Book,* 69 (1968), 543–549. (Hereafter the *American Jewish Year Book* will be referred to as *AJYB*.)

[2] See Jacob R. Marcus, "The Periodization of American Jewish History," *Publication of the American Jewish Historical Society,* 47 (September 1957–June 1958), 128–130.

[3] This is the group celebrated by Stephen Birmingham in his book *"Our Crowd": The Great Jewish Families of New York* (New York: Harper and Row, 1967).

[4] See Barry E. Supple, "A Business Elite: German Jewish Financiers in Nineteenth-Century New York," *Business History Review,* 31, No. 2 (Summer 1957), 143–178.

[5] See Marshall Sklare and Joseph Greenblum, *Jewish Identity on the Suburban Frontier: A Study of Group Survival in the Open Society* (New York: Basic Books, 1967), p. 35.

[6] *Ibid.,* p. 34.

[7] *Ibid.,* pp. 97–178.

[8] *Ibid.,* pp. 123–124.

[9] Benjamin B. Ringer, *The Edge of Friendliness: A Study of Jewish-Gentile Relations* (New York: Basic Books, 1967), p. 81.

While Ringer studies the problem of intragroup tension from the vantage point of length of residence rather than place of origin, German-East European cleavages are implicit in the material that he presents in Chapters 4 and 5.

10 *Ibid.*, p. 78.

11 *Ibid.*, p. 96.

12 For the history of these institutions (the David Einhorn Temple and the Max Lilienthal Temple) see Sklare and Greenblum, *op. cit.*, pp. 133–151, 162–166.

13 From an interview in the author's files.

14 The European Sephardic immigration did not come to an end during the colonial period; small numbers of European Sephardim have migrated to the United States during the past two centuries. But whether of European or Oriental origin, Sephardim constitute a small group in the contemporary American Jewish community. Furthermore, their impact on Jewish communal affairs (or on the affairs of the general community) is minor. While Sephardim live in all cities with a Jewish population of 100,000 or over, in no single such community is their influence very strong. In one smaller community they do, however, constitute a significant minority. This is Seattle, Washington where out of a Jewish population of 11,000 it is estimated that there are some 3,500 Sephardim (see William Greenberg, "Sephardim—as Others See Us," *The American Sephardi*, 2, No. 1–2 [1968], 66). It is significant that the most ambitious attempt to preserve the Sephardic heritage and to improve the Sephardic self-image is being sponsored by an Ashkenazic institution, Yeshiva University.

15 Morris Gross, *Learning Readiness in Two Jewish Groups: A Study in "Cultural Deprivation"* (New York: Center for Urban Education, 1967), p. 33.

16 The authors' rationale for ignoring these distinctions was appropriate to the times: "The effort has been to capture the core of continuity running through the Jewish culture of eastern Europe rather than the details in which localities and regions differed. Where forms are described, the most representative one has been selected; or only the basic features have been reported, minimizing the details that vary from place to place." Mark Zborowski and Elizabeth Herzog, *Life Is With People* (New York: International Universities Press, 1952), p. 21.

17 This statement is made with due regard to the pogroms, homelessness and dislocations that followed the defeat of Russia in

the Russo-Japanese War and the Revolution of 1905, as well as earlier dislocations. See Lucy S. Dawidowicz, *The Golden Tradition: Jewish Life and Thought in Eastern Europe* (New York: Holt, Rinehart and Winston, 1967), pp. 69–75.

18 Quoted in Bernard D. Weinryb, "Jewish Immigration and Accommodation to America" in Marshall Sklare (ed.), *The Jews: Social Patterns of An American Group* (New York: The Free Press, 1958), p. 12.

19 See Moshe Davis, *The Emergence of Conservative Judaism* (Philadelphia: The Jewish Publication Society of America, 1963), p. 318.

20 See Moses Rischin, *The Promised City: New York's Jews, 1870–1914* (Cambridge: Harvard University Press, 1962), pp. 144–168. Perhaps to counterbalance the popular image, Rischin emphasizes the secular and radical activities at the expense of the extant religious activities.

21 Charles S. Liebman, "Orthodoxy in American Jewish Life," *AJYB*, 66 (1965), 27–28.

22 See Weinryb, *op. cit.*, p. 12.

23 May N. Tabak, "My Grandmother Had Yichus," *Commentary*, April 1949, pp. 368–372, conveys some of the pathos involved.

24 See Sidney Liskofsky, "Jewish Immigration," *AJYB*, 51 (1950), 75; and Nathan Glazer et al., *The Characteristics of American Jews* (New York: Jewish Education Committee Press, 1965), p. 19.

25 See Ben Halpern, "America is Different," in Sklare, *The Jews*, pp. 23–39. We have, of course, oversimplified the American picture. For some of the shadings see Oscar Handlin and Mary F. Handlin, "The Acquisition of Political and Social Rights by the Jews in the United States," *AJYB*, 56 (1955), 43–98. It should be remembered, for example, that non-Protestants were denied full rights in New Hampshire until 1877.

26 Lucy S. Dawidowicz, "From Past to Past: Jewish East Europe to Jewish East Side," *Conservative Judaism,* 22, No. 2 (Winter 1968), 20–21. For figures on the frequency of voting by Irish, Jewish, and other ethnics see Jack Elinson, Paul W. Haberman, and Cyrille Gell, *Ethnic and Educational Data on Adults in New York City 1963–1964* (New York: School of Public Health and Administrative Medicine, Columbia University, 1967), p. 155.

27 The day schools established in the early days of the Republic had closed when the public school system was established.

[28] See Ernest Stock, "Washington Heights' 'Fourth Reich,'" *Commentary*, June 1951, pp. 581–588.

[29] See Gershom Scholem, "Jews and Germans," *Commentary*, November 1966, pp. 31–38.

[30] For the second group see Liebman, *op. cit.*, pp. 67–89.

[31] This ambivalence is depicted in Philip Roth's well-known story that has a suburban setting: "Eli, the Fanatic," *Commentary*, April 1959, pp. 292–309.

[32] Most Jewish organizations have been against the collection of data on the basis of religion. See Marshall Sklare, "The Development and Utilization of Sociological Research: The Case of the American Jewish Community," *Jewish Journal of Sociology*, 5, No. 2 (December 1963), 169–172.

[33] See Ira O. Glick, "The Hebrew Christians: A Marginal Religious Group," in Sklare, *The Jews*, pp. 415–431.

[34] Note the case of the convert in Park Forest who revealed his origin: see Herbert J. Gans, "The Origin and Growth of a Jewish Community," in Sklare, *The Jews*, p. 229.

[35] The one published study of the black Jews focuses on the group claiming *Falasha* descent. See Howard Brotz, *The Black Jews of Harlem: Negro Nationalism and the Dilemmas of Negro Leadership* (New York: The Free Press, 1964). The desire of some non-Falasha black Jews to press their claims for acceptance into the Jewish community has been complemented by the desire of some white Jews to speed such integration. Hence the establishment in New York City in 1964 of an organization known as *Hatzaad Harishon*.

[36] Louis Wirth, *The Ghetto* (Chicago: University of Chicago Press, 1928), p. 271.

[37] *Ibid.*, p. 273.

[38] *Ibid.*, p. 279.

[39] *Ibid.*

[40] Milton M. Gordon, *Assimilation in American Life* (New York: Oxford University Press, 1964), pp. 24–25. See also Marshall Sklare, "Assimilation and the Sociologists," *Commentary*, May 1965, pp. 63–67.

Chapter 2 ◉ Five Social Characteristics and Their Implications

The social characteristics of America's Jews help to determine what kind of group the Jews are, what problems they face, and what the prognosis is for their survival. In this chapter we shall discuss the five social characteristics—population size, geographic distribution, generation, secular education, and occupation—that are most relevant to understanding the nature of the Jewish group, its problems, and its prognosis for survival.

Population Size

While from the vantage point of world Jewry America's Jewish population is large, from the national demographic perspective Jews constitute only a minor segment of the total population. It was noted in Chapter 1 that prior to the start of the East European immigration Jews constituted less than 1 percent of the population. Although Jewish population size grew rapidly around the turn of the century, at no time have Jews constituted a major segment of the American population. The highest proportion of Jews relative to the population at large occurred in 1937 when the ratio reached 3.7 percent. By 1957 the ratio had slipped to 3.07 percent and by 1967 it had diminished to 2.92 percent (see Table 1). There is every indication that this downward trend will continue.[1]

The prominence of Jews in American society is much greater than their total number and relative size as a group suggest.

37

Table 1. Total, Gentile, and Jewish Populations, United States 1877–1967

Year	Total Population	Gentile Population	Jewish Population	Ratio of Jewish to Total Population
1877	46,353,000	46,123,913	229,087	0.49%
1888	59,974,000	59,574,000	400,000	0.67
1897	71,592,000	70,654,200	937,800	1.31
1907	85,817,239	84,040,054	1,777,185	2.07
1917	103,266,000	98,877,049	3,388,951	3.28
1927	119,038,000	114,809,971	4,228,029	3.55
1937	128,961,000	124,190,353	4,770,647	3.70
1947	144,126,000	139,126,000	5,000,000	3.47
1957	171,198,000	165,943,000	5,255,000	3.07
1967	197,863,000	192,083,155	5,779,845	2.92

SOURCES: Data through 1957 adapted and reprinted from Robert Gutman, "Demographic Trends and the Decline of Anti-Semitism," in Charles Herbert Stember et al., *Jews in the Mind of America* (New York: Basic Books, 1966), p. 354. Data for 1967 from Alvin Chenkin, "Jewish Population in the United States, 1967," *AJYB*, 69 (1968), 283.

And the conspicuousness of individual Jews is complemented by the significance of Judaism and Jewishness in American culture. Although Jews did not play a decisive role in early American history, part of their importance is explained by the crucial role of Judaism in the Christian past. Paradoxically then, the importance of Judaism, as well as the conspicuousness of the individual Jew, is intimately related to the Gentile American's connection with Christianity. While some Jews may view such connection more as a threat than as a boon, the place of Jews in the American pluralist scheme is not conceivable without it. In sum, the claim made by Jews that they are one of America's three great faiths can hardly be said to rest upon any statistical reality. It rests, rather, upon a symbolic importance—an importance that is in part dependent on the connection between Christianity and Judaism. Such symbolic prominence was present even before there were significant Jewish communities in America, for some of the country's earliest settlers viewed themselves as Christians with roots in an ancient Hebrew past—pilgrims who had arrived in a new Promised Land.

Yet the problems of group survival and group influence created for the Jewish community by its small size cannot be overlooked. Population size influences the extent to which politicians regard the desires and needs of a group. Population size influences the rate of intermarriage. And only if population size is sufficiently large can the specialized institutions that the Jewish community requires—such as rabbinical seminaries, teachers' colleges, and publishing houses—be created and maintained. Although some Jewish needs may be met by importing personnel or cultural objects from abroad, or by sending novices overseas for training, these are only temporary stratagems.

Population size depends upon births, deaths, and migration. For ethnic and religious groups four additional factors are operative: intermarriage, conversion, apostasy, and assimilation.[2] Statistics on these four factors are not easy to gather, and even when statistics are available their import is not altogether clear. As we shall point out, for example, intermarriage does not invariably lead to assimilation. Furthermore, the process of assimilation itself is exceedingly difficult to measure and evaluate. Assimilation is sociological death in the sense that the individual is lost to the group. However, sociological death is much more ambiguous than physical death; it is difficult to determine precisely the point at which the individual has assimilated. Thus it is easier to count births, deaths, and migration than it is to measure and evaluate intermarriage, conversion, apostasy, and assimilation. Yet the impact of these latter factors on Jewish population size is of increasing importance.

Table 2. Annual Rates of Population Increase Among Total, Gentile, and Jewish Populations, United States 1877–1966

Period	Total Population Increase	Gentile Population Increase	Jewish Population Increase
1877–1887	2.7%	2.7%	6.8%
1888–1896	2.2	2.1	14.9
1897–1906	2.0	1.9	9.0
1907–1916	2.0	1.8	9.1
1917–1926	1.5	1.6	2.5
1927–1936	0.8	0.8	1.3
1937–1946	1.2	1.2	0.5
1947–1956	1.9	1.9	0.5
1957–1966	1.6	1.6	1.0

SOURCES: See sources for Table 1.

Up to this time the most important fact about Jewish population size is that its increase has depended so heavily upon immigration. The highest rate of Jewish population growth coincides with the period of heaviest immigration, from 1877 to 1916. During this era the Jewish rate of population increase was much larger than the Gentile rate (see Table 2). Since the 1930s, however, the Jewish rate has lagged behind the Gentile rate.

To carry the comparison of the two groups further, it is readily observable that the Jewish rate of increase has been more dependent upon immigration than the Gentile rate. The peak of Gentile dependence on immigration was reached during the decade from 1907 to 1916 when 33.7 percent of Gentile increase was attributable to net migration; since that time only a minor portion of Gentile population increase has been attributable to migration (see Table 3). From 1947 to 1956, for example, the figure for Gentiles was 7.5 percent but during the same decade 57.3 percent of Jewish population increase was attributable to migration.[3]

Jewish immigration to the United States is now so small that it does not make a substantial contribution to increasing the absolute size of the Jewish population. And because mortality differences between Jews and Gentiles have greatly diminished in recent years, this particular factor is less important in affecting the relative size of the two groups than it was in the past. All of which leads to a consideration of the crucial issue of the Jewish birth rate.

Jewish fertility in the United States has never been high; it has never exceeded or even equaled the rate for non-Jews.[4] The earliest comparative statistics, gathered in 1889 in a Census Bureau study of ten thousand Jewish families, found that the Jewish birth rate was less than that of the population at large. And prefiguring the Jewish population problem it was found that foreign-born Jewish women had an appreciably higher birth rate than native-born women. Subsequent research found that the Jewish fertility rate remained lower than the Gentile rate. Thus a study conducted in Rhode Island in 1905 discovered that the average family size of native-born Jewish women was 2.3 children compared with 2.5 for native-born Protestants and 3.2 for native-born Catholics. A study conducted in Indianapolis in 1941 discovered that the fertility rate of Jews was approximately 25 percent below that of Protestants.

The Census Bureau's Current Population Survey of March 1957, which contained a question on religion, underlined these results. It was found that the cumulative fertility rate of Jewish women age forty-five and older was 19 percent below that of Protestants and 27 percent below that of Catholics. Furthermore, the privately conducted Jewish community studies of

Table 3. Increase and Net Migration of Jewish and Gentile Populations, United States 1888–1966

Period	POPULATION INCREASE		NET MIGRATION		RATIO OF NET MIGRATION TO POPULATION INCREASE	
	Gentile	Jewish	Gentile	Jewish	Gentile	Jewish
1888–1896	11,080,200	537,800	2,372,625	334,338	21.4%	62.2%
1897–1906	13,385,854	839,385	3,618,190	679,598	27.0	81.0
1907–1916	14,836,995	1,611,766	5,003,973	787,971	33.7	48.9
1917–1926	15,932,922	839,078	2,246,689	326,778	14.1	38.9
1927–1936	9,380,382	542,618	717,897	70,092	7.6	12.9
1937–1946	14,935,647	229,353	253,210	168,613	1.7	73.5
1947–1956	26,817,000	255,000	2,015,134	146,225	7.5	57.3
1957–1966	26,140,155	524,845	2,797,672	81,789	10.7	15.6

SOURCES: Figures for population increases are derived from Table 1. Figures for net migration, Gentile and Jewish, 1888–1956 are from Gutman, "Demographic Trends," p. 357. Jewish migration figures for the last decade are based on *AJYB*, 62 (1961), 64, and on estimates provided by United HIAS Service (see footnote 3 of this chapter for additional details). Gentile migration for the last decade was computed by subtracting the estimated Jewish migration from the total number of immigrants admitted to the U.S., as listed in the *Statistical Abstract of the United States*, 69 (1968).

the 1950s and 1960s were in agreement with the Census Bureau findings. Surveys of ten different communities found that the fertility ratio of Jews varied from a low of 450 to a high of 596 children under five years of age per one thousand women ages twenty to forty-four (see Table 4). The fertility ratio for

Table 4. Jewish Fertility Ratio: Selected American Cities

City	Year	Fertility Ratio*
New Orleans	1953	496
Lynn	1955	528
Canton	1955	469
Des Moines	1956	596
Worcester	1957	525
New Orleans	1958	510
Los Angeles	1959	560
South Bend	1961	494
Rochester	1961	489
Providence	1963	450

* The number of children under five years of age per thousand women ages 20 to 44.

SOURCE: Goldstein, *Providence*, p. 66. Adapted and reprinted from Sidney Goldstein, *The Greater Providence Jewish Community: A Population Survey* (Providence: General Jewish Committee of Providence, 1964).

the total white urban population in 1960 was 635 children per thousand women of the same age bracket. Some authorities contend that fertility differences between Jews and Gentiles are more apparent than real, that they are strictly a function of the demographic contrasts between the two groups. In this view the Jewish birth rate can be explained by social determinants of low fertility—including urban residence, high educational attainment of the wife, and white-collar occupation of the husband—that are characteristic of Jews. The 1957 Census Bureau survey seemed to hint at this conclusion when it demonstrated that Presbyterian fertility was no higher than Jewish fertility.

We will discuss the question of whether or not there is a

Jewish component in the fertility behavior of American Jews in Chapter 3. Let it suffice to say at this point that all portents indicate a continued reduction in the proportion of Jews to Gentiles. Unless countervailing forces prevail, this means a diminution in Jewish influence in the society. Perhaps the most serious implication of the population ratio implosion is the collective psychological condition that it may create. The realization by Jews that they constitute an ever smaller percentage of the population is capable of breeding a garrison mentality—the feeling among them that they are a small minority confronted by an overwhelmingly large majority against whom they are engaged in a long-term war for survival, a war in which the Jewish side will suffer many casualties. Even if the Jewish side prevails the weary survivors are only the remnants of a once-large army.

Geographic Distribution

Like population size, the factor of geographic distribution exercises a significant influence on the Jewish role in American life as well as being an important aspect of the problem of group survival. As we shall see, the strong geographic concentration of American Jews counteracts somewhat the problems that stem from their low population size and their declining ratio to the general population.

With respect to regional concentration four out of five American Jews live in the North. Some 58 percent reside in the Middle Atlantic States alone, as compared to 19 percent of the total population.[5] At a time when cities have become the focus of American life over 95 percent of American Jews live in urban areas. And so great is the concentration in a handful of cities that 77.8 percent of American Jews reside in ten population centers. Finally, a total of 46.5 percent of American Jewry is concentrated in the New York–Northeastern New Jersey Standard Consolidated Area, which is unrivaled as a Jewish population center (see Table 5). Los Angeles is the nearest competitor but it contains only 8.7 percent of the Jews of the nation.

At various times efforts have been made to halt or reverse these trends toward regional and urban concentration. The Galveston movement attempted to deflect the East European immigrants from eastern seaboard ports. The activities of the Industrial Removal Office were aimed at relocating those who landed on the eastern seaboard to the interior of the country.

Table 5. Jewish Population in Areas of Heavy Jewish Concentration

Area	Jewish Population	Percentage of U.S. Jewish Population
New York–Northeastern New Jersey SCA*	2,687,680	46.5%
Los Angeles	500,000	8.7
Philadelphia	330,000	5.7
Chicago	269,000	4.7
Boston SMSA	208,000	3.6
Miami	130,000	2.2
Washington, D.C.	100,000	1.7
Baltimore	100,000	1.7
Cleveland	85,000	1.5
Detroit	84,500	1.5
Total	4,494,180	77.8%

* New York State Portion of SCA: 2,390,625; New Jersey Portion of SCA: 297,055.

Note: Figures for New York–Northeastern New Jersey SCA are based on 1962 estimates. As Chenkin cautions, they were out of date at the time they were utilized.

sources: For New York–Northeastern New Jersey Standard Consolidated Area (SCA) see Alvin Chenkin, "Jewish Population in the United States, 1966," *AJYB*, 68 (1967), 231–233; for Boston Standard Metropolitan Statistical Area (SMSA) see Axelrod et al., *Boston*, p. 12; estimates for the other cities are from *AJYB*, 69 (1968), 285–289; estimate for total U.S. Jewish population from *AJYB*, 69 (1968), 283.

Finally, the Jewish Agricultural Society, sponsored by the Baron de Hirsch Fund, attempted to create an American Jewish farming class. But none of these projects succeeded in making any substantial modification in the geographic distribution of American Jewry.

Nevertheless the spectacular growth of the Jewish population of Los Angeles, and to a lesser extent of Miami, testify to the geographic volatility of American Jewry and suggests that concentration is not merely a function of the dead hand of the past. Furthermore, Los Angeles and Miami—as well as many cities having smaller Jewish communities—demonstrate that when Jews relocate they move in patterned ways, and that to a greater or lesser extent a Jewish component is involved in their decision. As a consequence, when Jews leave old areas of Jewish concentration they tend to establish new ones. Generally speaking they are uninterested in an area that does not have a Jewish community of some size or the promise of developing one.[6]

The factor of concentration is crucial. Without concentration it would be difficult to create a Jewish life that had continuity with past models. The more traditional the type of Jewish life which the individual chooses the more necessary concentration is: prohibitions on Sabbath travel necessitate that Jews reside within walking distance of a synagogue, dietary restrictions necessitate kosher butcher shops as well as grocery stores that carry specialized products, and educational needs require Jewish schools to be close at hand. However, while concentration is necessary for traditionalists it also plays a vital role for the many who lack such commitments. Thus it is essential to the preservation of Jewish identity for the children of families whose attachment to the Jewish group is nonideological. If a youngster from a nonideological background is reared in a close Jewish neighborhood located in a city of heavy Jewish concentration, his Jewish identity can develop easily. He can integrate himself into a Jewish peer group with ease. However limited is his formal socialization in Jewish culture he can come to view the world from a Jewish perspective.

Brownsville—the famous area in Brooklyn that was settled by highly diverse elements of the immigrant generation after 1890—was just such a neighborhood.[7] Alfred Kazin's account of his life there is a perfect illustration of the process of informal socialization leaning heavily upon the factor of geographic concentration. Kazin describes how the solidification of his Jewish identity took place despite the fact that his immigrant father was a freethinker. While the Jewish education to which Kazin was exposed consisted only of a few Hebrew lessons designed to enable him to appear in a synagogue and have a Bar Mitzvah, he came to feel that: ". . . we had always to be together: believers and nonbelievers, we were a people; I was of that people. Unthinkable to go one's way, to doubt or escape the fact that I was a Jew."[8]

The example of Brownsville, or even of some contemporary Jewish neighborhoods, highlights another essential aspect of the concentration phenomenon: concentration not only increases the contact between Jew and Jew but it also reduces the contact between Jew and Gentile. While a significant effect of concentration is that of encouraging Jewish life by making possible the existence of certain Jewish institutions and services, an equally significant effect is the establishment of a network of social relationships among Jews. These social relationships result in slowing the rate of acculturation. And when acculturation does take place it occurs in a Jewish setting. Since acculturation is a necessary—although not sufficient—precondition for assimilation, the factor of concentration thus works to slow the assimilation process. Finally, concentration has the effect of magnifying the Jewish role in American society. Were Jews more evenly distributed throughout the country their miniscule population size would mean that however prominent individual Jews might become, they would be of little significance as a group.

Generation

While Jews are generally described as one of America's more recent immigrant groups, only a minority of Jewish adults are foreign-born Americans. In middle size and larger communities the proportion of foreign-born adults is commonly in the 20 to 30 percent range. In smaller Jewish communities the proportion of foreign-born is insignificant. As a rule, the larger the Jewish population the higher the proportion of foreign-born. For example, in Milwaukee the foreign-born number 28 percent of the adult population but in New York City the proportion reaches 37 percent (see Table 6).

Table 6. Foreign-Born Jewish Adults in Three Cities

City	Adults Foreign-Born*	Foreign-Born Over Age 70**
Milwaukee	28%	79%
New York City	37	76
Providence	26	81

* 20 years of age and older.
** New York City over age 65.
SOURCES: For Milwaukee and New York City, see Chenkin in *AJYB*, 69 (1968), 273. For Providence see Goldstein, *Providence*, p. 35.

Although the foreign-born are still a statistically important group they constitute an aged population. In Milwaukee some 79 percent of foreign-born adults are age seventy and over; in Providence the figure is 81 percent. Thus the influence of the foreign-born in the world of work is small as many are no longer members of the labor force. And while the foreign-born may dominate Jewish institutions that serve their own needs, their influence on institutions designed to meet the needs of the total Jewish community is waning.

The distinction between the foreign-born and the native-born is crucial for understanding the sociology of American Jewry. The two groups not only have contrasting age-profiles but they differ sharply with respect to such social characteristics as occupation and education. Furthermore, the attitudes and values of the two groups are significantly different.

This is not to say that the foreign-born are all alike—there are wide variations among them, as, for example, in religious practices. These variations are immediately apparent in New York City where the large size of the Jewish population means that population diversity is more pronounced than elsewhere. In Brooklyn—the borough that has attracted the highest percentage of the foreign-born—there are Jewish neighborhoods where Hasidim predominate, others where Orthodox Jews predominate, and still others where Jewish secularists are strong. Nevertheless, upon close sociological inspection similarities may be discerned between the foreign-born members of all three of these population segments. They are Yiddish-speaking, they have similar attitudes toward non-Jews, and they share the same food preferences despite differences about the validity of Jewish dietary laws. The reason for such similarities is clear. Most foreign-born Jews coming from eastern Europe were reared in a recognizably Jewish culture. Regional variations existed within eastern Europe but these variations became part of Jewish culture itself. Despite ideological diversity and subsequent acculturation in America the mark of the original cultural experience has remained.

How did foreign-born Jews react to the generation gap? Significantly, the overwhelming majority of foreign-born expected their children to be different from themselves. They accepted as inevitable fact that their children were going to be reared in a culture that was American—in other words, not Jewish. Confronted by what they experienced as the power of American culture, their tendency was to seek accommodation. As noted in Chapter 1, only the Hasidim and the ultra-Orthodox refused to accommodate. These two groups did not countenance any distinctions between themselves as foreign-born members of the first generation socialized in a foreign culture, in contrast to their children as native-born members of the second generation, and hence potential candidates for socialization in a new and alluring culture. The refusal of Hasidim, for example, to abide a generation gap has precipitated an open and deliberate rejection of America. In attempting to preserve and transmit their original culture they stress the wearing of distinctive clothing and hair styles, the use of Yiddish as the vernacular, prohibitions against exposure to the mass media, and a highly organized subcommunity designed to minimize contact with outsiders whether Gentile or non-Hasidic Jews.[9]

Some Hasidim—especially the followers of the Skvirer Rebbe —believe that cultural transmission is impossible in the city. Despite Brooklyn's thick Jewishness they feel that the integrity of their culture can only be preserved by geographical isolation. Viewing Brooklyn as part of an urban world in which social control cannot be effectively exercised, Skvirer Hasidim purchased a plot of land in Rockland County, New York, in 1954. There they succeeded in establishing their own community of New Square. Some members of the community commute by special bus to carefully selected jobs in New York City while others are employed in the community itself. Socialization of the native-born generation—for whom the community was essentially created—is tightly controlled.

Table 7. *Generation of Boston Adults in the Jewish and General Populations*

Generation	Jewish	General*
First generation	22%	18%
Second generation	50	27
Third generation and later	26	50
Not ascertained	2	5
Total	100%	100%

* Includes Jews.

source: Axelrod et al., p. 36. Adapted and reprinted from Morris Axelrod, Floyd J. Fowler, and Arnold Gurin, *A Community Survey for Long Range Planning—A Study of the Jewish Population of Greater Boston* (Boston: Combined Jewish Philanthropies of Greater Boston, Inc., 1967).

The problem of cultural transmission between the first and second generation can still be observed in some neighborhoods of Brooklyn, as well as in other boroughs of New York City. More typically, however, the current problems of American Jewry revolve around the question of the transmission process between the second and third generation, and increasingly between the third and fourth generation. In Boston, for example, only 22 percent of the adult Jewish population are members of the first generation but 50 percent are members of the second generation, and already 26 percent are members of the third generation (see Table 7). Thus for some time the typical Jewish household in Boston has consisted of second generation parents and third generation children. Households consisting of third generation parents and fourth generation children are also common.

Despite the increasing number of adults who are members of the third generation, as a group Jews are still new Americans. In some major cities their late arrival in the United States is obscured by the fact that they are old residents of the city, having been followed by certain other European ethnic groups as well as by Puerto Ricans, Appalachian whites, and southern Negroes. But the Boston statistics highlight the newness of the Jew. While some 50 percent of Gentile Bostonians are members of the third or fourth generation only 26 percent of the Jews are in the same category.

Secular Education

The great majority of Jewish immigrants who came to the United States possessed only the most rudimentary secular education, if any at all. Only after 1905, and particularly after World War I, was there a substantial group of East European arrivals who possessed a secondary or higher education, and only after 1933 did German Jews who had attended a *gymnasium* or a university immigrate to the United States. Given this comparative absence of secular education, the transformation of the Jewish group has been enormous: in the space of about six decades Jews have become one of the best educated segments of the American population.

This transformation may be studied by referring either to national or local statistics. Local statistics are preferable: national figures tend to maximize Jewish-Gentile differences inasmuch as they do not control for such relevant variables as region and size of community. In Milwaukee, for example, 13 percent of Jewish adult males are at the bottom of the educational ladder, having only an elementary school education or less (see Table 8). A total of 34 percent have attended college, and an additional 18 percent have had some graduate training. On the other hand, some 37.3 percent of Milwaukee Gentiles are at the bottom of the ladder. Furthermore, only 20.5 percent of the Gentiles, in contrast to 52 percent of the Jews, received college and graduate training.

Table 8. *Level of Education, Adult Males in Milwaukee and Providence, Jewish and General Population*

EDUCATION	JEWS		GENERAL POPULATION	
	(Age 20+) Milwaukee	(Age 25+) Providence	(Age 25+) Milwaukee SMSA*	(Age 25+) Providence SMSA*
Elementary School or less	13%	13.7%	37.3%	43.0%
Some High School	} 35	8.5	18.8	23.2
High School Graduate		27.5	23.4	18.8
Some College	} 34	14.2	9.8	6.7
College Graduate		14.1	} 10.7	} 8.2
Postgraduate	18	19.7		
No Information	—	2.2	—	—
Total	100%	100%	100%	100%

* Note: The general population figures for Milwaukee SMSA and Providence SMSA include Jews. However, in these particular communities the resulting bias is small and operates to narrow the disparities between Jews and Gentiles.

SOURCES: Data for the Jewish population is from Mayer, *Milwaukee*, p. 45 and Goldstein, *Providence*, p. 72. Data for the general population is from the 1960 U.S. Census. Adapted and reprinted from Albert J. Mayer, *Milwaukee Jewish Population Study 1964–1965* (Milwaukee: Milwaukee Jewish Welfare Fund, 1967).

Sharp contrasts exist in other communities as well. While only 22.2 percent of the Jews in Providence failed to graduate from high school the corresponding figure for the general population is 66.2 percent. Figures from these and other communities suggest that Jews have climbed the educational ladder with great rapidity, that they have done so much more quickly than other subgroups, and that their rise has been so meteoric that they have caught up to—and in some cases have surpassed—those who trace their origins to the oldest and most favored segments of the American population. During the space of six decades Jews have shifted from a modal educational level of grade school or less to a modal educational level of at least some college, with a significant proportion earning a graduate or professional degree.

If we are to gain a fuller understanding of changes in the level of secular education among Jews we must turn to New York City. Not only does New York have a larger percentage of foreign-born individuals than either Milwaukee or Providence but it also is the single place in the country where there still is a Jewish working class. Furthermore, it has always been the center of Jewish religious traditionalism in the United States. New York City also has many dense Jewish neighborhoods where the impact of the general culture—with its stress on the value of secular education—should not be felt as keenly as in smaller communities. These factors should work to place New York Jews behind those of the rest of the country as well as to make them educational underachievers in comparison with certain segments of the Gentile population of the city.

The foreign-born Jews of New York are indeed a poorly educated group with respect to secular education: some 50.6 percent of them have received only a grade school education or less (see Table 9).[10] Among native-born Jews, however, the situation is entirely different: a mere 5.7 percent of them have received only a grade school education or less, while a total of 62 percent have received higher education (37.9 percent have attended college and 24.1 percent have taken graduate studies). Just as foreign-born Jews are distinguished by their educational deprivation so native-born Jews are distinguished by their educational achievement.[11] In fact the native-born

Table 9. Education, Adult Males, New York City, by Ethnicity

Education	Negro	Puerto Rican	Irish*	Italian*	Other Catholic
Some Grade School or less	20.8%	35.2%	12.5%	21.1%	10.7%
Grade School Graduate	10.8	13.2	15.0	16.8	11.3
Some High School	28.3	25.3	25.0	23.4	25.4
High School Graduate	20.0	16.5	20.0	20.4	22.6
Some College	14.2	4.4	17.5	12.4	15.3
College Graduate	4.2	3.3	7.5	2.2	7.3
Postgraduate	1.7	2.2	2.5	3.6	7.3
Total	100%	100%	100%	100%	100%

* Note: Persons are classified as "Irish" or "Italian" only if they or their fathers were born in Europe. Anyone of third or later generation Irish or Italian background is classified "Other Catholic" or "Other Protestant," as the case may be.

SOURCE: Elinson et al., Ethnic and Educational Data, p. 14. Adapted and reprinted from Jack Elinson, Paul W. Haberman, and Cyrelle Gell, Ethnic and Educational Data on Adults in New York City 1963–1964 (New York: School of Public Health and Administrative Medicine, Columbia University, 1967).

Five Social Characteristics and Their Implications · 55

Table 9. (Continued)

Education	Other Protestant	Native-Born Jews	Foreign-Born Jews	All Jews	Total
Some Grade School or less	4.7%	1.7%	39.4%	14.4%	16.7%
Grade School Graduate	16.8	4.0	11.2	6.5	11.9
Some High School	16.8	14.9	13.5	14.4	21.0
High School Graduate	22.4	17.2	13.5	16.0	19.3
Some College	15.9	24.1	13.5	20.5	15.3
College Graduate	7.5	13.8	3.4	10.3	6.8
Postgraduate	15.9	24.1	5.6	17.1	9.1
Total	100%	100%	100%	100%	100%

have achieved so much that they have outdistanced even the "Other Protestants," a group composed of whites largely of old American descent. In contrast to 62 percent of the Jews only 39.3 percent of the "Other Protestants" have received a higher education. We must conclude, then, that factors which retard the educational rise of other groups—religious traditionalism, working class background, and isolation from the general culture—do not seem to affect native-born Jews very strongly. Jews even outdistance the "Other Protestants," a group where these factors constitute a minimal influence.

We can gain a more precise understanding of the rapidity of the Jewish advance in New York City by comparing the education of the native-born with that of their fathers. A total of 89 percent of these sons surpass their fathers in educational attainment (see Table 10). Furthermore, widespread Jewish educational mobility has had profound effects: instead of moving one or two steps ahead of their fathers, a noticeable proportion of the native-born have moved many steps ahead of them. For example, some 27.1 percent score in the highest mobility bracket. In most cases this means that the father failed to receive a grade school diploma but the son achieved a baccalaureate or graduate degree.

The explanation for this education explosion has usually followed this line: the young Jew decided to pursue an education since he saw the advantage to be gained from doing so. His motivation was the desire for mobility, more particularly the urge to leave his working class origins. He was able to utilize education as an avenue to mobility because Jewish culture stressed religious learning. But he was no longer interested in sacred studies. For example, while the study of Jewish law no longer had any attraction secular law became interesting for him. He decided to enroll in a law school. Not only would he be able to advance to middle class status by becoming a lawyer, but he would be able to escape the prejudice he would encounter if he attempted to join the ranks of the corporate bureaucracy. As an attorney he would be able to work as a free professional and be judged on merit alone.

At a minimum this line of reasoning assumes that men act out of rational calculation; at a maximum it suggests that

Table 10. Male Educational Mobility, New York City, by Ethnicity

| | EDUCATIONAL MOBILITY* | | | | | |
| | UPWARD | | | | DOWNWARD | |
	+5 to +7	+3 or +4	+1 or +2	0	−1 or −2	−3 to −7
All Men	8.2%	22.4%	41.5%	20.6%	6.0%	1.3%
Negro	4.3	23.7	38.7	22.6	7.5	3.2
Puerto Rican	2.5	13.6	51.9	25.9	3.7	2.5
Irish	3.0	30.3	27.3	36.4	3.0	0.0
Italian	3.3	30.0	46.7	15.8	4.2	0.0
Other Catholic	6.4	19.1	48.4	19.1	5.1	1.9
Other Protestant	3.0	19.0	47.0	20.0	9.0	2.0
Native-Born Jewish	27.1	33.5	28.4	5.8	4.5	0.6
Foreign-Born Jewish	3.8	9.0	35.9	43.6	7.7	0.0

* *Educational Mobility:* The difference between respondent's educational level and his father's educational level. Educational levels were ranked: none = 1; some grade school = 2; grade school graduate = 3; some high school = 4; high school graduate = 5; some college = 6; college graduate = 7; postgraduate = 8.

Upward Mobility: Respondent's educational level higher than father's.
Downward Mobility: Respondent's educational level lower than father's.
Zero: Respondent's educational level same as father's.
SOURCE: Elinson et al., *Ethnic and Educational Data*, p. 26.

Jews act out of base motives, that they debase learning from an elevated pursuit to a business proposition. The theory does not explain why the parents of Jewish girls should have afforded their offspring anything more than the minimum education required by public law. It does not explain why immigrants, and more especially the children of immigrants, should have been so attracted to intellectual and academic pursuits at a time when opportunities were so few and prejudice was so strong.[12] Finally, the theory does not explain why so many members of the third generation coming from middle and upper class families have been so interested in undergraduate and graduate study, and why their parents have encouraged them in this direction. Frequently such education results in alienating a son from the occupation pursued by his father. And even if the son does enter the family business his expensive education may prove to be as much a liability as an asset.

A more meaningful approach is the following: Jewish culture embraced a different attitude toward learning from that which characterized the dominant societies of eastern Europe. This Jewish attitude was part of the value-system of the immigrants. It pertains to learning in general, though in the traditional framework it is most apparent with respect to the study of religious subjects. Learning is seen as a positive good—the more learning the more life. Indeed, without learning man is little better than an animal. Learning is the process that transforms the individual into a human being; inasmuch as all normal people are capable of learning, all are capable of such a transformation.

These attitudes apparently set the stage for the educational explosion that occurred among Jews in the United States; if there was calculation regarding the economic return that could be realized from education, such calculation necessarily took place within this framework. But the period of explosion is over: the level of education cannot rise much higher, since over four out of five are enrolled in college. And while the disparity between Jewish and Gentile educational levels will continue for some time, the differences between the two groups are already being narrowed. Because the national interest makes it necessary to raise the educational level of the American population,

educational disparities between Jews and Gentiles will ultimately shrink, if not disappear. We should remember, however,
that Jewish educational mobility started well before the age of
compensatory education, educational incentives, preferential
programs, and educational recruitment from minority groups.
Furthermore, the Jewish attitude to learning predates Sputnik,
even as it predates the encounter with American culture.

If the educational rise of American Jews has made them a
kind of model for others, their accomplishments have, of
course, been accompanied by many benefits to themselves as
well as to the society. At the same time, however, the rise has
created severe problems of group adjustment and survival, as
we shall stress when we discuss Jewish education in Chapter
5. Throughout most of East European history the educational
aspirations of Jews were concentrated on the area of religious
studies. In the United States, however, learning generally became secular learning. For most, Jewish studies came to be
pursued for only a brief time during childhood and then only
on a supplementary basis. As a consequence the culture of the
individual became American, or more exactly a Jewish variant
of American culture. Because the culture of the individual was
so American, Jewish culture began to stagnate. The result can
be seen in the fixation on such sentimental reconstructions of
shtetl life as "Fiddler on the Roof."

In its more acute phase the educational rise involved something more serious than bathos, as it involved Jews adopting
the culture of the West, including its anti-Semitic aspect. In
its less acute phase the rise meant the creation of a group of
intellectual Jews who were on one hand devastatingly critical
of the Jewish community but on the other hand were not
seriously interested in its reform. Fastening particularly on
the excesses of the *nouveaux riches* and more generally on
Jewish ethnocentrism and provincialism, such Jewish intellectuals have been incapable of discovering any redeeming
features in American Jewish life. Ironically, while declaring
that the American Jew is beyond redemption, they share his
sentimentalism toward the *shtetl* and toward the good old days
on the Lower East Side and in other such immigrant neighborhoods. But unlike the Jewish middle and upper classes, their

feelings in this respect serve as a justification for rejecting the contemporary Jew and the community which he has created.[13]

The Jewish community has made attempts to deal with problems of group adjustment and survival brought on by the explosion in secular education among American Jews. The most notable of such efforts is one that has been established on the campuses themselves: the development of the B'nai B'rith Hillel Foundations. By 1969 some 250 of these groups had been established at American universities. The first Hillel Foundation was established in 1923 at the University of Illinois. Interestingly enough, it was formed at the suggestion of a non-Jew, Edward Chauncey Baldwin. As a professor of Biblical literature, Baldwin had an opportunity to evaluate the knowledge of his Jewish students with respect to Jewish studies. Appalled by their ignorance and indifference, he suggested the project to Jewish leaders in Champaign. Prominent Jews in Chicago were later contacted and in 1924 the project was taken over by B'nai B'rith. In 1963 the work of the Foundations was expanded to include faculty as well as students. Not only had the number of Jewish faculty increased greatly since the Foundations' establishment but it had become apparent that the attitudes of an important segment of the faculty toward their Jewishness were as ambiguous as those of some of the students. As we shall see in Chapter 5, the most recent development is the introduction of Jewish studies into the university curriculum.

Occupation

If Jews came to the United States with little in the way of secular education they also arrived without capital or marketable skills. According to one government report the average Jewish immigrant in 1900 landed with nine dollars compared with an average of fifteen dollars for all immigrants.[14] They also had very little to offer in the way of skill. The German Jew solved the problem of making a living by choosing the occupation of peddler. Peddling became for him what manual labor was to other groups: an occupation which needed little in the way of expertise, capital, or powerful connections. Like the manual laborer the lot of the peddler was not a happy one; the letters and memoirs of German immigrants are full of descriptions of the physical strain and psychological deprivation that peddling involved.

Arriving later than the German Jews, a smaller percentage of East Europeans took up peddling. Those who did tended to confine themselves to the city since opportunities in the countryside had started to decline. The East European counterpart of peddling was operating a machine in the clothing industry. In 1900 this was the largest single occupation of East European immigrants, with 34 percent being so employed (an additional 23 percent were blue-collar workers in other industries).[15] Many of these individuals had not worked in the garment trades in Europe but they chose the industry because it was located close at hand, because it required dexterity more than brute strength, and because they could more easily find work in an industry dominated by Jews. For a time garment manufacturing in the United States became an industry in which East European Jews were the workers and German Jews were the bosses.

The perils of peddling and the trauma of the sweatshop are now part of the folklore of the American Jewish community. Some Jews—generally immigrants, and generally residents of New York City or former New Yorkers—still work at blue-collar occupations, mostly in unionized industries where working conditions are above average. Many other Jews—younger, middle age, and some older—continue to make their living in industries with which their families were originally connected. However, they are not occupied at working class jobs; they function rather as salesmen, managers, or proprietors. Outside of New York City in particular, the Jewish roots of certain industries are now reflected more in the composition of its executive and sales forces, and sometimes of its union officialdom, than in the composition of its total labor force. The garment industry is the most noted example.

The data do not allow us to state with precision exactly how far the East European immigrants who came here before World War I, and their descendants, have moved up the occu-

Table 11. Occupations of Adult Male Jews in Selected Cities

Occupation	Boston*	Detroit**	(Age 20+) Milwaukee	(Age 25+) Providence	(Age 20+) N.Y.C.
Professional	32%	23%	22%	20.7%	25.7%
Managers and Proprietors	37	54	35	40.7	28.2
Clerical	3	⎫ 13	⎫ 26	4.5	⎫ 19.2
Sales	12	⎭	⎭	20.9	⎭
Blue Collar	14	10	15	12.1	26.9
Not Ascertained	2	—	—	1.1	—
Total	100%	100%	100%	100%	100%

* All male Jews in labor force.
** Adult male family heads.

SOURCES: Axelrod et al., *Boston*, p. 44; Mayer, *Milwaukee*, p. 34; Goldstein, *Providence*, p. 89; Elinson et al., *Ethnic and Educational Data*, p. 47.

pational ladder. But the main outlines of the picture are clear: the majority of East Europeans have left the working class and have moved into middle and upper class occupations. Only in New York City is there a substantial Jewish working class, and some of its members are fairly recent immigrants.

While in 1900 some 57 percent of male East European immigrants were blue collar workers, by 1963 the figure for the Jewish population of New York City was 26.9 percent. At about the same time in four other cities a maximum of 15 percent were members of the working class (see Table 11). In 1900 some 2.9 percent of the East European male immigrants were professionals; in the 1960s the figure varied from a low of 20.7 percent in Providence to a high of 32 percent in Boston. These facts are particularly instructive, because the blue-collar group and the professional group are far removed from each other in the occupational spectrum. The great reduction in the percentage of Jews in the blue-collar group, together with the large increase in the professional group, is a convincing demonstration of the high occupational mobility of Jews. It suggests that relatively few sons of working class fathers have inherited the paternal occupation.

Among Jews in the 1960s, managers and proprietors were the largest single occupational group in each city.[16] This category includes individuals of the most diverse sort: owners of large retail chains together with proprietors of neighborhood shops, senior officials of nationally known enterprises together with managers of marginal businesses. In spite of this variability there is little question that the situation today is vastly different from 1900. At that time the majority of East European immigrants who were managers or proprietors operated very small enterprises—sometimes nothing more than the proverbial "hole in the wall," and sometimes merely an open-air stall.

Jewish occupational mobility is further highlighted by comparisons between Jews and the population at large. In our five cities—Boston, Detroit, Milwaukee, Providence, and New York —we find that the percentage of the general population comprised of blue-collar workers varies from 50.1 to 59.3 percent (see Table 12). Thus the proportion of the general population

Table 12. Occupations of Adult Males in Selected Cities

Occupation	Boston SMSA	Detroit SMSA	Milwaukee SMSA	Providence SMSA	N.Y.C.*
Professional	14.8%	11.9%	12%	9.2%	16.2%
Managers and Proprietors	11.6	9.1	8	10.5	16.7
Clerical	9.1	7.7	⎱ 26	8.1	⎱ 15.5
Sales	8.4	7.4	⎰	7.4	⎰
Blue Collar	50.1	59.3	54	57.9	51.6
Not Ascertained	6.0	4.3	—	6.9	—
Total	100%	100%	100%	100%	100%

* New York City, age 20 and over.

SOURCES: For Boston and Detroit see appropriate data in 1960 U.S. Census reports. For Milwaukee, Providence, and New York City see sources cited in Table 11.

that is now working class is about the same as that of East European Jewish immigrants in 1900. Furthermore, the proportion that are professionals in the general population varies from 9.2 percent in Providence to 16.2 percent in New York City. In most of the cities, then, proportionally twice as many Jews are professionals as in the population at large. With the exception of New York City proportionally three or four times as many are managers and proprietors as in the population at large.

As favorable as these figures seem, they can easily lead to oversimplification. To use our previous example of the Jewish lawyer, we cannot assume that Jews are randomly distributed throughout the legal profession. Of course there is never a random distribution, if only because of family connections, differences in legal training, and individual interests—interests that are in part a reflection of group history and culture. But for Jews there is the strong additional factor of discrimination. However, the long-standing practice of discrimination in prestigious law firms is now waning. Even assuming that discrimination will continue to decline, it will take some time for the character of the firms to change and for Jews to be fully represented in the most profitable and prestigious segments of the legal profession.

The situation experienced by Jewish lawyers applies to other occupations as well. Jewish managers, for example, work predominantly for small and middle-size firms. Many of the firms are Jewish-owned. Jewish managers are conspicuously absent from the ranks of the higher managers and officialdom of the 500 largest corporations (except those few firms originally owned by Jews). It is also apparent that the situation of Jewish proprietors is not uniformly favorable. Some are small merchants who are under severe pressure from expanding shopping centers, discount houses, and chain stores, and from shifts in consumer preferences. Others are small merchants located in Negro neighborhoods. Such merchants are highly vulnerable to theft, violence, and looting as well as to the demands for the expansion of black-owned business. The vulnerability of the Jewish merchant in the Negro neighborhood is matched by his counterpart in the professional group: the

Jewish teacher and school administrator. Such educators are under sharp attack by Black Power advocates of community control.

Like educational mobility, occupational mobility has brought great benefits to the Jewish group. It also has brought severe problems of group adjustment and survival.[17] Occupational mobility entails class mobility; in the process of shifting from the working class to the middle class and the upper class, Jews have made drastic changes in their culture. The new cultural patterns that they adopted were not generally Jewish patterns —they were patterns from the larger culture. True, Jews adopted and relinquished cultural patterns selectively, with the consequence that the culture of middle class Jews is not identical with that of their opposite-numbers among Gentiles. Nevertheless in many cases continuity between old and new cultural patterns is weak.

The occupationally mobile Jew may be said to be a victim of his own success inasmuch as he feels compelled to surrender old cultural patterns as inappropriate to his new position. In doing so, however, he does not feel that he is compromising either his identity as a Jew or his integrity as a human being. Because cultural patterns are generally substituted in bits and pieces rather than as a total set of values, he is unaware of how fast and how far he is moving. But in the end, he creates an identity problem for himself: in what sense is he still Jewish? And even if he feels that he is different from his Gentile neighbor, in what sense can his child—who has had so little contact with the Jewish working class and its culture— feel a sense of identity?

The acculturation that we have been describing is experienced by all people who have been involved in the process of social mobility. But as we have seen acculturation raises special issues for minorities, including the problem of their group adjustment and survival. We may note that in most of the communities we have studied some 20 to 25 percent of adult Jewish males are professionals. It is apparent that in the next few decades this figure will increase greatly. For example, in Detroit already 42 percent of the male Jewish family heads ages twenty to thirty-four are professional men. (The speed with which Jews have been moving toward professional occupations is apparent from the fact that only 2 percent of male Jewish family heads age sixty-five and over are professionals.) Not only does this mean that Jews are approaching the upper limit of the occupational spectrum but it also suggests that many younger Jewish professionals serve predominantly Gentile instead of Jewish clientele (indeed it would be impossible for them to serve exclusively Jewish clientele even if they wished to do so, inasmuch as a broader public is necessary to generate sufficient demand for their services). Some younger Jews not only have a Gentile clientele but they are doing what few American Jews ever did before: they are working as salaried professionals employed in large Gentile-dominated corporations.

The implications of working in such corporate structures can be realized if we look at the problem in perspective. Economic survival within the working class required minimal shifts in values. One could survive by working hard for the required number of hours. Little commitment to one's work was required. Furthermore, while mobility in the traditional Jewish industries might entail long hours and considerable ingenuity, the value shifts required were minimal. Contacts with the Gentile world were usually of short duration and were narrowly limited to financial transactions.

The new occupational world of the corporation, or indeed of any large scale enterprise, requires acceptance of the values of the general culture. Contacts between Jews and Gentiles are no longer limited to brief exchanges of goods or services but rather require diffuse and extended interactions in which the ability to move easily in a Gentile social world is a major determinant of success. Those who judge the acceptability of an upwardly mobile person are those who have already "arrived," largely Gentiles. The threat of rejection hastens the elimination of many Jewish-Gentile distinctions, not only those that are functionally incompatible. In the new occupational world the will to resist the values of the general culture is encountered only among individuals whose Jewish commitment is extraordinarily high.

While the problem posed by mobility and acculturation is clear in the giant Gentile-dominated corporation, even the person who makes his living in a Jewish-owned company may no longer live in the same self-contained world as before. He may be active in civic affairs, in the alumni activities of his college or graduate school, or in the work of a trade association. And in the event that his company is acquired by another, he may find himself an employee of a giant Gentile-dominated corporation after all.

The problem posed to the Jewish community by the new occupational world is highlighted by the situation of the Jewish academician. Not only is he a professional man who works in a Gentile setting but he belongs to a community as well—the academic community. Certain traditional Jewish values—once they are secularized and universalized—are close enough to the values of the university to facilitate movement into the academic community. Jews have also found a greater degree of social acceptance within the academic community than elsewhere. Finally, academicians have a stronger professional identity than certain other professionals.[18]

The problem of maintaining a Jewish identity among academicians comes not so much from the possibility of a sudden rejection of that identity but rather from a diminished involvement in and commitment to the Jewish community. Gradually such commitment becomes less meaningful than commitment to one's profession and to the academic community. In the end commitment to the Jewish community may come to be replaced by commitment to the academic community, and to the value that the academic community places on universalism over particularism. That this is already reflected in Jewish academic families is suggested by a recent study of interreligious dating among college students. It was found that the group that considered itself most likely to intermarry were the children of academicians. Thus some 29 percent of Jewish students whose fathers were academicians considered it likely that they would intermarry in contrast to 16 percent of those from professional families, 11 percent of those from business families, and 9 percent of those from blue-collar families.[19] Furthermore, a larger proportion of Jewish students from academic families were participating in interreligious dating.[20]

In summary, Jews constitute a relatively small group in the total American population, though their numerical inferiority is to some extent compensated by their concentration in a handful of metropolitan areas. But perhaps the outstanding characteristic of their demographic situation is that despite the recency of their arrival in the United States, on such crucial indicators as secular education and occupation Jews rival the oldest and most successful segments of that privileged group which is sometimes invidiously referred to as the "WASPs." Even in their birth rate Jews resemble highly privileged segments of the Protestant group, such as the Episcopalians and the Presbyterians.

Jews, then, appear demographically to be old Americans; the educational level that they have achieved and the occupational profile that they present are more characteristic of an established segment of the population than of a new one. The recentness of Jewish arrival makes this accomplishment remarkable. It is the more spectacular considering the discrimination with which Jews have had to contend in the United States. And the rise appears even more amazing in the light of the persecution and demeaning treatment to which the Jew was subjected before he came to America, as well as by the attempted genocide of Jews in Europe. The latter event took place during the same period in which the rise was proceeding in the United States.

There is another side to the success of the American Jew. While the rise guaranteed that the group would not present problems of social disorganization it helped to bring in its wake serious problems of identity and continuity—problems that are in their own way as resistant to solution as the familiar pathologies that other minorities confront, such as poverty, educational deprivation, and family disorganization. As a consequence the demographic situation of American Jewry can be viewed from two contrasting perspectives: as a triumph over obstacles and an unmixed blessing, or as a success story filled with ominous implications for the future survival of the group.

Notes

[1] While general population statistics derive from official sources, Jewish population statistics generally originate from private sources. Most of the Jewish population statistics that we utilize

have been collected by the Council of Jewish Federations and Welfare Funds (CJFWF) and are published in the *American Jewish Year Book*. The statistics originate from the local affiliates of the CJFWF. In some cases local informants are also consulted. In only a relatively few instances are the statistics derived from an actual survey of Jewish population sponsored by a member federation. And when such surveys are implemented they do not routinely build-in the expensive and time-consuming procedures that assure population estimates of the highest quality. The problem is compounded by the fact that some of the largest communities have never been surveyed.

The question of the validity of Jewish population statistics is a reflection of the broader issue of the quality of the data that is available on American religious groups. In this respect the Jewish situation seems better than many others. If CJFWF population statistics are not by and large the result of local censuses they do appear to have greater validity than the material issued on behalf of certain other religious groups. At the very least the Jewish statistics are derived from the accumulated wisdom of the local federations. These agencies are well-organized, they conduct annual fund-raising campaigns, and the question of population-size is of considerable interest to them.

However, confidence in the validity of CJFWF population statistics is decreased by the upward trend that they indicate. From what we know of the birth rate, death rate, and net migration rate, it seems unlikely that these factors not only balance out the impact of intermarriage, conversion, apostasy, and assimilation, but produce a population increase.

2 For a discussion of some of these factors see Erich Rosenthal in *Future Directions of American Jewish Life and Their Implications for Jewish Community Centers* (Proceedings of a Conference Sponsored by the National Association of Jewish Center Workers and the National Jewish Welfare Board, Lakewood, N.J., January 6–9, 1963), pp. 49–63.

3 In November 1943 the Immigration and Naturalization Service discontinued the practice of ascertaining the identity of Jews. (For an analysis of the issue see Yiddish Scientific Institute— YIVO, *The Classification of Jewish Immigrants and its Implications: A Survey of Opinion* [New York: YIVO, 1945].) Since 1943 Jewish migration statistics have been supplied by United HIAS Service and are based on the number of immigrants aided by this organization. HIAS assists in only one relocation. However, an undetermined number of Jews enter the United States on a second, and hence privately financed, relocation. Also, some Jews

coming to the United States do not seek agency assistance. Thus recent immigration statistics are minimal estimates and the dependence on migration during recent years is greater than indicated in Table 3.

4 For details about the studies cited here see Calvin Goldscheider, "Fertility of the Jews," *Demography*, 4, No. 1 (1967), 196–209.

5 *AJYB*, 69 (1968), 284.

6 There is evidence that suggests that very small Jewish communities—generally consisting of a handful of merchants and one or more professional men—are sharply on the decline. Their decline can be traced to assimilation, to young people who settle in other places, and to families who move to larger communities in order to rear their children in a more Jewish environment.

7 See Alter F. Landesman, *Brownsville: The Birth, Development and Passing of a Jewish Community in New York* (New York: Bloch Publishing Co., 1969).

8 Alfred Kazin, *A Walker in the City* (New York: Harcourt, Brace and Co., 1951), p. 60.

9 The stress of Hasidim on cultural transmission has meant that greater rigidity must be introduced into the cultural system. For example, since arriving in America many Hasidic groups have instituted stricter rules with respect to the separation of the sexes. Their justification is that the American environment is more erotically stimulating than the environment they knew in eastern Europe.

10 It should be noted that some foreign-born Jews may have received some secular education in the course of receiving a Jewish education. And even those without any secular education had been exposed to intellectual training by virtue of their Jewish education.

11 Some of the native-born Jewish respondents are the children of out-of-towners. New York City probably attracts a disproportionately large group of native-born, well-educated Jewish immigrants. On the other hand the survey minimizes the educational level of the native-born, for the sample is limited to the city itself. The city appears to have a larger proportion of native-born persons with limited education than would be true for the metropolitan area as a whole.

12 One of the most sensitive autobiographies of this type of Jewish academic is Morris Raphael Cohen's *A Dreamer's Journey* (Boston: Beacon Press, 1949).

13 The most suggestive statement can be found in "Under Forty:

A Symposium on American Literature and the Younger Generation of American Jews" which appeared in the *Contemporary
Jewish Record*, 7, No. 1 (February 1944), 3–36 and in the sym-
posium "Jewishness and the Younger Intellectuals," which ap-
peared in *Commentary*, 31, No. 4 (April 1961), 306–359. For
a sociological statement from the same perspective see Melvin
M. Tumin's article "Conservative Trends in American Jewish
Life," *Judaism*, 13, No. 2 (Spring 1964), 131–142; reprinted
in Peter I. Rose [ed.], *The Ghetto and Beyond: Essays on Jewish
Life in America* (New York: Random House, 1969), pp. 69–82.
For a sociological study from this perspective see Judith R.
Kramer and Seymour Leventman, *Children of the Gilded Ghetto*
(New Haven: Yale University Press, 1961). See also Leventman,
"From Shtetl to Suburb," in Rose, *op. cit.*, pp. 33–56.

14 Quoted in Nathan Glazer et al., *The Characteristics of American
Jews* (New York: Jewish Education Committee Press, 1965),
p. 21.

15 These figures are calculated from data in Nathan Goldberg,
Occupational Patterns of American Jewry (New York: Jewish
Teachers Seminary and People's University Press, 1947), pp.
15–16. The data are based on material from the 1900 United
States Census and refer to immigrants from the Russian empire
living in cities of 250,000 or more. As Goldberg demonstrates
the great majority of such immigrants were Jewish.

16 Since the category "managers and proprietors" is not comparable
with the one used in 1900, a comparison cannot be made.

17 In some cases the effects of occupational mobility are distinct
from educational mobility but frequently the two are strongly
related.

18 See Harold L. Wilensky and Jack Ladinsky, "From Religious
Community to Occupational Group: Structural Assimilation
Among Professors, Lawyers, and Engineers," *American Sociological Review*, 32, No. 4 (August 1967), 541–561. This article
contains significant data and interpretations of the effect of
occupation and work setting on religious identity. Wilensky and
Ladinsky also suggest that such effects must be understood in
the light of the processes of self-selection and anticipatory
socialization. Further work on the problem will involve sys-
tematic consideration of these processes.

19 David Caplowitz and Harry Levy, *Interreligious Dating Among
College Students* (Processed, Bureau of Applied Social Research,
Columbia University, 1965), p. 53.

20 *Ibid.*, p. 41.

Chapter 3 ◉ Family
and Identity

Hardly a month passes without the appearance of a new work of fiction that in one way or another deals with the Jewish family. The popularity of the subject has produced treatments of the Jewish family on many levels of sophistication and taste. As a consequence a number of what may generously be called humorous books on the Jewish family have appeared. However vulgar these books may be, they seem to have one feature in common with serious works of fiction about the Jewish family: the mother is portrayed as the most imposing and threatening member of the family; the central problem of the book is the child's struggle to emancipate himself from her domination.[1]

The very abundance of such interpretations underlines the paucity of substantial research studies on the American-Jewish family. The lack of social science treatments, in turn, makes it difficult to place the fictional literature in perspective. The reason for the dearth of social science writing is clear: the Jewish family constellation has not created social problems in the general society. In fact it has done just the opposite: the Jewish family seems to have solved problems rather than caused them. And the foremost problem that it has solved is that of motivating the young toward achievement.

There are those who claim that the price has been too high —that such achievement has been purchased at the cost of sound mental health. While a "Moynihan Report" on the Jewish family would certainly focus on the problem of emotional disorder, it is dubious that it would be able to demonstrate that the Jewish family structure is a serious threat to mental health. For example, one large scale study has indicated that while

Catholics and Protestants exceed Jews in the most favorable mental health category, Jews are found less frequently in categories where symptoms are severe enough to impair normal functioning.[2] Instead of emphasizing the presence of neurotic elements in Jewish family life the authors suggest ". . . the possible presence in the family unit of an impairment-limiting mechanism that operates to counteract or contain in some degree the most pathogenic life stresses."[3]

Without additional studies both from the perspective of the humanities as well as from the social sciences, we cannot proceed as confidently as we would like. However, while it is not incumbent upon us to complete the task of analyzing the Jewish family—and the relationship between family, personal identity, and group belongingness—neither are we free to desist from making a beginning.

The Obligation of Marriage and Family Life

Just as it is difficult to separate the ethnic and religious components of Jewish identity, any attempt to divide sacred and secular in the Jewish family is a delicate business. In Jewish tradition marriage and family life is not viewed as a compromise between the holy and the profane, between the spirit and the flesh, between the requirement to perpetuate this world and the need to prepare for the next. Rather, to marry and to establish a family is a *mitzvah*, a religious commandment. To perform a *mitzvah* is also to do good and to increase the supply of happiness in the world. And, according to traditional conceptions, the performance of a *mitzvah* adds to one's merits for the world to come.

In Jewish culture the obligation of marriage and family life is prescribed for everyone. Even he who aspires to the very highest levels of spirituality is commanded to marry; if he does not do so his spirituality is suspect. One scholar formulates the Jewish tradition in the following terms:

> Marriage is a wholesome fulfillment, a sacred bond, an inherent good, a divine command. . . . Marriage

in the Jewish view is the good, the normal, the ideal. For rabbi or laymen, for high priest or scholar or saint. . . .

Marriage is a step in the unfoldment of *homo religiosus*. It represents man's capacity to live beyond himself in perfect union with another. The ideal is to transcend oneself so that the *I* encompasses the married partner in mutual love. It is a significant step in the life-long religious task of an ever expanding circumference of self-investment.[4]

So firm is this view that widows or widowers who are past the age of fertility, and who no longer experience insistent sexual urges, are perfectly free to remarry. There is nothing gauche in their behavior. Rather, by their marriage they are acting in the way that good Jews should.

For a modern industrial society an extraordinary proportion of the American population marry. Because both the general culture and traditional Jewish culture encourage marriage we would expect that, all other things being equal, a large proportion of the Jewish population would marry. The case of New York City offers an excellent opportunity to study this matter. Although the availability of endogamous mates is greater there than any other place, we find that in the age group of twenty to thirty-four years native-born Jews rank higher than any other ethnic group in the proportion who have never been married: a total of 48.1 percent are single. But in the thirty-five to forty-nine age group they rank the lowest: a mere 3.4 percent have never been married. (Foreign-born Jews achieve an even lower figure: 2.4 percent of them have never been married.) Thus native-born Jews marry later than their peers but when they reach what they consider an appropriate age they outdistance all others. And they prevail despite the handicap of their educational attainments, for the higher the level of education the stronger is the tendency to remain single. Furthermore, their behavior is all the more remarkable if it is assumed that a pattern of late marriage should work to reduce the chances of marrying.[5]

American Jews, then, still observe the Jewish commandment to marry. However, the basis of their marriages is more
in keeping with the norms that they have learned in the
United States rather than those of their tradition. The position of traditional culture is clarified by the person of the
shadchan (marriage broker). Although a favorite butt of
Jewish humor his role reveals a great deal about the stance
of traditional Jewish culture toward love and marriage. *Shad-
chanut* is based upon the presumption that marriage is both
a religious obligation and a rational decision. Any two decent
people can marry: it is not the attraction between boy and girl
that is paramount but the suitability of their family lines.
Marriage is an alliance between families rather than an
arrangement between two individuals. In sum, the idea of
romantic love is deviant rather than normative in Jewish
culture.

Arranged marriage—as typified by the *shadchan* as well
as by his many amateur competitors—could exist only as long
as the idea of romantic love remained submerged. When Jews
became modernized romantic love surfaced and arranged marriage went underground. A leading historian characterizes the
shift to modernity as follows:

> Whereas in the traditional society, a couple who fell in
> love before getting married needed some moral-rational
> camouflage to justify their union, it was now the other
> way round; even marriage contracted solely on the basis
> of objective considerations were made to appear as if
> they had come about through the personal attraction of
> the couple to one another.[6]

There is no better instance of the shift in attitudes toward
marriage than that exemplified by Moses Mendelssohn (1729–
1786). The great leader of German Jewry during the period
of the transition to modernity, Mendelssohn sought to convince himself and others during his courtship that Cupid was
responsible for the match. He refused to follow rituals that
might associate him and his bride with the traditional pattern
of arranged marriage:

Mendelssohn . . . apparently was introduced to his future wife by mutual friends, but he later tried to give the impression that the match had come about entirely spontaneously. In seemingly trivial matters, such as refusing to undertake to give his bride gifts formally stipulated in advance and in ignoring the set style in writing to his betrothed, he wished to stress the personal element in everything pertaining to the marriage institution. In displaying this attitude, he departed, in any case, from accepted practice and rejected it in principle. In this, Mendelssohn was simply expressing the growing trend. Almost overnight marriages arranged by matchmakers lost their special propriety. They did not disappear, but they had to adapt themselves to the new ideal. The matchmaker had to do his work unobtrusively. The dowry became a matter negotiated behind the scenes, and the couple pretended to be a pair of lovers whom fate had thrown together.[7]

If traditional norms were unacceptable in Germany two centuries ago Jews of today can certainly be expected to reject anything that smacks of arranged marriage. Thus even the assistance of parents and relatives may be spurned, for the young person may feel that such assistance casts doubt upon his resourcefulness and attractiveness. In some cases help may not even be proffered, for native-born parents may have so thoroughly internalized the romantic-love ideal as to feel that it is inappropriate to intervene. But whether help is offered and rejected or not offered at all, the young person still experiences a pressure to marry from his family and friends. Those who find difficulty in locating a partner may be driven to utilizing the services of commercial organizations. Such organizations bring some order into the market; ironically, in the name of romantic love they provide a substitute for the professional or amateur *shadchan*. But because they operate outside of the concept of *mitzvah* and without entangling interpersonal alliances, they are free to perpetuate vulgarities and cruelties unknown in traditional society. According to *Newsweek* magazine:

. . . the Catskills' largest matchmaking mill drew a capacity 2,800 unattached men and women during its recent singles gathering. And while the high-rise Concord [a Catskill hotel] was stacking four stags to a room, more than 1,600 singles were camped in ersatz Tyrolean cottages at neighboring Grossinger's, the circuit's second largest stagorium. What it all proves once again is that the mating game is becoming the national pastime, and nowhere is it played with more military calculation—and quiet desperation—than on winter weekends in the Borscht Belt, less than 100 miles north of Times Square. . . .

A key confrontation on a singles weekend arrives with Saturday breakfast. In the Concord's stadium-size dining room . . . the atmosphere is as romantic as a bottling plant—but to singles it looks like the world's largest marriage factory. Accordingly, the master of their fates is maitre d' Irving Cohen, who decides who sits near whom. Cohen requires seconds to size up a stag's approximate age, education and motivation, then assigns the single to a table where tastes should be compatible. To help him keep track, Cohen identifies each guest with a color-coded peg stuck in a war plan of the dining room. . . .

In fact the mingling begins in the registration line on Friday night and continues compulsively through Sunday checkout when, according to Grossinger's veteran Richard Tepper "the girls practically have their phone numbers pasted on their foreheads."[8] (Copyright Newsweek, Inc., January 15, 1968)

Whatever the cruelties, the singles weekend provides an example of acculturated Jews who seek to respond to Jewish tradition and the American norm—both of which stress the desirability of marriage—as well as to conform to the ideal of romantic love. But as we shall see in Chapter 6, loyalty to the ideal of romantic love may at times mean disloyalty to the Jewish norm of endogamy. The singles weekend at a Catskill hotel is one of many arrangements designed to forestall this possibility—because the clientele is homogeneous it is possible to fall in love and at the same time to be assured that the object of one's affections will be a fellow Jew.

Family Size

Traditional Jewish culture emphasizes the desirability of the large family. Fathers and mothers of many children are esteemed. But as we noted in Chapter 2 the birth rate of American-Jewish women has been comparatively low. The process of family limitation among American Jews has its roots in the fertility behavior of the first generation. But it was not until the second generation that newer conceptions of family size made deep inroads. Accordingly, in the second generation the birth rate dropped so precipitously as to have serious implications for Jewish population size as well as for group continuity.

We do not know precisely how Jews managed to change so rapidly from the high fertility pattern that they followed in eastern Europe in the nineteenth century to the one that they adopted in the United States. The barriers against such a shift were formidable. There was the thrust of Jewish culture with its emphasis on the desirability of the large family. There was also the barrier of *halachah,* with its prohibition against mechanical contraception except in cases where prescribed reasons for its use could be adduced and rabbinic sanctions be obtained. It is apparent that these regulations were not only ignored by the Jewish public at large but were also violated by many who considered themselves observant Jews. Apparently, a particularly wide gap existed between the regulations of the Jewish sacred system with respect to birth control and the new self-conceptions developed by the American Jew.

The end result was that the topic of birth control became taboo in the Jewish community. Until very recently it was not discussed in the Jewish press, or from the pulpit or the lecture platform. Laymen avoided the question with rabbis and rabbis refrained from confronting laymen with it. When religious leaders did discuss the stance of Jewish tradition toward the use of contraceptive devices, their discussions were generally confined to the privacy of rabbinical conventions, technical journals, and collections of *responsa*. Each of the three wings of American Judaism treated the problem in its distinctive fashion. Reform rabbis ignored the problem of the relationship between fertility and Jewish survival and exempted the question of contraception from the area of the sacred, implying that a decision about family size was a private concern. Conservative leaders followed, but at a distance. Orthodox spokesmen could hardly go as far in the direction of secularization. Rather, they preferred to concentrate on other religious issues such as maintaining the practice of *kashrut*.

By the second generation Jews had won the reputation of being the most ardent and efficient contraceptors in the American population. Unlike sizeable numbers of Protestants and Catholics, they did not delay practicing contraception until after their first child had been born. Furthermore, they chose the most efficient means of contraception. Finally, they had fewer contraceptive failures than others. In one authoritative study Jewish contraceptive virtuosity so impressed the investigators that they used language unusual for traditionally reticent demographers:

> The degree to which Jewish couples practice more effective contraception than either Protestants or Catholics both in the periods preceding and following first pregnancy strains credulity. Not only do the Jewish couples of this sample rely more exclusively on the most effective methods, but they apparently manage these methods with unusual efficiency.[9]

One way to explain the modest fertility rate of the American Jew is to state that there is nothing exceptional about the Jewish birth rate—that it only appears to be small. Thus if certain factors that have an important bearing on fertility are controlled—urban residence, wife's educational attainment, husband's occupation, and family's social class—Jewish behavior would hardly deviate from the norm. In this view

Jewish exceptionalism is only a function of the Jewish demographic situation: Jews have so few children because they are so heavily urban, so high in social class and occupational rank, and so many of their women have been afforded educational advantages.

This approach has serious limitations. Not only is it questionable that this view can explain all of the variance between Jewish and Gentile fertility behavior but it does not tell us how Jews managed to disregard the teachings of Jewish tradition with respect to birth control. And even if such variance is explained, what have we proven? For example, if second-generation Jewish women had fewer children because they were so highly educated, we are still left with the question of why so many of them were given an education. Neither Jewish tradition nor the American culture to which their immigrant parents were exposed encouraged such high educational aspirations for females.

The other mode of approach is to argue that a Jewish component is significant in explaining low Jewish fertility. But what is this elusive component? A recent study utilizes a factor suggested several decades ago by Nathan Goldberg, a demographer who specializes in the area of Jewish studies.[10] According to this theory Jewish fertility is a function of Jewish status. Jews are discriminated against. They realize that they must surpass Gentiles if they are to compete with them. Furthermore, their minority status induces feelings of insecurity. The net result is that they defer marriage, and when they do marry they have small families. They have so few children because they feel the need to give each child maximum advantages, thus enabling their offspring to compete with the more fortunately situated Gentiles.

There are many objections to this theory. If it were correct, Jews in Israel who are the sociological opposite-numbers of American Jews should have a considerably higher birth rate. But in spite of living in a country where Jews are the majority and thus need have no fear of suffering discrimination, the birth rate of such Israelis is not very different from that of their American cousins.

A more tenable explanation has been offered. It suggests

that low Jewish fertility is a result of mobility drive rather than of minority status. According to one sociologist:

> A relationship between low fertility and rapid social mobility has been postulated in the theory of social capillarity, according to which a family must be small if it is to rise in the social scale. The Princeton Fertility Study is the first to reveal empirically the operation of social capillarity in the Jewish case, finding that a major factor governing the fertility behavior of the Jewish couples in the sample survey was "a perceived incompatibility between sending children to college and having large families." Low fertility, therefore, has been an important means for rising in the social and economic scale for Jews.[11]

Unless we contend, as an advocate of the previous theory might, that Jews are interested in rising precisely because they constitute a minority, we must examine the operation of social and cultural factors to explain mobility drives. If we extend the perspective of Nathan Glazer and others we might hypothesize that Jews have been so driving because psychologically they already belonged to the middle class. In an American setting where economic opportunities prevailed, Jews were driven to achieve in class position what they had already achieved in culture. At the first opportunity they proceeded to enter the middle class.

The size of the Jewish family is no doubt related to the drive for social mobility. But while mobility drive may be a necessary condition for moving from a large family orientation to a small one, it is not sufficient to explain the shift. We must consequently look at changing self-conceptions, focusing particularly on changing conceptions of self held by the Jewish woman.

In explaining why she has fewer children than her mother, as well as a smaller family than her Gentile counterpart, the Jewish woman—particularly those of the second generation where the smallest families are encountered—generally espouses the argument that she wants to give each child what he is entitled to: a maximum of love, attention, and advantages. In a sense the mother maintains that she has so few children because she loves children so much.

It cannot be assumed that the explanation for fertility behavior lies in the woman's altruistic desires for her children's welfare—a more revealing line of inquiry is to analyze what she wants for herself. Traditionally the Jewish woman has seen herself as a maternal figure whose status derived from her role as mother and homemaker. Within the short space of a generation a decisive change took place. Instead of "living for her children" as the expression had it, the Jewish woman of the second generation "owed it to herself" to receive an education, to develop personal grooming, to build social relationships with friends as well as with kin, to interest herself in organizational activity, to travel, and (for a much smaller group) to pursue an advanced degree and/or a career.[12]

All of these new needs which the Jewish woman so speedily developed were discrepant with the large family pattern. In a sense she now "owed it to herself" *not* to have a large family. A large family would inhibit social mobility of course, but more to the point it would prevent the achievement of certain new personal aspirations. A large family would mean continued subordination to the demands of others; it would interfere with self-realization. Thus a new orientation to the role of motherhood was developed—to be the mother of a large family was to be a beast of burden, an animal yoked to the treadmill, a primitive.

While a new image of the female role evolved, the Jewish woman was unprepared to complete her liberation. She did not wish to forgo the status of mother. Not only did personality needs impel her to have children, but motherhood was also a status esteemed in the general culture. Furthermore, Jewish culture had left its mark upon her. Jewish culture considers childlessness a grave affliction, even a punishment. It is beyond belief that anyone would choose to be childless.

The Jewish woman proceeded to square her new desires with her cultural background. Hence the ideal of a small family was born—a family that preferably had two children, hopefully a boy and a girl. Some were even content with a single child. In either case the ideal of a small family would allow the woman to consider herself a Jewish wife and mother and at the same time fulfill her needs for education, relaxation, career, and display.

If the downward trend in fertility that the second generation woman evidenced had continued, Jews would now constitute even less than their present 2.92 percent of the American population. Sometime around World War II the downward trend was arrested. In fact, during the post-World War II era, Jewish fertility—which has come to be increasingly based on the reproductive behavior of the third generation—showed a moderate rise over previous decades. The three-child family became as respectable as one- and two-child families. Some couples even surpassed the ceiling of three children, thereby risking the disapproval of their middle-aged or elderly parents. However, because of the deficit resulting from the fertility pattern of an earlier generation, as well as because of the impact of other processes such as assimilation, higher birth rates have not meant a rise in overall Jewish population.

Why do some Jews today have **more** children than did their parents? Is their decision connected with Jewishness in the sense that they have undergone a reevaluation of their religious principles? Are they affirming a desire for group survival? While such motives cannot be entirely discounted, the somewhat higher fertility of younger Jews does not appear to be connected with Jewishness in any direct sense. In fact a case can be made for precisely the opposite conclusion. The fertility of younger Jews can be seen as related to a higher level of acculturation rather than a more intensive Jewishness. From this perspective when younger Jews have more children than their parents it is because they are more "American," more suburban than urban. Among the things that they have adopted from the general culture is its family size.

An additional perspective is provided by the fact that many younger Jews are born into the middle class and hence do not have to strive to achieve a desirable position. They do not connect social mobility with the small family pattern. Indeed, it would be unrealistic of them to do so; limiting family size to one or two children is hardly the way to move from the middle class to the upper class. Added to these social perspectives there is a possible psychological factor: some younger parents who are the offspring of small families may feel negatively about the experience. Having grown up in the intense atmosphere of a one- or two-child household they prefer to avoid rearing their own children in such a setting. This leads us, then, to the all-important topic of the relationship between parents and children in the Jewish family.

Parents and Children

The image of Jewish family life that exists in popular culture suggests that there is great warmth between parents and children and that the parent-child relationship is characterized by respect and affection. Families are closely knit, observing Jewish holidays and rituals together. Families are stable and sober. They care about each other.

Fictional treatments validate the idea of closeness but many novelists view the Jewish family from an entirely different perspective. While they see closeness they fasten upon its neurotic aspect. The parent—infected with the disease of closeness—passes it on to his child. The child, once infected, is condemned to a life of guilt as he tries to attain responsible adulthood and fulfill his desire for independence. He may seek emancipation from guilt feelings through psychoanalysis or other forms of therapy, but parents, and particularly his mother, have left their mark upon him. The most that he can hope for is that the chain will be broken in the next generation, thus enabling his children to be free of the guilt feelings that he must bear.

It is safe to say that the normative Jewish family is neither the cozily secure unit suggested by the popular stereotype nor the hotbed of neurosis characterized by certain novelists. In fact we might ask if there is anything really distinctive about the Jewish family. It is possible to respond with the same answer that some give as the explanation of Jewish fertility behavior, namely that given the particular socioeconomic level that Jews occupy there is nothing exceptional in their behavior. Thus the American Jewish family can be viewed as a hybrid of the American middle class family. From this perspective the general public becomes interested in the revelations of the Jewish writer or in the barbed wit of the Jewish comedian because marginality permits Jewish writers and comedians to see their own families in an especially penetrating manner. The public experiences the shock of recognition because the Jewish families being portrayed are so much like those found generally in the American middle class.

The other perspective is to view the American Jewish family as having a much more distinctive form. In this view the Jewish family is not simply one more version of the American middle class family. Rather, it is a version of the *Jewish* family that happens to have certain distinctive American characteristics. The actors in the family drama may be unaware of their distinctiveness: they may not realize that the roles that they play have historical antecedents, and they may be only dimly aware of the fact that they differ from their suburban neighbors. This second perspective—that views the family as having continuity with the Jewish past—seems the more profitable way of understanding the American Jewish family.

The American middle class family has been compared to a pad from which the child is launched into adulthood. Of course it is difficult for the parent to arrange for the launching of his child. But however great the psychological drain his duty is to proceed, for he and the child are two distinct entities. If the parent succeeds in his role, he arranges a launching that results in the child going into his own distinctive orbit. Yet this orbit should cross that of the parent on certain occasions and at stated intervals. For example, it is desirable for adult children to spend holidays such as Thanksgiving or Christmas with their parents. But if this is difficult communication by telephone will substitute. In any case, the thrust of the family system is the emphasis on the distinction between the generations and the establishment of mutual independence.

In the Jewish family we see much more emphasis on extension rather than distinction. Parents and children are not really distinct entities. For example, an injury to the child is an injury to the parents. In fact, it is often felt that the injury would have been better visited upon the parents. Since the child is by definition weak and foolish, the injury could be better sustained by the parent, who is by definition strong and wise. Furthermore, there is an emphasis on providing nutrition for the child so that he will be able to cope with the environment. However physically vigorous the child may be (and however debilitated the parent) the child is seen as dependent. And as masterful as the child may be when he achieves maturity, he is viewed as lacking the experience and wisdom that his parents possess. Regardless of age children remain children.

The emphasis on keeping the child emotionally dependent and the tendency toward extension rather than distinction does not result in a powerless child however. These very factors give the child the opportunity to tip the balance of power within the family in his favor. The irony of extension is that the parent may become dependent on the child; if the child is an extension of the parent then the good reputation of the parent rests upon his success in rearing his children. However eminent the parent may be in his business or profession and however high his status in the community, if he does not succeed as a parent he is an abject failure.

The clue to parental dependence is supplied by the word *nachas,* a Hebrew term for pleasure or gratification.[13] While it is possible to receive *nachas* in many ways, there is only one true and abiding source of *nachas:* that which is received from children. Or put another way, if one does not have *nachas fun kinder* all other pleasures and gratifications are empty. Thus by their power to either give or withhold *nachas,* children are transmuted from a condition of powerlessness to one of overwhelming strength. Since only he can supply *nachas* the child has the power to consign the parent to a life of quiet desperation.

The parent is sensitive to the threat however. Seeking to assure himself *nachas* he tries to stimulate its production.

Thus he offers the child what are sometimes termed the "advantages" or, in common American-Jewish parlance "everything," as in the expression: "they gave their son everything." "Everything" means the best of everything from the necessities to the luxuries: it includes clothing, medical attention, entertainment, vacations, schools, and myriad other items. It does not include love or attention, for it is taken for granted that the child is being given emotional support. By being open-handed, by sacrificing for the child, the parent reduces his vulnerability. After all, only an ingrate would withhold *nachas* from a generous parent. And if *nachas* is withheld, then it is clear to everyone that it is the child who is the aggressor and the parent who is the innocent party. The parent who lacks *nachas* has at least this one small bit of consolation.

Those on the other side of the ethnic fence—the Gentiles —may esteem togetherness but at the same time they are critical of the Jewish family. Having a less dependent relationship with their children and lacking a *nachas*-oriented culture, they see the Jew as engaged in spoiling his child. They fear that in the process he may spoil their own offspring, who may come to demand the same advantages bestowed upon his Jewish peers. And if the Gentile lives with the fiction that he is continuing to follow the simple ways of his rural and small-town ancestors, he may project onto the Jew the responsibility for those permissive aspects of contemporary culture that undercut this older life. Particularly in the better suburbs where patterns of child-rearing are of central concern, objective differences in child-rearing patterns can become indistinguishable from anti-Jewish stereotypes. All of these trends are present among Gentiles in Lakeville:

A young housewife who is living among Jews for the first time observes that "the few Jewish children I've met are kings and queens of their house." A Catholic who recently moved to Lakeville makes this criticism: "I don't think that Jewish children are being prepared for life in a heterogeneous community. They are taught that they are the 'chosen people' and not disciplined, and they're always Mama's angel." Young Jewish children in Lakeville are almost invariably believed to be spoiled by an overly generous allowance and an unlimited supply of playthings, indulgences which in turn engender a false sense of superiority. . . . The complaints on this score proliferate. The Jewish child who receives a dollar allowance at the age of five; the Jewish teenagers who drive their own Thunderbirds . . . give lavish parties, are waited on hand and foot by servants, and judge their Gentile peers accordingly. Meanwhile, the children of our respondents are made unhappy or else have their own values distorted by the Jewish example. As a well-informed businessman who has lived in Lakeville all his life sums up the matter: "There is a heightened sense of competition within the schools. It's more bad than good. It's competition directed toward the material ends rather than toward education for education's sake. Competition shows itself again in possession of the material things. It creates competition with a distorted sense of values. My daughter came home from a Jewish home and asked why we didn't have seven telephones." [14]

Despite its special character the structure of parent-child relationships in the Jewish family is fated to move toward the American middle class family model, with its stress on distinction rather than extension and on the mutual independence of parents and children. The source of such a change is more than a pervasive acculturation or a simple imitation of Gentile models. Rather, it emanates from two specific sources. The first is the high educational level of Jews. Such education frequently produces an urbanity and sophistication that takes a dim view of traditional family relationships and is very much at odds with Jewish parents' orientation to *nachas*. Efforts to stimulate *nachas* are regarded as a crude form of bribery. The second source that works to undermine older patterns is the sympathy of Jews toward modern psychology, especially with regard to its utility as a therapeutic technique. Of all segments of the American population Jews display the greatest faith in psychotherapy and make the most extensive use of it.[15] Because all schools of psychological thought stress the reduction of dependence (whether on the part of parents or children) they are necessarily critical of the structure of the Jewish family and of its special culture.[16]

Whatever new relationships may be predicted, the cohesion of the Jewish family has been remarkable, especially considering the presence of extraordinary potentials for estrangement among its members. The most obvious of such forces is the process of social mobility, which has been so rapid among Jews. Mobility can estrange father and son, grandfather and grandchild, uncle and nephew. There is no doubt that mobility greatly complicated the relationship between the first generation and the second. Although this older type of intergenerational stress may no longer be as large a threat as before, there is still the problem of intragenerational estrangement: members of the same family may have different rates of mobility, and such differentials may serve to estrange siblings or to complicate the relationship between cousins. In sum, while social mobility has placed strains on the Jewish family, considering the potential of its disruptive effects the Jewish family has retained a surprising degree of closeness.

A second, and related source of estrangement, is educational mobility. As we have seen Jews are now among the best educated segments of the American population despite their comparatively recent arrival in the United States. Enormous educational contrasts between generations have become commonplace in the Jewish community: an imigrant who lacked a grammar school diploma might have a son or daughter who attained a bachelor's, master's, or doctoral degree. And it was even less exceptional for second generation parents who possessed only a grammar school or high school diploma to have an offspring with similarly high educational achievements. Again, however painful the conflicts that educational mobility engendered, such mobility does not seem to have severed the relationship between the generations.

A third source of strain is the generation gap, which exists in all modern countries. Because cultural norms are always changing, parent and child are hardly ever socialized in precisely the same milieu. For immigrant groups the sharpest generation gap is experienced by the first and second generations. The immigrant has been socialized in a "foreign" culture. While he may adapt himself to the new culture the values of the old one are deeply imprinted on his personality. The child, however, carries little such cultural baggage, for his socialization takes place in the new culture. So wide is the gap between the generations that normal socialization processes are upset. Instead of the parent being the master of the cultural milieu and introducing the child to it, the process is reversed: the child is the master and consequently serves as cultural mentor to his parents.

The problem of the generation gap is of course not specific to the Jewish group. However, it seems reasonable to assume that the gap was particularly wide in the Jewish community, considering that the religious component of Jewish culture has roots in the East rather than the West. Gentile immigrants had at least been socialized in a Western culture and the religious component in their culture was generally closer to American norms than was true for the Jewish group.

In addition to the generation gap and the potentially disruptive forces of social and educational mobility, some Jews have been exposed to additional source of strain with respect to family cohesion: the threat of radical politics. The threat of radical politics to family unity resides in the fact that the child comes to participate in a world that is different from that of his parents. Family unity can even be undermined in cases where the parent is sympathetic to his child's political orientation. The requirement that the radical "live his politics" means that the child must set family loyalty aside: his primary obligation is to his movement rather than to his parents. In extreme cases the movement begins to function as a surrogate family. Inevitably, the ties which bind the individual to his kin are loosened.

Jewish radicals are not typically the children of conservative parents. Many radicals of the second generation, for example, were the offspring of leftists immigrants and have consequently been termed "red-diaper babies." Ironically, in such cases family unity might be threatened by a child who became acculturated to American norms and hence turned conservative! Nevertheless, the Jewish radicals of the Depression era were predominantly members of the second generation who, if anything, were more consciously radical than their parents. But whatever the similarities or distinctions between the generations there is nothing to suggest that such radicals severed their relationships with their parents or with their extended kin. Again we find an instance of high vulnerability, but an apparent survival of kinship bonds.

Will the New Left accomplish what the Old Left did not? It is too early to make any definitive assessment of the impact of contemporary radicalism on the Jewish family. While it is apparent that present-day Jewish students participate in radical movements on the campus as did the previous generation, we know little about the manner in which they relate to their families, and how they compare in this respect with their Gentile peers. In the absence of definitive research our assumption is that Jewish student radicals have not severed their ties with their parents, or Jewish parents with their radical children.

Mark Rudd, formerly the leader of the Students for a Democratic Society at Columbia University, provides a dramatic illustration of the Jewish student radical who desires to revolutionize society while at the same time seeking to continue a relationship with his middle class parents. Rudd in fact developed his early politics in the womb of his family: "My grandmother owned a candy store in the Central Ward of Newark, and I used to visit her all the time. The area was turning black and I was stunned by the poverty."[17] During high school days Rudd ". . . urged his father to pay his Negro employees higher wages. . . ." While developing contempt for his high school (the Columbia High School of Maplewood, New Jersey) and for his suburb, which he derided as populated by individuals whose only concerns were money and comfort, Rudd's scorn never extended to his parents. According to a reporter who interviewed him in 1968: "Mark Rudd speaks of his parents with respect and affection."

Columbia officials viewed Rudd as the complete revolutionary, a kind of later-day Lenin. The then vice-president and provost of the university, David Truman, characterized Rudd as follows:

> He is totally unscrupulous and morally very dangerous. He is an extremely capable, ruthless, cold-blooded guy. He's a combination of a revolutionary and an adolescent having a temper tantrum. No one has ever made him or his friends look over the abyss. It makes me uncomfortable to sit in the same room with him.

But to his mother Mark Rudd was a source of *nachas*—a devoted son who had not forgotten his family:

> Mrs. Jacob Rudd pointed out the picture window of her brick ranch house to a colorful rock garden. "My revolutionary helped me plant those tulips last November, my rebel," she said with motherly pride.

Since Rudd could not leave the barricades at Columbia in the spring of 1968 and return home to celebrate Mother's Day, the family held their reunion on Morningside Heights:

> On Mother's day, last weekend, his parents went to the Columbia campus and brought a veal parmigiana dinner, which the family ate in their parked car on Amsterdam Avenue.

However deeply felt this scene, Rudd's subsequent career as a Weatherman illustrates the threat of New Left politics to the unity of the Jewish family. Wanted by the police in connection with a series of bombing episodes, Rudd is no longer able to participate in family celebrations even should he wish to do so. As a hunted man, loyalty to his movement must inevitably replace his older attachment to his family. Rudd's fellow Weathermen in fact now constitute his family, for it is to them that he must look for sustenance, protection, and emotional support.

Kinship Relationships

The ideal household of the American Jew, like that of the middle class generally, consists of parents and their minor children. While children may continue to interact with their parents after marriage they do not continue residence in the parental home. The three-generation household common in Europe, which consisted of grandparents, parents, and children, is rejected by the American Jew.

When the household does not conform to the parent-minor children prototype, the resulting ambiguity may make the actors unsure of themselves; they may experience guilt feelings and become hostile toward each other. One such problem was alluded to earlier: the son or daughter who reaches adulthood but is unmarried. Such an offspring must decide whether to continue living at home or to establish an independent household. If the child remains at home he is a source of embarrassment; his singleness suggests that the parent has failed in some way. If the child opts for his own household he is also a source of embarrassment. According to traditional conceptions a household consisting of a single young adult is not a valid family unit.

Another source of strain is created by aged, infirm, or widowed parents. The passing of the tradition of the three-generation household, as well as the lengthening of the life span, forces a resolution of the problem of whether children should invite their parents to live with them. Many apparently prefer that their parents continue to live apart from' them. This conclusion is suggested by the rapid increase of homes for the Jewish aged sponsored by Jewish communal bodies and by commercial interests, and by the proliferation of other arrangements such as hotels for senior citizens catering to a Jewish clientele. The only other possibility—doubtful at best—is that the great majority of aged persons who reside in such settings have been invited by their children but have rejected such hospitality. In any case, according to traditional norms parents and adult children should form a single household. The child is obligated to care for his aged parents and institutional care is appropriate only for the childless or for those parents who have been unlucky enough to have their children predecease them.

The problem of what obligations are owed to aged parents is of course a general one in contemporary life. Ambiguities in this connection among Jews should not be interpreted as meaning that Jewish kinship relationships are rapidly withering away. It cannot be assumed that if the child does not personally shoulder the responsibility for the care of aged parents that his relationship with more remote kin is nonexistent. For example, considering the class level and educational status of most American Jews, the concentration of extended kin who reside in the same communities seems remarkable. Furthermore, the amount and intensity of interaction among such persons reaches extraordinary levels. One investigation in a well-to-do suburb of Chicago found that 78 percent of the Jews, in contrast to 14 percent of the Protestants and 35 percent of the Catholics, had at least twelve households of kin in the metropolitan area. Moreover, some 71 percent of the Jews, in contrast to 16 percent of the Protestants and 33 percent of the Catholics, reported regular interaction with at least five households of such kin.[18] It is not unreasonable to suggest, then, that Norman Rockwell's sentimental pictures of kinship gatherings that appeared for many years in *The Saturday Evening Post* might now more properly depict a Jewish rather than a WASP family. While familism is comparatively absent among middle class Protestants who reside in giant metropolitan areas it is very much present among Jews.

However, some Jews who are amply endowed with relatives living close-by do not espouse the values of familism. An avant-garde exists that believes that kinship obligations should be confined primarily to the nuclear family. Rather than viewing interaction with the extended family as a form of gratification these individuals feel it to be an imposition that arbitrarily limits freedom of choice. They believe that extended-family obligations restrict the full development of individual interests and stunt the growth of a mature personality.

A study of the attitudes of the social work staff and of the clientele of the Jewish Family Service of New York highlights the gulf that separates this avant-garde from other Jews.[19] Clients of this agency are predominantly lower middle class. A sizeable minority pursue working class occupations. Their educational attainments are modest by Jewish standards: only 7 percent have studied for an advanced degree. The parental backgrounds of the social workers are rather similar to that of their clients but they have had very different life experiences. All of the social workers have studied for an advanced degree. Their occupational conditions differ radically from those whom they serve. Furthermore, in keeping with the emphasis of many Jewish family agencies they are strongly oriented to psychiatric counseling and see themselves primarily as therapists.[20]

We find that while 63 percent of the clients of the Jewish Family Service of New York agree with the statement "It's selfish for someone to cut himself off from his relatives," only 16 percent of the social workers feel the same way. And relatively few of the social workers evince any enthusiasm for efforts to maintain or increase the cohesion of the extended family. Some 58 percent of the clients agree with the statement "It is a thing of pride and joy to have a family circle or cousins club," but only 16 percent of the social workers feel the same way.[21] Social workers would thus magnify individualism at the expense of extended-kinship relationships. (They would also favor limiting certain involvements with and obligations to immediate kin.) Whatever the extent to which such values are transmitted to clients and succeed in moving them away from familistic orientations, the social workers demonstrate that there is a segment of the Jewish group which prefers a family pattern similar to that of middle and upper class Protestants.

To be sure, the social workers are not entirely consistent; considering their ideology, they are more involved with their relatives than they should be. For example, some 53 percent of them have taken more trips and vacations with kin than with friends.[22] And when the chips are down they prefer to turn to family rather than friends. Asked who they would want to take care of their own minor children in the case of their death, 83 percent of the social workers said that they would prefer kin rather than friends, despite the knowledge that their kin would surely not be capable of rearing their children in as enlightened a manner as their friends.[23]

While members of the avant-garde do not sever family ties, nevertheless their lack of affirmation of the extended-family idea cannot be dismissed lightly. Despite the fact that Jews have such high rates of family interaction, these rates are noticeably lower than before. The decline is most conspicuous in the upper class and the upper reaches of the middle class. The Lakeville study is instructive in this connection:

> . . . while the change [toward less interaction with family members] represents a long-range development in the social order, the surprising thing is that even the present Lakeville generation has witnessed a measurable shift in familial interaction. When our respondents were children 39 per cent of their parents spent more time socializing with relatives than with their friends. Only some 5 per cent of our respondents, however, spend more time with relatives than with their friends. And the children of our respondents will apparently be even less family minded. While some 59 per cent of our respondents saw their cousins more than once a month when they were children and 46 per cent did so at least once each week, the comparable figures for the children of our respondents are 38 per cent and 22 per cent, respectively.[24]

While the shift to interaction with friends rather than with relatives is magnified in Lakeville where the very prosperous and the very well-educated predominate, it is apparent that even the horizons of those situated on the middle and lower rungs of the Jewish social and educational ladder are no longer confined entirely to the world of the family. Thus only 29 percent of the clientele of the Jewish Family Service of

New York agree with the statement "One usually has more in common with relatives than friends." And only 32 percent agree with the traditional sentiment that "Friends can't give you the love you can get from relatives."[25] Although they are family-centered these working and lower middle class Jews are aware of the difference of the kinship pattern in the general culture from their own. It appears that although they are very much family-centered, they hesitate to advance the claim that their pattern of family relations is superior to that of the general culture.

The Transmission of Identity

However significant all of these changes are for the evolving character of the Jewish family, they have their most profound implications in connection with the transmission of Jewish identity. The extended family that interacts regularly and follows a pattern of mutual assistance and mutual obligation constitutes a kind of natural community. One may acquire Jewish identity by being reared in such a community and partaking of its interactions, obligations, and celebrations. One's Jewishness flows out of the fact that all members of the extended family are Jewish. Furthermore, Jewish friends and neighbors help to reinforce what the kinship group has already taught—that the family is a microcosm of the Jewish people and that, conversely, the Jewish people comprise a kind of huge extended family.

The changing significance of the family, and particularly the fairly recent declines in the frequency and intensity of interaction with the kinship group, means that identity can no longer be acquired solely through this traditional institution. But new forms do arise as substitutes. The friendship clique comprised of Jews is one example. However, while the clique may serve as an equivalent identification function for adults it generally cannot do so for the young. A close parental friend may sometimes become a friend of the family as well, but the relationship of the friend to the child is generally not of sufficient intensity and longevity to be a substantial factor in identity-formation

An additional reason why the family can no longer serve as the natural community for Jews involves the relatively new practice of intermarriage, which is discussed in Chapter 6. The number of families in which the extended kinship group is religiously and ethnically homogeneous is sharply on the decline; because of intermarriage Gentiles are now found in the majority of extended Jewish families. Furthermore, intermarried couples do not invariably sever their ties with Jewish kin, and Jewish kin do not respond in keeping with tradition—they do not invariably exclude the intermarried. While it is entirely possible that the maintenance of kinship ties may prevent or retard the assimilation of the Jewish partner, the maintenance of ties with the intermarried may have the unanticipated effect of diminishing the extended family as a natural community. The introduction of Gentiles into the family circle necessarily imperils the function of the extended family in the formation of Jewish identity. The child who interacts with Gentile aunts and uncles as well as with Jewish ones, with Gentile cousins as well as with Jewish cousins, must form his Jewish identity elsewhere than in the community of the extended family.

As we shall see in the two chapters that follow, American Jewry has a highly developed communal structure as well as a firmly established network of Jewish schools. Potentially, this system is capable of serving individuals from highly diverse family backgrounds. But however significant the communal network and the school system are as building blocks, they are a kind of superstructure resting upon the foundation of the family—for it is the family that has been the prime mechanism for transmitting Jewish identity. This system of identity-formation is currently on the decline. The emerging crisis of the Jewish family in identity-formation is in part due to the newer limitations on the family as a socialization agent—limitations that affect all other Americans as well. But it is also traceable to the specific factors that we have analyzed, such as the high acculturation of many Jewish parents, the diminished interaction with Jewish relatives, and the presence of Gentiles in the Jewish kinship network.

If it is doubtful whether the Jewish family can continue

to maintain its function of identity-transmission, it is not clear how the family can be replaced. Although the familiar complaints of the Alexander Portnoys that we reviewed at the begining of our analysis—the syndrome of the dominating mother, the powerless father, and the consequently neurotic offspring—are frequently assumed to be *the* problem of the contemporary Jewish family, it is the shrinking contribution of the family to Jewish identity-transmission that constitutes its essential weakness.

Notes

[1] The most notable deviations from the mother-child pattern are Herbert Gold, *Fathers* (New York: Random House, 1967); Isaac Rosenfeld, *Passage from Home* (New York: Dial Press, 1946); and Saul Bellow, *Herzog* (New York: Viking Press, 1964).

[2] See Leo Srole et al., *Mental Health in the Metropolis* (New York: McGraw-Hill, 1962), p. 305.

[3] *Ibid.*, p. 319.

[4] Eugene Mihaly, "The Jewish View of Marriage," *CCAR Journal*, (October 1954), p. 33.

[5] For the statistics see Jack Elinson, Paul W. Haberman, and Cyrille Gell, *Ethnic and Educational Data on Adults in New York City 1963–1964* (New York: School of Public Health and Administrative Medicine, Columbia University, 1967), pp. 9–10, 84. It appears that if data were collected for the entire metropolitan area rather than for the city alone the figures of 3.4 percent and 2.4 percent would be reduced even further. Newer suburbanites such as Jews—particularly if they are in the thirty-five to forty-nine age group—are almost never unmarried.

[6] Jacob Katz, *Tradition and Crisis: Jewish Society at the End of The Middle Ages* (New York: The Free Press, 1961), p. 268.

[7] *Ibid.*

[8] *Newsweek*, January 15, 1968, p. 52.

[9] Charles F. Westoff et al., *Family Growth in Metropolitan America* (Princeton: Princeton University Press, 1961), p. 102.

[10] See Sidney Goldstein and Calvin Goldscheider, *Jewish Americans: Three Generations in a Jewish Community* (Englewood Cliffs, N.J.: Prentice-Hall, 1968), pp. 135–136.

11 Erich Rosenthal, "Jewish Fertility in the United States," *AJYB*, 62 (1961), 22–23.

12 In its extreme version in the second generation the woman moves to a narcissistic preoccupation with self. She has an overwhelming interest in her clothes and appearance. She spends much time at cards. She patronizes restaurants extensively. She is extremely competitive with other women in terms of home furnishings and clothing, she is greatly dependent on household help, and she has a poor sexual adjustment. For a psychological analysis see Alexander Grinstein, "Profile of a 'Doll'—A Female Character Type" in *The Psychodynamics of American Jewish Life*, Normal Kiell (ed.), (New York: Twayne Publishers, 1967), pp. 79–93. Grinstein believes that traditional Jewish culture and family structure, as they are manifested in the immigrant home, produce the "doll":

> The European and Jewish tradition of the importance of the male . . . dominate the attitude in the household. Boys are to be educated, and the goal of "my son, the doctor" is no myth in its importance to the self-esteem of the hardworking and self-sacrificing mother. In their unconscious the son was frequently equated with the mother's phallus. The consequence of the mother's ambition for her sons and preferential treatment of them often results in a bitter sacrifice of the daughter's personality. The obeisance demanded of the daughters to their brothers' expected accomplishments serves to perpetuate a feeling of repressed aggression and secret contempt within these girls. Specific defenses must then be erected to cope with these emotions. Their excessive preening and exhibitionism which make unconscious use of the familiar equation body = phallus, represents one way in which these girls attempt to solve their problem of intensified penis envy, as well as their extreme jealousy of their brothers who were so much more valued by their mothers than they were. (pp. 87–88.)

13 *Nachas* belongs to that class of Hebrew words that are part of the Yiddish language. It is one of a small number of such terms that is still understood by some individuals who are not Yiddish-speaking. It has survived despite the fact that it has neither a religious nor a vulgar connotation.

14 Benjamin B. Ringer, *Edge of Friendliness: A Study of Jewish-Gentile Relations* (New York: Basic Books, 1967), pp. 71–72.

15 See Jerome K. Myers and Bertram H. Roberts, "Some Relationships Between Religion, Ethnic Origin, and Mental Illness," in

Marshall Sklare (ed.), *The Jews: Social Patterns of An American Group* (New York: The Free Press, 1958), pp. 551–559; and Srole, *op. cit.*, pp. 317–319.

[16] Only among the sociologists do we see an attempt to look for positive consequences of Jewish family structure. See especially Zena Smith Blau, "In Defense of the Jewish Mother," *Midstream*, February 1967, pp. 42–49; reprinted in Peter I. Rose (ed.), *The Ghetto and Beyond: Essays on Jewish Life in America* (New York: Random House, 1969), pp. 57–68.

[17] *New York Times*, May 19, 1968. The quotations that follow are from the same source.

[18] Robert F. Winch, Scott Greer, and Rae Lesser Blumberg, "Ethnicity and Extended Familism in an Upper-Middle Class Suburb," *American Sociological Review*, 32, No. 2 (April 1967), 267.

[19] Hope J. Leichter and William E. Mitchell, *Kinship and Casework* (New York: Russell Sage Foundation, 1967).

[20] Some 19 percent of the social workers are Gentile. Some 2 percent of the clients are Gentile but all are married to Jews. The study does not specify how many of the Gentile social workers have Jewish spouses. In any case, attitudinal differences between social workers and clients are too large to be accounted for by contrasts in ethnic background. *Ibid.*, pp. 209–212, 254–262.

[21] *Ibid.*, p. 217.

[22] *Ibid.*, p. 241. The figure for clients was an overwhelming 97 percent.

[23] *Ibid.*

[24] Marshall Sklare and Joseph Greenblum, *Jewish Identity on the Suburban Frontier: A Study of Group Survival in the Open Society* (New York: Basic Books, 1967), p. 252.

[25] Leichter and Mitchell, *op. cit.*, p. 222. In addition to clients and social workers, the JFS project includes a substudy of a small group of respondents drawn from a service run by the agency for the aged. Responses of the aged are much more traditionalistic than those of the clients. For example almost twice as many of the aged (some 63 percent) agree with the statement: "Friends can't give you the love you can get from relatives."

Chapter 4 ◉ Community and Identity

While the family is basic, it exists within the larger context of community. In fact one assumption of the Jewish family system is that all Jews share a common ancestry. The Jew is thought to be connected with all other Jews and the Jewish community is often viewed as a kind of extended family. So strong is the principle of family-community that according to Jewish tradition those who have no Jewish ancestry—the proselytes—are considered to be reborn upon their conversion; they have discarded their Gentile ancestry in the process of becoming Jews.

Conceding that the Jewish community rests upon an extension of the kinship principle, some will argue—in keeping with the line of reasoning developed by Louis Wirth in *The Ghetto* (see Chapter 1)—that the elaboration of a specifically Jewish communal structure is primarily a result of exclusion by the majority group. Another point of argument will be that even when such exclusion was not rife the Christian character of general societal institutions encouraged Jews to develop a separate structure. Jewish communality, however, has been necessitated by the demands of the Jewish religion and the character of Jewish culture as much as it has been stimulated by outside forces. To obey that religion and to follow that culture meant to elaborate a structure distinct from the general society. The structure that developed did not always parallel that of the general society, for it reflected the special character of Jewish culture.

What occurs when Jews come to a new country where the processes of acculturation and secularization occur rapidly, and where the institutions of the general community are ostensibly secular and nondiscriminatory? Surprisingly, a concept of Jewish communality remains and a network of Jewish institutions has come to be established. Some claim, as has the sociologist Milton Gordon, that such persistence is supported ". . . by the principle of psychological inertia, comfortable social immersion, and vested interests."[1] No doubt social institutions are sticky, even institutions imported from abroad. But vested interests cannot keep them vigorous once the time for their decline and demise has arrived. Peculiarly enough, Jewish organizations seem to flourish in contemporary American life. Not only do old agencies persist but new ones are established. And organizations spring up despite the fact that the American Jew has become steadily less dependent on Jewish agencies.

Why then does an organized Jewish community persist? Why are new Jewish agencies established at a time when dependence on them ebbs? The answer resides in the fact that community persists because identity persists. Community serves the need for identity, and while serving it also stimulates a feeling of identity.

Community and Subcommunity

If Jewish identity has motivated the establishment of a communal structure and is in turn stimulated by it, its structure did not follow any established formula. The model known to East European Jews gave explicit recognition to the separateness of the Jews; autonomy was conceded by the larger government in defined areas. While the German model placed less emphasis on Jewish autonomy, it had strong roots in traditional society and in the social structure of the period before Jewish emancipation. Jews who came to the United States did not generally feel a commitment to replicate European models for they did not wish to live under the authority of lay officials and rabbis. Nevertheless, European models—rooted in the medieval conception of corporate rights and responsibilities—provided essential preparation for the communal structure that the American Jew was to build.

If American social organization did not encourage groups who wished to establish themselves as full-fledged communities, and if European models were considered neither achievable nor desirable by American Jews, American society did offer an alternative: the subcommunity. The subcommunity is a community of sentiment rather than of coercion. It exists within the interstices of the social order and accommodates itself to that order. The subcommunity is a community of association. Such associationalism can be strong: the subcommunity may be the prime focus of the individual's social attachments. Nevertheless, it is not accorded official standing; the rights of the individual are derived from his status as a citizen rather than from his status as a member of a group. Furthermore, loyalty to the subcommunity is presumed consistent with loyalty to the community. In the remote situation in which loyalty to community and subcommunity conflict, society expects that the subcommunity will modify its program, defer its demands, and demonstrate its loyalty to the concept that the needs of the community have primacy. However, if the subcommunity feels imperiled, if it believes that compromise will be counterproductive, or if its morale is high, it may refuse to concede such subordination.

The feelings of Jews about their identity, their desire to maintain their group, and their strong communal tradition were all elements that helped them to create a subcommunal structure. This structure appears to be the most elaborate of any American ethnic group. For example, organizations exist to aid the aged and the young, the physically sick and the mentally ill. A multitude of Jewish agencies have been established to serve the most diverse purposes: some are concerned with local problems, others with national needs, while still others are geared to the needs of Jews overseas, especially in Israel. Jewish organizations are not only distinguishable by their programs but by their constituencies as well: they may appeal to distinctive age, sex, class, status, and brow-level groups. Furthermore, Anglo-Jewish weeklies are published in all but the smallest communities. They exist side by side with a network of Jewish magazines that are geared to a nationwide audience. And in addition to the press, the organi zations, the welfare agencies, the synagogues, and the community centers, the subcommunity provides a final facility for its members: the Jewish cemetery. Old Jewish cemeteries must be maintained and new Jewish cemeteries must be established to meet current and future needs.

While the structure is highly elaborate it is not characterized by completeness or regularity. Subcommunal structure is sprawling and inchoate: because its development rests more on individual initiative rather than on bureaucratic planning, it is necessarily irregular. And because the structure is powered by the need to maintain identity—a need that is experienced differently among the varied segments of the group—the norms of rationality operate poorly if at all. Jewish communal experts have devised ambitious plans to bring coordination, to reduce duplication, and to satisfy unmet needs. Outside experts have also been called in on occasion, including in one instance a Gentile academician who was assumed to be above the battle of competing organizations. However, the ambitious blueprints of planners have rarely been put into effect.[2] The coordination that has taken hold has developed pragmatically rather than academically.

The philanthropic field, especially the area of local social services, is the earliest and most successful example of coordination. The services have been noncontroversial—whatever one's orientation to Jewish identity there was consensus about the need to help the Jewish orphan, the Jewish elderly, the Jewish sick, the Jewish unemployed, the Jewish family in trouble. Hence agencies came to be established to meet these problems. In some of the largest communities separate sets of agencies were founded by German Jews and by East European Jews. The need for collaboration between the agencies soon became apparent, particularly as the growing fiscal requirements of the proliferating agencies necessitated a joint campaign for funds. The joint campaign, and the consequent federating of the agencies, was made possible by the emerging awareness on the part of both Germans and East Europeans that whatever their differences they were members of a single collectivity.

During the past sixty years Jewish "federations" have been

established in every community of significant size. Although the original impetus was to increase the efficiency of fund raising for local needs and to bring some order into the pattern of local services, the federations have become much more than fiscal or disbursing instrumentalities. Bringing individuals together for fund-raising purposes inevitably resulted in heightening their sense of community. And the success of the federations served to further reinforce the sense of community. In addition, the professionals employed to organize the campaigns were influential; they were experts in community organization and social planning. They too sought to increase the sense of community, for they realized that such feelings were essential to the success of their efforts.

Perhaps the largest single impetus to the sense of community as expressed through the instrumentality of the federation occurred when the federations took on the responsibility of raising funds for national and overseas Jewish needs. In the past two decades federation activities have centered on support for welfare needs in Israel. Each federation consequently allocates a substantial proportion of its annual campaign receipts to the United Jewish Appeal (UJA), the major agency delegated to raise funds for overseas and refugee assistance. In addition, material assistance is given to Israel in other ways than through the federations. Many of the larger welfare, cultural, educational, and religious agencies in Israel have enlisted supporters in the United States and each agency consequently receives support from its organization of "American Friends." In recent years there has also been an emphasis on extending material assistance outside of the philanthropic framework. The Bonds for Israel program is the outstanding example of the emphasis on assisting Israel through investment rather than philanthropy. Nevertheless, the federations are still the leading American-Jewish instrumentality for financial support of Israel, and their significance on the local scene has been magnified accordingly.

Because of the emphasis on fund raising and social planning each federation seeks to gather a complete list of local Jewish residents. In addition, some collect demographic data of residents of their community. And as we noticed in Chapter 2 and elsewhere, there are also federations that are even more thorough and scientifically oriented—they periodically sponsor large-scale surveys designed to gather detailed information on the social characteristics of the local Jewish residents, on their patterns of Jewish identity, and on their attitudes toward matters of Jewish concern. While information on the local Jewish population is essential to the operation of a federation, the symbolic significance of such information is as important as its day to day utility. The files on the Jewish population—or, as is more usual now, the computer tapes— symbolize the fact that the subcommunity is an organized entity rather than an abstraction.

The growth of subcommunal structure is also evidenced by the way in which the federations cooperate with each other. Part of this cooperation takes place on the national level through the coordinating body known as the Council of Jewish Federations and Welfare Funds (CJFWF). But perhaps the most revealing index to the growth of subcommunal structure is the interchange between one federation and another. For example, when information is received in the office of the Jewish Federation of Detroit that family "X" has left the city and relocated in Rochester, N.Y., Detroit will notify Rochester accordingly. The assumption behind this practice is that the subcommunity constitutes an entity to which the individual owes a continuous loyalty and obligation, and to which he may look, in turn, for the satisfaction of his needs.

The concept of need is ever-changing. Federations are now moving beyond the conventional social welfare needs that originally brought them into being. For example, some are beginning to implement programs to alleviate the alienation from Jewish life that is evident in the New Left and other segments of student youth. However, such efforts reveal that agencies find it exceedingly difficult to deal with problems outside of the ken of philanthropism. Alienation can only be conquered by commitment—that is to say by ideology. The principle behind the federations has been that it is nonideological—that it stands only for those things that all Jews, regardless of ideology, can agree upon.

The urban crisis is an even more striking illustration of

another type of limitation inherent in the federation structure. One of the most significant local issues confronting the Jewish community is what should be done about families who live in changing, crime-ridden neighborhoods. Secondarily, there is the problem of businessmen whose livelihood has been severely affected by the rise of the Black Power impulse. After a halting start several federations have initiated small-scale programs to alleviate these conditions. Some of the programs are aimed at stabilizing neighborhoods and improving police protection while others looked toward assisting residents in moving to other areas. Some federations have also sought to counsel merchants about relocating their establishments in different neighborhoods. But the federations have not moved decisively, massively, or significantly. Their problem is understandable: the effect of the urban crisis on the Jewish householder, merchant, or teacher cannot be mitigated by the old expedient of philanthropism. The only effective remedy is political rather than philanthropic—the agency must cast tradition aside and organize a power bloc that will compete with other blocs, and use its leverage with a wide variety of local, state, and federal government bodies.

On the national level, if not the local, the political aspect of subcommunal problems has long been apparent. Three large national agencies devote themselves to the highly political area of intergroup relations or "community relations" as it is generally termed. These are the Anti-Defamation League of B'nai B'rith (ADL), the American Jewish Committee, and the American Jewish Congress. All three have offices in major cities. In addition, most federations subsidize a local intergroup relations agency ("community relations council" as it is generally termed). Furthermore, a number of the major national Jewish organizations sponsor various projects in the field of intergroup relations. All of these bodies belong to a coordinating organization, the National Community Relations Advisory Council (NCRAC).

Sentiment about Israel has also been a strong spur to the establishment of coordinating efforts on the national level. Thus the Conference of Presidents of Major American Jewish Organizations was founded to coordinate support for Israel on the political front as distinct from the philanthropic arena. Efforts to alleviate the plight of Russian Jews are coordinated by the American Jewish Conference on Soviet Jewry.

With this brief overview of the character of the subcommunity we shall proceed to an in-depth analysis of three contrasting types of Jewish organizations. The first is the congregation, the most widely diffused and numerous of all Jewish associations. The second is the community center, which is found in all significant centers of Jewish population. The third is the social service agency. In this connection we shall analyze three significant types of services: hospitals, family and child care agencies, and old age homes. However, before we can understand the congregation—and also the community center and the social services as well—we must study how the Jewish religion is practiced in the United States.

The Jewish Religion in America

Jewish tradition teaches that the Jews became a group only by their having embraced the Torah. Thus in classical perspective religion is recognized as the foundation of group identity. American Jews seem to follow this tradition. Increasingly they have come to understand their group identity in religious terms. However, they have not arrived at this position purely out of respect for tradition. Their feelings have also been influenced by factors such as the desire to survive as a group; the belief that survival can best be assured by a group identity that is based on religious commitments; and the impact of a culture that assumes that all men have a religion and believes that religion is good, and that regards separatism on the basis of a religious commitment as justifiable, even admirable. Finally, the ever-present need to explain Jewish identity to the general community has created an additional incentive for affirming religion as the foundation of such identity.

OBSERVANCE AND THE JEWISH HOME. If Jews increasingly

have come to think of themselves as religionists this does not mean that they are prepared to act accordingly. There are in fact some very formidable obstacles to their making a serious religious commitment. We noted earlier (in Chapter 1) that a substantial segment of those who arrived in the United States during the great wave of East European immigration were at best nominally Orthodox. They had already felt the impact of secularization before they left Europe and the process gained considerable momentum in the United States. Thus the experience of many native-born Jews—even those who are members of the second or third generation—has been to grow up in a household where the hold of secular values was strong.

Secularization brought the usual challenges that members of other religions experienced. But its impact was sharpened by certain problems traceable to the special character of Judaism. For example, in traditional Judaism the arena of the sacred is extremely wide. Under the influence of secularization the American Jew was challenged to fashion a sacred-secular dichotomy. As a consequence he exempted much of what had formerly been considered holy from the operation of sacred norms. Furthermore, many Jewish observances were disharmonious with the environment—they had been fashioned in the East and consequently were at odds with Western culture. Additionally, while the thrust of Jewish religious culture is sacramental the thrust of American religious culture is moralistic.[3] As acculturation proceeded Jews began to doubt the necessity of upholding the *mitzvot*. Furthermore, Judaism is distinguished by the lack of any real system of differential religious obligations as between laity and clergy—identical behavior is expected of both layman and rabbi. Under the influence of secularism, however, a distinction came to be recognized. The rabbi became a religious specialist charged with observing norms from which the layman was excused.

As the impact of these processes was felt the need to define oneself as an individual who upheld religious values despite apparent secularity became more pressing. Consequently, the designations of "Reform" and "Conservative" emerged; as a reaction the term "Orthodox" also entered the popular vocabulary. Reform came to stand for a Judaism in which a sacred–secular dichotomy had been implemented and the area of the sacred narrowly defined; where Western culture was observed and religious practices in conflict with that culture were either discarded or were reshaped to conform with norms of the larger culture; where sacramentalism was downgraded and moralism (or "prophetic Judaism") upgraded; and where rabbi and layman were accorded different roles. Orthodoxy came to stand for a Judaism that maintained strong continuity with tradition. Conservatism came to stand for a Judaism located at some loosely defined point between Orthodoxy and Reform.

Whether accurately or not, the majority of American Jews would describe their grandparents as Orthodox. But they would not describe themselves as Orthodox, and increasingly they would not describe their parents as being such. In Boston, for example, 44 percent consider themselves to be Conservative, 27 percent to be Reform, and 14 percent to be Orthodox.[4] With the possible exception of New York City where the Orthodox group is generally assumed to be somewhat stronger, these figures seem to be typical for most communities in the Middle Atlantic and New England states. In the South, the Middle West, and the West, the percentage considering themselves Reform tends to be higher.

In explaining why Reform and Conservatism have made such strong gains some Orthodox spokesmen maintain that their success is based on a formula of making Judaism easy. They contend that Reform and Conservatism attracted those who were looking for a Judaism that would demand the least amount of sacrifice. But if we view the problem from a more sociological perspective it appears that the crucial issue is Judaism's sacramental emphasis, and the inability of many a modern Jew to embrace the totality of the Jewish sacred system.[5] Instead of receiving all that has been handed down to him, such a Jew seeks to discover what *mitzvot* he can still adhere to out of the vast sacramental heritage. Whatever the particular results of such a confrontation, the *mitzvot* that many a contemporary Jew finds meaningful may not conform to the criteria internal to the religious system. Thus the tenets that were hallowed in traditional life may conflict sharply with contemporary culture, and those that were formerly of secondary importance may now achieve primacy because they fulfill important needs.

In sum, then, the modern Jew selects the *mitzvot* that are subjectively possible for him to identify with. He is guided by a new personalism rather than by an old prescriptionism. Of course his personalism is not truly individualistic: it is influenced by the prevailing culture, by his class, by his education, his spouse, his children, his parents, his friends, his neighbors, his community. These influences help assure that selection from the sacramental heritage will not be a random one, and that a limited number of observance-patterns will emerge that will be characteristic of entire population segments.

An analysis of any single observance or set of observances would illustrate the problem that individuals have, on one hand, in identifying with Jewish tradition and, on the other, of maintaining a feeling of identity should they choose to neglect or reject the observance. For example, the dietary laws are a striking illustration of Judaism's sacramental tradition. They invest the routine and mundane act of eating with sacred significance and they provide the believer with recurring opportunities to show his obedience to God's will. Having no hygienic or other instrumental purpose, their sole justification is that they are pleasing in God's sight. Furthermore, their observance affects the individual in the most profound ways. Observance of the laws may influence choice of friends, neighborhood, occupation, and spouse. Finally, they give the home an indisputably Jewish character.[6]

There is no simple answer to the question of what constitutes full observance of *kashrut* (the system of dietary laws), for there are considerable variations in strictness even among observant Jews who seek to follow the system both outside as well as inside the home. But it is indisputable that certain basic aspects of the system are observed by only a minority. In as conservative a community as Providence only 32 percent say that they use separate dishes in the home for milk and meat.[7] Even this modest figure does not characterize a cross section of the community. While 53 percent of the first generation use separate dishes for milk and meat, only 25 percent of the second and 16 percent of the third generation do so. Unless there is a sharp change on the part of younger people (we must remember that by now a significant percentage of them have been reared in homes where the laws were disregarded to a greater or lesser extent), it can be assumed that in the future *kashrut* will be observed by an even smaller minority of Jews.

While basic aspects of the dietary laws are disregarded by many, other observances are followed by a clear majority. The best examples are the Seder on Passover and the lighting of the *menorah* on Hanukkah. In Providence, for example, some 79 percent attend a Seder each year and 74 percent light the *menorah*. Furthermore, there are no strong differences between the generations with respect to these observances. Why, then, do some home observances live while others die, or are retained only by a special group? Observance seems to result from the pull of two forces: the pervasive impact of the modern, Christian, and secularist environment, and the desire to express Jewish identity and continuity in familiar forms. But which forms? Five criteria emerge in explaining the retention of specific home rituals. The highest degree of retention will occur when a ritual: (1) is capable of effective redefinition in modern terms; (2) does not demand social isolation or the adoption of a unique life style; (3) accords with the religious culture of the larger community while providing a "Jewish" alternative when such is felt to be needed; (4) is centered on the child; and (5) is performed annually or infrequently.

To review these criteria in detail:

1. *Capable of effective redefinition in modern terms.* We might expect that neither Hanukkah nor Passover would be attractive to the American Jew. These holidays center around the celebration of a miracle: in the case of Hanukkah, the cruse of oil normally sufficient for one day that lasted for eight days; in the case of Passover, the exodus from Egypt accomplished by Divine intervention. However, the miraculous elements inherent in both holidays are capable of redefi-

nition: both holidays are interpreted to symbolize man's un-
quenchable desire for freedom. The focus is no longer on
God's benevolence but on the struggle of the ancient Jewish
people and their heroic leaders to overcome slavery in the
case of Passover and religious intolerance in the case of
Hanukkah.

As the dietary laws attest, not all reinterpretations are
equally successful. One familiar reinterpretation of the dietary
laws is that they have hygienic significance. But the idea has
had little appeal for individuals who live in a publicly enforced sanitary environment, and who, furthermore, conceive
of food prohibitions as primitive taboos.

2. *Does not demand social isolation and the following of a
unique life style.* If the Jew were to observe the full routine of
traditional rituals he would find himself following a separate
and highly distinctive life style. Valuing his acculturation
and disinclined to lead a distinctive way of life he is attracted
to those rituals that demand minimal separation and deviation from the general community. By way of contrast Hasidim
seek to retain even those aspects of culture, as for example
East European Jewish dress, which have no basis in *halachah*.
Among the reasons why such dress is retained is that it constitutes a distinctive style and thus serves to separate Jews
from Gentiles, and Hasidic Jews from other Jews.

3. *Accords with the religious culture of the larger community while providing a "Jewish" alternative when such is felt
to be needed.* This criterion refers to convergent characteristics in each of the major American religions that form the
basis of the "tri-faith" culture which has been noted by many
commentators. The aspects of Hanukkah observance currently
emphasized—the exchange of gifts and the lighting and display of the *menorah* in the windows of homes—offer ready
parallels to the general mode of Christmas observance as well
as provide a "Jewish" alternative to the holiday. Instead of
alienating the Jew from the general culture, Hanukkah helps
to situate him as a participant in that culture. Hanukkah, in
short, becomes for some a Jewish Christmas.

4. *Centered on the child.* Both the Passover Seder and the
lighting of Hanukkah candles have traditionally been among

the most child-centered observances in the Jewish calendar. Not only is the Passover Seder a personal religious experience for adults but it also has the purpose of conveying to the next generation the experience of the Exodus. While the ritual of Hanukkah is not explicitly child-centered, its mode of celebration inclined in this direction even before the encounter with America; witness *dreydl* (spinning-top) games[8] and the giving of Hanukkah *gelt* (money) in Europe. In essence, then, the recitation of the Haggadah and the lighting of the *menorah* constitute religious acts performed by adults to satisfy personal religious requirements as well as ritual occasions that are made doubly meaningful by the participation of the young.

While the retention of these rituals may be stimulated by the child's eagerness, the motivation of the parent does not rest on his child-centeredness alone. These occasions appeal to the parent because they accord with his desire to transmit Jewish identity to his offspring. Hanukkah and Passover, which provide ready-made forms and techniques for involving the child at major points in their celebrations, carry the imputation and the hope that when the child becomes a parent he will be performing these rituals for himself and for *his* children.

The mood of a child-centered holiday must be appropriate. Passover and Hanukkah have special appeal in this connection, for both commemorate joyous occasions. Their tenor is in keeping with the norms of optimism, fun, and gratification that the general culture holds with respect to the atmosphere in which children should be reared. And the parent feels that having provided his child with "positive" associations with Jewishness, the child will have no cause to reject his heritage.

5. *Performed annually or infrequently.* The fact that both Passover and Hanukkah are annual rather than weekly or daily occasions undoubtedly serves to maintain their observance. Sabbath rituals and customs—such as the lighting of candles, the preparation of a special meal, the attendance at the meal by all members of the family, the recitation of *Kiddush*—involve a kind of regimen. While they are not to

be compared with the significance of the decision to avoid work and other proscribed Sabbath activities, they do make regular demands on each member of the family. Thus their appeal is primarily to the more pious. But the lighting of the *menorah* (even if done faithfully on eight successive evenings) and the holding of a Seder (even if it includes the reading of all of the Haggadah—the book read at the Seder) are unusual occasions. Coming once a year they are a relief from the routine.

Infrequently performed rituals harmonize more with the secular component in modern American life than daily or weekly rituals. Secularization affects the scope of religion. It restricts the application of religion to fewer and fewer areas of the individual's life. It results in limitations on the regular and routine performance of religious observances. Given the pervasiveness of secularization, the yearly ritual will persist more than the seasonal, the seasonal more than the monthly, the monthly more than the weekly, the weekly more than the daily. Secularization undercuts the emphasis of Jewish sacramentalism on the sanctification of the routine and imperils the continuation of those rituals which do not celebrate an extraordinary occasion.

In summary: the observance of religious ritual in the American Jewish home is geared to the celebration of selected aspects of certain occasions on the Jewish calendar, observance is personalistic in orientation, and holidays are emphasized rather than the sanctification of routine. The resulting pattern reflects a home that has been strongly affected by secular culture.

worship. In traditional Jewish society worship takes place in the home. Women pray at home as well as the synagogue, and although it is considered preferable for men to pray with a congregation or quorum of ten adult males (*minyan*), convenience may dictate that on weekdays adult males recite morning, afternoon, or evening prayers in private at their homes (or if more suitable, at their places of work). While this tradition has survived among some Orthodox Jews and undoubtedly reinforces the Jewish character of their homes, worship has increasingly come to be centered in the synagogue. (A *minyan* may of course be convoked in the home, but at present this is common only during the initial period of mourning for the dead.) An analysis of synagogue attendance will give us greater insight into the religious habits of the American Jew as well as provide an introduction to the sociology of the American synagogue.

Table 13. *Frequency of Synagogue and Church Attendance in Greater Boston*

Frequency of Synagogue or Church Attendance	Jewish	General
More than once a month	17%	65%
Once a month or every few months	21	11
Only on High Holy Days	39	6
Less often or never	23	18
Total	100%	100%

Note: Because in this survey the general population includes Jews, the extent to which the 6 percent who attend services "only on High Holy Days" represent Jewish respondents in the "general" population is unclear. It is possible that this figure includes some Gentiles who construed the question to refer to holidays such as Christmas and Easter.
SOURCE: Axelrod et al., *Boston*, p. 139.

Many investigators have collected statistics on the question of attendance at worship. Their findings all point in the same direction: Jews attend religious services very infrequently. Furthermore, Jewish behavior is not a simple response to the prevailing culture, for Gentiles attend church much more faithfully than Jews attend synagogue services. Even if we grant that at times comparisons across religious lines may be misleading, it is undeniable that attendance statistics underline the heavy impact of secularization on American Jewry. In Boston, for example, some 39 percent of the Jewish population worship only on High Holidays while another 23 percent attend less often or never (see Table 13). Since we may safely assume that those who pray in private attend public worship frequently, we are justified in concluding that the experience of worship on a daily, weekly, monthly, or even seasonal basis is unknown to the majority of Boston's Jews.

The pattern of attendance that is restricted to High Holiday worship is a very striking phenomenon. Why does the person who is basically a nonworshipper feel compelled to come to the synagogue on these particular days? Have the High Holiday services in some way become defined as exercises which are obligatory upon the individuals who are ethnic survivalists? Or, to put it another way, is absence from synagogue unacceptable to the nonworshipper because he would feel that by staying away he was betraying the group, that he was disowning his ancestors in general and his immediate forebearers in particular? The hypothesis requires further study. What does seem apparent is that the High Holidays suggest the operation of one of our criteria for ritual retention: the greater persistence of certain annual and infrequently performed rituals. Their endurance also underlines the break with prescriptionism: according to traditional norms attendance at weekly Sabbath services is highly important, and the commandment to observe the Sabbath is in no sense inferior to the requirement to observe the High Holidays. In any case a full explanation of the significance of High Holiday attendance must await the results of an inquiry on this singular phenomenon.

Some 17 percent of Boston Jewry may be considered regular attendees inasmuch as they go to services more than once a month. While in a distinct minority regular attendees constitute a crucial group—it is they who keep the system of Sabbath services alive. Their attendance is also important in maintaining the daily services that are conducted in some congregations. Paralleling the case of *kashrut*, they exercise a subtle influence over their less-devout peers: their maintenance of the services constitutes a kind of indirect pressure upon those who acknowledge the desirability of attendance but do not themselves come to worship. And by maintaining the system they also provide the Jewish public with a structure to which they may return when they feel the need to do so. On the other hand, by maintaining the system they

Table 14. Frequency of Synagogue and Church Attendance in New York City

Ethnicity	RELIGIOUS SERVICE ATTENDANCE					
	More than once a week	Once a week	Once a month or a few times a month	A few times a year	Once a year or less	Never
All Adults	7.4%	30.7%	17.2%	22.7%	13.3%	8.7%
Negro	7.2	24.1	30.7	16.9	15.9	5.2
Puerto Rican	5.2	37.5	24.0	9.9	15.1	8.3
Irish	18.9	61.1	7.8	5.6	3.3	3.3

Grouped totals (braces): All Adults 55.3, 62.0; Negro 66.7; Puerto Rican 87.8

				Total			
Italian	6.6	50.7	20.5	77.8	13.2	5.2	3.8
Other Catholic	11.1	53.4	11.3	75.8	10.8	9.5	3.9
Other Protestant	5.0	21.9	24.8	51.7	21.5	15.3	11.6
Native-born Jewish	3.0	2.8	5.8	11.6*	47.9	23.8	16.6
Foreign-born Jewish	11.3	11.7	10.8	33.8*	44.1	12.2	9.9

* Total for all Jews attending once a month or more: 19.8%.

SOURCE: Elinson et al., *Ethnic and Educational Data*, p. 147.

alleviate whatever guilt feelings are experienced by their less-devout peers.

The contrast between Jewish attendance and attendance among the total population in Boston is sharp: while only 17 percent of the Jews attend regularly 65 percent of the population at large do so. Thus there is nothing comparable in the general population to the very considerable percentage of Jews who appear year after year for one, two, or three services. But there is one similarity between the Jews and Bostonians in general: the proportion who rarely or never attend. Some 18 percent of the total population are in this category in comparison to 23 percent of the Jews.

While the large number of Catholics in Boston (more specifically the large number of Irish) may serve to raise non-Jewish attendance figures over what they would be in other communities of similar size, there is nothing to suggest that the religious behavior of Boston Jewry is particularly deviant. In New York City only 19.8 percent attend once a month or more (see Table 14).[9] Furthermore, regular attendance is much more common in the first generation than in later generations. Thus while 33.8 percent of foreign-born Jews are regular attendees only 11.6 percent of the native-born fall into the same category. But even foreign-born Jews are less faithful worshippers than the most secularized of the non-Jews: 51.7 percent of the group designated as "Other Protestants" are regular worshippers.[10] And the "Other Protestants" are no match for the Irish, some 87.9 percent of whom go to church once a month or more.

THE AMERICAN SYNAGOGUE. From the attendance statistics of New York City, Boston, and numerous other communities we might expect that the American synagogue is a struggling institution that is banished to the periphery of Jewish life and located predominantly in neighborhoods where the foreign-born reside. Nothing could be further from the truth. The American synagogue is a vital institution; it is by far the strongest agency in the entire Jewish community. Many hundreds of new synagogues—Reform, Conservative, and Orthodox— were built as a consequence of population movement after

World War II. The process continues. As new Jewish neighborhoods and suburbs develop, new synagogues are established or old synagogues are transferred to new locations. Not only have synagogues been built in areas where Jewish life is intensive but sooner or later they are organized even in places that attract the more marginal Jewish families.[11] The number of synagogues, the value of their buildings, and their location in all areas where the Jewish population totals more than a handful of families all attest to the predominance of this institution in American Jewish life.[12]

We already know that only a minority of American Jews can bring themselves to patronize the synagogue with any degree of regularity in connection with its function as a house of prayer. Yet the continuing construction of new buildings, as well as the prosperity of established institutions suggests that the American synagogue must be more than a house of prayer. To help us discover its real nature, we must first know what proportion of America's Jews are affiliated with a synagogue.

There are no reliable nationwide statistics on affiliation. The most notable aspect of synagogue affiliation is that it varies greatly with the size of the Jewish population. In small communities affiliation commonly reaches well over 80 percent, despite the high intermarriage rates characteristic of such communities. In Flint, Michigan, for example, where the Jewish population is under 3,000, a total of 87 percent of the Jews in the community are affiliated with a synagogue.[13] In communities of intermediate size (10,000 to 25,000 Jewish population), the level of affiliation is lower—commonly over 70 percent are synagogue members. Thus in Providence the figure is 77 percent, in Springfield it is 76 percent, in Rochester, N.Y. 71 percent, and in Camden it reaches the exceptionally high figure of 82 percent.[14] In large Jewish communities the rate of affiliation is much lower, commonly running at about 50 percent of the Jewish population. Thus in Detroit 49 percent are affiliated while in Boston the figure is 53 percent.[15] New York is *sui generis*—while no study is available observation suggests that the affiliation rate is measurably lower than it is in any other large city.

Unlike the observance of many *mitzvot*, which as we have seen tend to be concentrated in one segment of the population, synagogue membership is widely diffused. Irrespective of community size, membership is common in all segments of the population, with the following exceptions: it is somewhat more concentrated among the prosperous as well as among those with children between the ages of five and fifteen. Significantly, the rate of affiliation among the foreign-born is no higher than among the native-born. Even in the large cities where the rate of affiliation is so low, most nonmembers have belonged to a synagogue at one time or another. Former members include, for example, the widow who resigned after her husband's death and who now lives in reduced circumstances, or the prosperous family that dropped out after their children had a Bar Mitzvah or Confirmation. Furthermore, some of those who have never been affiliated will do so in the future. This is the case with many young marrieds who will join when they move from city apartments to suburban homes, or when they have children old enough to enroll in a Sunday or Hebrew School.

Whatever criticisms former members may have, and whatever the situation of those who have never affiliated, it is hard to find a principled opponent of the American synagogue.[16] Those who are outside of the synagogue are not firm opponents of the institution. Absence from the membership rolls does not generally represent a clear commitment to any rival institution. It does mean of course that the individual has been strongly influenced by the secularization process. But any critical observer would be quick to point out that most synagogue members have been vitally affected by the same process.

The lack of principled objection to the synagogue and the affiliation of diverse segments of the population must be added to our previous findings about wide differences in affiliation rate between smaller and larger communities. There is little to suggest that Jews in smaller communities are more sacred in their orientation than their metropolitan cousins. In fact a case can be made for precisely the opposite conclusion: that they are more secular in orientation, and much less traditional in their thinking. Why then do those who reside in smaller communities affiliate with greater frequency?

The smaller the community the clearer is the threat of assimilation and the clearer it is that the future of Jewish life rests upon the personal decision of each individual Jew. The decision to affiliate with a synagogue, then, means to vote yes to Jewish survival. And the smaller the community the more literal the voting metaphor: since every individual in the small community is asked to join, he is forced into casting his ballot. A refusal to join means placing himself in the assimilationist camp unless of course he has provided clear-cut evidence to the contrary by becoming intensely involved with some alternative Jewish agency. The larger the community the less chance of solicitation by significant others, the less pressure to make a decision for survival, and above all, the more remote the threat of assimilation.

Clearly in the largest communities, especially in New York, synagogue membership does not have high symbolic significance. Since many people lack the feeling that Jewish identity requires synagogue membership, nonaffiliation does not mean a vote for assimilation. Conversely, one's resignation from a synagogue is not interpreted as meaning disloyalty to the group. In the metropolis, then, the synagogue must appeal on the basis of its instrumental as well as symbolic functions. However, a substantial proportion of the population finds the synagogue unessential to its needs. These people have little interest in the classical functions of the synagogue—religious services and study by adult males of Jewish texts. Nonclassical functions that the synagogue has added also do not attract them. Their children may be too young or too old for Hebrew School or Sunday School. Furthermore they are not interested in the social activities provided by the synagogue, for they already are a part of a satisfying clique. Generally their group is entirely Jewish and dates back to friendships that were cemented in adolescence or early adulthood. Others not attracted to the synagogue's social activities because they have a rich social life within their family circle. Finally in the largest communities a host of organizations and causes of a specifically

Jewish nature are available outside of the orbit of the synagogue.

Whether situated in a large or small community the synagogue is focused upon Jewish survival. It need not have been so—conceivably the synagogue in America could have followed a different course and insisted that as a religious institution it was an end in itself rather than a means for Jewish survival. Such a stance would exclude those who were strongly secular in orientation, or at least require that they accept a subordinate position. But there is religious justification for the synagogue moving in the direction it has: in Judaism the preservation of the Jewish people as a group is an act of religious significance.

The American synagogue has accepted the secular Jew on his own terms; the institution has been more concerned with transforming him than with erecting barriers to his admission. In most congregations membership is open to all; no test of the applicant's religious attitudes or observance of *mitzvot* is required. While in many Reform or Conservative congregations an applicant for membership is generally sponsored by a member of the synagogue or by one of its officials, this is only for the purpose of screening those who have an objectionable moral reputation. The exceptions to the rule are certain Orthodox congregations that are interested in an applicant's observance of *mitzvot*. Such institutions prefer to restrict their roster to those whose behavior is in conformity with certain selected religious norms.

Since the typical American Jewish congregation is formed by local initiative rather than by the authority of a central body, every synagogue is free to determine its own program and ritual.[17] Furthermore, because the polity—the form of religious organization—among American Jews is congregational rather than episcopal, each synagogue is the equal of all others. Residents join together to hold religious services and to establish a school for their children. They raise the funds necessary to build an edifice and to hire a professional staff. The synagogue is organized in the form of a corporate body that holds periodic membership meetings at which the affairs of the institution are discussed and officers and board members elected. The board is responsible for determining the policies of the institution, although on strictly religious questions, as well as in certain other areas, the advice and consent of the rabbi is commonly solicited.

The prototype of the contemporary American synagogue is the "synagogue center." This is the synagogue that compromises with the culture while serving the need for Jewish identification. Recognizing the impact of acculturation this type of synagogue expands its program far beyond the traditional activities of prayer and study. It seeks encounter with the Jew on his own secular level and it strives to reculturate him. The content and procedures of religious services are adapted to give them greater appeal, with Reform synagogues, Conservative synagogues, and Orthodox synagogues each handling the problem of cultural adaptation in characteristic fashion. Although traditionally there is no sermon during the weekly Sabbath service, part of the process of adaptation involves the introduction of this feature. Thus the sermon has become a standard feature of the weekly service in Reform, Conservative, as well as in some Orthodox congregations. The sermon is employed as an instructional as well as a hortatory device.

All synagogues sponsor some kind of program of adult Jewish study, although its character, and the importance attached to it, varies greatly from congregation to congregation. With the exception of some Orthodox synagogues women are free to participate in the program. In many places the traditional textual approach to study has been modified or supplemented. New kinds of courses have been introduced. But Jewish learning for children rather than for adults constitutes the real focus of the congregation's educational efforts. With the exception of certain Orthodox synagogues all congregations sponsor a Jewish school. While the majority of those who attend are of elementary school age, most schools aim to retain their youngsters after the high point of the educational experience: Bar Mitzvah, Bat Mitzvah, or Confirmation.

For the less-committed the opportunity for Jewish education is a strong inducement to affiliate. In most newer neighborhoods of the city, and in the suburbs, the only available Jewish religious schools are those conducted under congregational auspices. Some congregations make membership mandatory for enrollment, while others adjust their tuition fees to provide a financial incentive for membership.

Another important motivation for affiliation is the desire of secular-minded Jews to attend religious services on the High Holidays. While daily services, Sabbath services, and festival services are open to all, the demand for seats on the High Holidays is so large that admission is commonly restricted to ticket holders. In some congregations tickets are distributed only to members while in other synagogues they are sold to the public, but at a higher price than that made to members. Since most High Holiday services today are conducted under the auspices of a synagogue, the institution is in a position to attract individuals who might not ordinarily be interested in an affiliation. The phenomenon of "mushroom synagogues"—opened during the High Holidays by private entrepreneurs—is on the wane and the phenomenon is rarely encountered in more prestigious neighborhoods. It has been replaced by the practice of established congregations that hold overflow services for the High Holidays, or of Reform congregations that conduct services on a double shift.

Most congregations sponsor a variety of clubs for high school youth, young adults, young marrieds, adult women, adult men, and the elderly. These organizations provide the synagogue member with another tie to the congregation. They are particularly crucial for individuals who are not strongly involved in the classical functions of prayer and study. Generally the organization composed of adult women (the "sisterhood") is the most vital of these clubs. Membership in the clubs is so widespread that in the intermediate size Jewish community they enroll far more members than any other Jewish organization. In Providence, for example, 53.2 percent of all men age fifty to fifty-nine are members of a synagogue-affiliated club, as are 55 percent of the women.[18] Recreational and associational opportunities are not limited to the synagogue affiliates, however. There are congregational socials and parties, dinner dances, specialized activity groups, and fund-raising drives. All strive to increase the interaction among members. In the New York area in particular many synagogues provide a variety of athletic facilities.[19]

The contemporary synagogue is a large institution by traditional standards. While older Jewish neighborhoods in the largest cities may contain a dozen or more small congregations in addition to two or three large ones, an average synagogue in a newer neighborhood of a metropolis or suburb will generally enroll over 500 families. Congregations of this size have many members who confine their participation to specialized activities, or who participate very irregularly. Given the large size of most congregations and the specialized, irregular, or even nonparticipation of members, the printed word becomes a vital part of congregational life. Thus most congregations publish a bulletin at regular intervals. The bulletin contains the time of services and the topic of the weekly sermon, the schedules of the clubs, information about adult education lectures and courses, and news of the school. Of equal if not greater significance are the personals columns of the bulletin. Births and deaths are announced, donors are listed, names of active workers are publicized, and significant milestones in lives of members and their families are featured, including birthdays, wedding anniversaries, graduations, and promotions.

While synagogues of the more traditional variety contrast sharply with the synagogue-center type of institution, it is the synagogue characteristic of modern Israel which places the contemporary American synagogue in boldest relief. The core of the program of the Israeli synagogue is the traditional activities of prayer and study. Worship activities are centered on the three daily services and the Sabbath service. Some men remain after the daily services, or come early, for the purpose of studying various sacred texts. They do this either by themselves, in pairs, or in groups. Most synagogues are small. Each has its officials, its leaders, and its congregants. However, individuals think of themselves as praying at a particular synagogue rather than being affiliated with it in any formal sense. Most synagogues do not have a professional staff—

rabbis are employed by a central authority rather than by a particular congregation. While attendance and participation at services and in the study circles ebbs and flows, and although at certain holidays worshippers appear who are absent at other occasions, the interaction of the group of men who pray and study together constitutes the foundation of the institution.

Unlike the United States, then, the synagogue in Israel offers little other than the classical functions of prayer and study of the sacred system by adult males. Unlike the United States, its existence and prosperity is not interpreted as a promise of Jewish survival at a time when the acculturation process is so advanced as to make survival difficult to assure. And unlike the United States, the Israeli synagogue is not perceived as an emblem of Jewish identity or as the guarantor of the Jewish future. Rather, the nationhood of Israel is viewed as assuring Jewish survival. In essence, then, the synagogue in Israel has little symbolic significance; it exists as an end in itself rather than as a means to an end. Because it does not occupy the unique role that it does in the United States, the Israeli synagogue is a much weaker institution. It reaches a much smaller proportion of the population than its American counterpart.

Even if the American synagogue is generally a means to an end rather than an ultimate value, it is still a religious institution. As such it is subject to evaluation by a unique yardstick —the yardstick of spirituality. Critics of the synagogue, while conceding that it makes a valuable contribution to Jewish life, are prepared to argue that it is nonetheless more of a liability than an asset. Some maintain that the American synagogue protects the individual from the demands of the Jewish religion as much as it exposes him to them. In a scathing indictment of the American synagogue Rabbi Eugene Borowitz, a leading Reform thinker, has commented:

> . . . the average synagogue member . . . comes . . . to join the synagogue because there are few if any socially acceptable alternatives to synagogue affiliation for one

who wants to maintain his Jewish identity and wants his children to be Jewish, in some sense, after him. Though this is not the only motive or level of concern to be found within the synagogue today, the Jew who does not rise above such folk-feeling unquestionably and increasingly represents the synagogue's majority mood. More than that, however, it must be said that he also represents the synagogue's greatest threat. . . . His newfound affluence and his need for status within the community have made the big building with the small sanctuary, the lavish wedding with the short ceremony, and the fabulous Bar Mitzvah celebration with the minimal religious significance well-established patterns among American Jewish folkways. . . .What does it say of Jewish life in America when Reform Judaism appeals because it demands so little but confers so much status? when people blandly proclaim that they are nonobservant Orthodox Jews; when Conservative Judaism makes a virtue of not defining the center so that it may avoid alienating those disaffected on either side.[20]

Borowitz believes that the synagogue should become a more sectarian institution, that it should be transformed to become an end rather than a means, and that it should relinquish its function of providing identity for the secular-minded, ethnically oriented Jew. Proponents concede that this policy will mean that many who presently belong will feel compelled to sever their affiliation (or, if not, have it severed for them), but their eventual assimilation is viewed as the price which must be paid for the survival of Judaism. Proponents hope that the loss of the masses will be compensated, at least in part, by the affiliation of those who—they claim—have remained outside or at the margin of congregational life because of an understandable distaste for the American synagogue. As Borowitz sees it:

Clarifying Jewish faith might bring many to the conclusion that they cannot honestly participate in Judaism and the synagogue. . . . No one wishes to lose Jews for Judaism, but the time has come when the synagogue must be saved for the religious Jew, when it must be prepared to let some Jews opt out so that those who remain in, or who come in, will not be diverted from their duty to God. As the religion of a perpetual minority, Judaism must always first be concerned with the saving remnant, and so long as the synagogue is overwhelmed by the indifferent and the apathetic who control it for their own nonreligious purposes, that remnant will continue to be deprived of its proper communal home.[21]

More ethnically oriented religionists have proposed less drastic remedies. One such idea is the *havurah,* a local group composed of individuals who belong to congregations but find such institutions to be so lax and undemanding that they require other avenues to express their Jewishness. It is claimed that banding together and forming a fellowship or *havurah* will protect and advance the spiritual life of those individuals who are ready for a richer religious diet than the synagogue makes available:

> The *havurah* is certainly *not* intended either to supplant the congregation or even to downgrade it. There is no doubt that the congregation serves many vital functions. . . [but its] insufficiency inheres. . . in the heterogeneous character of the constituency. And the main aspect of that insufficiency lies in the fact that belonging to congregations is often no more than an innocuous gesture. . . . Rabbis assume that the vast majority will attend only three times a year. Little— often nothing—is actually required besides the payment of dues. No commitment is asked; none is generally given.
>
> Now, while this may appeal to the escapists and the irresponsible, it does not appeal to those who are looking for a place in which they can take their Judaism seriously in the company of likeminded Jews. Thus, *commitment* is the key to one of the essentials of *havurah*.[22]

The American synagogue is considerably more differentiated than its critics assume. Population size and density permitting, a variety of congregations are commonly established. Even when such congregations are similar in ideological preference they cater to different segments of the community. Such population segments are generally distinguishable by secular differences such as class position and level of general education but frequently they are also separated by differences relating to Jewishness: levels of acculturation, differing conceptions of spirituality, and contrasting degrees of observance of the *mitzvot.*

Lakeville, for example, is served by four Reform synagogues. All of the congregations are distinctive. One of them—the Samuel Hirsch Temple—is highly individual in its approach. In its conscious effort to break with the synagogue-center type, it has been called a synagogue for people who do not like to join synagogues. For a long time the congregation resisted constructing a synagogue building, because the leaders did not want to become involved in the type of activity that a building would entail. Furthermore, the Samuel Hirsch Temple in Lakeville has banned all clubs, and thus it does not have a sisterhood or men's club. The congregation has sought to confine its program to the traditional activities of worship and study, though these activities are of course conducted in a style that differs markedly from the traditional approach.[23]

Differences in the Reform group are paralleled and even accentuated among traditionalists. Far Rockaway, New York, for example, is a community that is as Orthodox in reputation as Lakeville is Reform. Beneath its seeming uniformity there is great diversity among the many small synagogues in the area, and considerable difference between the two largest institutions: the White Shool and Congregation Shaaray Tefila:

> The White Shool has developed primarily as a synagogue for the young layman who was once a yeshiva bochur [student in a school for advanced Talmudical learning]. . . . It is unique as an American synagogue in that it numbers among its congregants about thirty-five ordained, non-practicing rabbis. The congregation has no chazan [cantor] but instead uses a battery of its

own unusually gifted baaley-tefilah [prayer-leaders] who "work" in rotation. . . . [The rabbi] not only gives more classes. . . than the average rabbi, but he offers them on a generally much higher level. In some areas —such as Gemorah [Talmud]—he may give shiurim [classes] on the same subject to different groups at different levels. . . like the European Rav, the largest part of the rabbi's time is given over to learning Torah and preparing shiurim. . . while a relatively small portion is devoted to the social duties and obligations which take up ninety per cent of the average American rabbi's time.

Shaaray Tefila is tailored . . . to serve the total Jewish community rather than being primarily geared to the intensively Torah-educated Jew. Shaaray Tefila's decorous, dignified service, led by a capable chazan, gives the synagogue and its divine worship an air of sacred reverence and respect for the Almighty. Many White Shool'ers, however, whose own synagogue breathes an atmosphere of an informal camaraderie prevalent in a "second home," feel uncomfortable in the dignified atmosphere of Shaaray. . . . On the other hand, most Shaaray'ites would feel ill at ease in the White Shool, where a considerable amount of conversation goes on during the service. The White Shool, to them, is an "overgrown shtibel" [an intimate setting for prayer and religious study] and far too undecorous.[24]

As we noticed earlier those who wish to change the American synagogue are tempted to do so either by going outside of the synagogue or by somehow convincing established institutions of the error of their ways and seeing to it that they implement higher standards of spirituality. But another option is open to the elitists: they are free to establish their own synagogues. This option is afforded by the congregational structure of American Judaism, guaranteeing as it does the independence of the local synagogue. If this option is exercised the burden of proof will then be on the elitists for they will be compelled to demonstrate the superiority of their institutions over the standard American synagogue center. Since the individual Jew is able to exercise freedom of choice such new congregations will find themselves competitors in the open market of affiliation. The American Jew, then, is free to remain unaffiliated, to retain his present affiliation, or to establish a new institution that offers him a more congenial spiritual atmosphere.

The Jewish Community Center

Since one or more synagogues are located in each neighborhood or suburb of substantial Jewish population, the synagogue is the most visible organization of the Jewish community. Despite the fact that a significant proportion of the Jewish population is unaffiliated with the synagogue, and that some who belong have only the most tenuous connection with the institution, the synagogue is by far the dominant Jewish agency on the local level. Yet despite its importance the synagogue is only one of many Jewish agencies that constitute the organized Jewish community.

The existence of widely different types of organizations reveals the diversity in American Jewish life—diversity that provides options that would be absent in a community that was clearly either religious or ethnic in its structure. Some of the extra-synagogual organizations neatly supplement the synagogue, because their programs express religious values. Others, however, express values that are outside the conventional religious framework. Inasmuch as the Jewish religion is so ethnically oriented, competition between the synagogue and the ethnically oriented organization tends to be indirect. Furthermore because of the close nexus between Jewish religion and Jewish ethnicity, the ethnically oriented organization need not be considered irreligious by the religious. In fact only the ideologically oriented or the sociologically sophisticated individual may discern that the diversity of organizations provides a series of options for those who desire a Jewish affiliation. Generally, the reaction of the Jewish man on the street is that all Jewish organizations are good, for they all do "good work."

The Jewish community center constitutes one option—in this case an option to affiliation with the synagogue. Center members are free to either join a synagogue or to remain outside organized religious life; the center does not require affiliation with a synagogue as a qualification for membership. In fact, one need not be Jewish to join a Jewish community center: the National Jewish Welfare Board (the national coordinating body of the centers) recommends that membership in the center should be open to all residents of the community.

Jewish community centers exist in all major centers of Jewish population. But the institution is popular enough that it is even found in cities where the Jewish population numbers less than 2,000, as for example in Columbia, South Carolina, Duluth, Minnesota, and Holyoke, Massachusetts. In communities of under 50,000 Jews the center generally operates out of a single building. In the larger cities there are frequently multiple units: there is a central building with branches located in the principle Jewish neighborhoods. In New York the picture is more complex. There is a chain of affiliated centers (the Associated YM and YWHAs) as well as a network of independent centers, each based in a particular area of Jewish concentration.

The extent of center membership in contrast to synagogue membership in any given community is not easily discerned. The non-Jewish membership must be subtracted from the center's enrollment; in 1967 the proportion of non-Jewish membership on a nationwide basis was 9.5 percent, almost double what it had been a decade earlier.[25] Furthermore while synagogue membership is customarily tabulated by family units, center membership is counted on an individual basis. In any case it is readily apparent that the affiliation rate with centers is much lower than the rate for synagogues. Only in the smaller communities can the affiliation rate of the center compare with that of the synagogue. In the smaller communities where the synagogue affiliation rate is commonly over 70 percent the majority of families may also belong to the center. In the larger communities, however, where the affiliation rate with synagogues may drop to 50 percent, the affiliation rate for centers is quite small; centers may enroll only 2 to 10 percent of the Jewish families of the community.[26] This disparity in affiliation rate exists despite the fact that synagogue membership dues and building assessments are more expensive than comparable fees in centers.

Finally, what proportion of center members are also synagogue members? This question has never been studied but it is apparent that while in the smallest communities center membership and synagogue membership may be almost interchangeable, in the largest communities it is not at all unusual to find a center member who has no link with the synagogue. And of course the larger the community the less chance there is that the synagogue member will belong to a Jewish community center.

Unlike the synagogue, the center is a modern invention. Some centers trace their beginnings to clubs established by youthful male immigrants who arrived in the United States from Germany in the nineteenth century. The first such club was established in Baltimore in 1854. These organizations, and their counterparts for women, generally emphasized culture and uplift, though without the stress on religious values characteristic of the YMCAs that were founded during the same era. These German-Jewish "Young Men's Hebrew Associations," or YMHAs as they came to be designated, flourished only briefly. Economic advancement and acculturation diminished their appeal. Private clubs for the upper classes and lodges for the middle classes became the vogue; community-wide organizations designed to meet cultural and recreational needs had to compete with the satisfactions derivable from more exclusive associations. And the notion of *Kultur* came to be challenged by less demanding recreational pursuits.

The immigration of East European Jews renewed the movement and led to the establishment of neighborhood centers, many of the settlement house variety. Some settlement houses conceived of themselves as Jewish institutions, dedicated to the welfare of the subcommunity. Others stressed service to people who happened to reside in the "ghetto" rather than to Jews in particular. However conceived, all were dedicated to teaching the immigrant the language and culture of America and to stressing what America required of him.

While the ancestry of the center movement traces back to the YMHA and the Jewish settlement house, the contemporary community center does not resemble its predecessors. Typically it is located in a "better" neighborhood or suburb and is an imposing structure of modern design. It offers something for every age and taste. There is a nursery school for those under six and a golden age program for retired and elderly members. There is a sports and health-club program for those of every athletic persuasion, from basketball or handball for those geared to strenuous pursuits to the sauna and masseur for the more sedentary. A selection of hobby groups, discussion groups, and classes is designed to appeal to individuals of the most varied sensibilities, and there is a club department geared to the interests of young people of elementary and high school age.

The question of the ideology of the center movement has been debated for many years. During the settlement house era there were occasional criticisms of the Americanization program: Was it in the best interest of the immigrant to Americanize him and thereby remove him from his cultural roots? Did not the stress on Americanization imply an unsupportable belief in the superiority of American culture? The same queries were of course being asked in the general settlement house movement. However, there was one aspect of the controversy that was specifically Jewish—the possibility that the end product of the effort might be ethnic and religious assimilation rather than Americanization. This possibility was raised by Solomon Schechter, the famed rabbinical scholar who came to the United States from England in 1902 to head the Jewish Theological Seminary of America. Soon after his arrival Schechter was placed on the board of the Educational Alliance, the great settlement house located on New York's Lower East Side. Opposed to what he found to be the thrust of the institution and frustrated in his efforts to effect change, Schechter wrote the following in his letter of resignation:

The great question before the Jewish community is not so much the Americanising of the Russian Jew as his Judaising. We have now quite sufficient agencies for his Americanisation. But the problem is whether we are able to keep the immigrant within Judaism after he has become Americanised. Nor is there any need on our part of civilising him, as the general phrase is. Our public schools are overcrowded with Russian young men and women, and so are our Colleges. . . .

Time and economic conditions compel the immigrant to grow constantly in his Americanism and to develop it, unfortunately not always for his good. . . . there cannot be the least doubt that what the immigrant loses quickest in this country is his Judaism. . . . However, my views on this and cognate matters are not shared by the Board. Heaven knows, we never had too much Hebrew [taught at the Alliance] . . . but even this little is to be reduced in favour of something which is called Ethics and Religion. . . . I have sufficient experience to know that it will terminate in representing the religion of the Settlement kind, made up of obsolete philosophies, intermixed with sociology and political economy, interspersed with epigrams from Emerson, obscure lines from Browning, and exclamations about evolution and progress, proving that we, the heroes of modernity, are the promise and fulfillment of civilisation. I have heard and read enough of this sort of lecture to know that . . . it is an "unsectarian religion" bringing us nearer with every day to the abyss; or the great "melting pot," which will devour Judaism ruthlessly as soon as the social prejudice on the part of our neighbours will sufficiently relax.[27]

Schechter was ahead of his time; the board of the Educational Alliance remained convinced that the problem before the Jewish community was that of building American identity, not Jewish identity.

Attention shifted away from the immigrant in the 1920s and toward adolescents and young adults who were members of the second generation. Inculcating the duties of citizenship and teaching the English language gave way to stressing the idea of leisure, the pursuit of hobbies, and the development of the body—all concepts strongly deemphasized in Jewish culture. The 1930s brought the Depression and the growth of anti-Semitism both in the United States as well as abroad. The resulting crisis served to postpone questions of ideological clarification. At the conclusion of World War II, however, the problem could no longer be avoided. Was the Jewish community center a nonsectarian agency charged with enhancing the growth and development of the individual by providing social group work services to people who happened to reside in Jewish neighborhoods? Or was it an agency dedicated to Jewish survival—or in more general terms to enhancing the Jewish growth and development of the individuals whom it served? If the answer was the latter, the method of social group work would be incidental to the purposes of the agency.

Inevitably a study was commissioned. It resulted in the submission of the "Janowsky Report."[28] The report called upon the centers to advance the Jewish component in the lives of the center's members. On the assumption that acculturation had made the Jew "American," it advocated what Schechter had termed "Judaising." Those who favored emphasis on nonsectarian aspects protested the report but by the 1940s this position was on the defensive. Acculturation had proceeded at such a rapid pace that only those to whom survival was irrelevant could still maintain that the traditional programs should be continued. Furthermore, the survivalists—who had been labeled as segregationists for many decades—managed to turn the tables upon their opponents. They charged that those who were oriented to nonsectarian programs were the true segregationists inasmuch as they defended the existence of Jewish institutions that had no distinctive Jewish purposes. Survivalists maintained that a Jewish institution that lacked Jewish purposes was necessarily segregative, and that it should either become Jewish in program as well as in name or be terminated with all deliberate speed.

While the Janowsky Report indicated a direction it did not

provide the answer to how the program of the center was to be shifted. Despite the innumerable resolutions that have been passed in recent years, "Jewish programming" as it is described in the center movement has made limited progress. Some trace the situation to negative attitudes of center staff to Jewish identification. Others emphasize that the commitment of the staff to traditional social work ideology makes them hesitant to advocate values to their clientele. Still others believe that the real roadblock is the ignorance of staff about Jewish culture. Finally, a number believe that the problem resides in the apathy, ignorance, or hostility of the membership of the centers.

Whatever the importance of each of these explanations, the overriding fact is that the center should now be the preeminent institution in the Jewish community. As Jews have become more secularized the center should have emerged as a logical option to the synagogue. Indeed it should have largely replaced the synagogue. But judged by any yardstick—the size of membership, the amount of resources, or institutional morale—the synagogue is far ahead of the center.

The problem of the center revolves around its vision of building a secular Jewish culture. To build such a system means splitting the Jewish atom of religion and culture; because Jewish culture is so suffused with religiosity its development in isolation from religion is extremely difficult. This complication aside, if a specialized culture is to flourish the individuals who desire it must separate themselves from the general community to a substantial extent. This condition is not generally fulfilled in the American Jewish community, and even those who are strong advocates of a Jewishly oriented center have hesitated to advocate such separation. In fact the major push toward separatism has come from the direction of the religious forces in the community.

The 1940s was already very late to attempt to rescue the secular Jewish culture that had flourished briefly during the immigrant era. The cornerstone of this culture was the Yiddish language. But the centers did not attempt to strengthen or preserve the use of Yiddish as a language. Ironically enough, by its emphasis on Americanization the center movement had contributed to the sharp decline in the use of Yiddish and thus had helped to decrease the possibility of developing the very secular Jewish culture that it later came to espouse.

Currently some centers are seeking to develop a connection with Israel as an alternative to their abortive efforts to create an American Jewish culture. Prior to the establishment of Israel, and even during the 1950s, the center movement never had strong linkages of this type. The difficulty of developing an American Jewish culture without separatism, plus the appealing image that Israel presents, has made the option a logical one. Nevertheless, it is questionable whether the attempt can solve the center's problem of developing a secular alternative to a synagogue-based Jewish life.[29]

We are now in a position to understand the greater appeal of the synagogue over the center. The synagogue, by its very existence, symbolizes Jewish identity. However far the individual may be from realizing the ideals of the synagogue, it offers an unambiguous model with respect to Jewish identity. The center, on the other hand, offers very little in the way of a model—in the absence of a secular Jewish culture it functions more as a service institution than as a model for identity. And in the absence of an identity model even the secular-minded Jew is motivated to turn to a sacred institution. Some would add that he is assisted in this choice by the tendency of the general culture to define the Jews as a religious group.

The superior numbers, resources, and morale of the synagogue group have motivated some of its ideologically oriented supporters to publicly express their attitudes toward the center.[30] Such criticism defines the center as an ethnic institution that emphasizes recreational activities of a nonsectarian type and in the process undermines the effort to move Jews either toward increased Jewish identity or greater Jewish religiosity. Critics claim that recreational needs can either be satisfied by synagogue-sponsored programs or in truly nonsectarian settings. The center movement has responded by declaring that it serves many individuals who do not belong to synagogues and thereby provides them with their only link to the Jewish community. Center supporters also stress that the institution offers activities that the congregations are not equipped to provide. The centers further claim that while the synagogue only serves those of its own persuasion the center is an institution that serves all kinds of Jews: Reform, Conservative, Orthodox, and those who are outside of the religious life of the community. By providing a nondenominational Jewish meeting place the centers maintain that they promote cohesion in the subcommunity and supply a model for Jewish unity.

Social Services

HEALTH CARE. The Jewish community maintains an intricate network of social services. Indeed the network is so extensive that in theory the individual Jew need not make use of the resources of the general community: he may live out his life within the framework of the subcommunity. However, the services provided by the Jewish community cannot be viewed only from the standpoint of the recipient. They perform equally vital functions for those who support them, those who direct them, and those who take pride in their existence.

Many Jewish hospitals have become widely known in the general community, and thus the area of health services is the most visible part of the Jewish communal network. The strong health consciousness found in the Jewish community has been complemented by the health consciousness found in the general community. This has helped to stimulate the growth of a network of hospitals that includes general hospitals, hospitals for the chronically ill, hospitals for the mentally ill, and hospitals that specialize in particular diseases. Other health services include convalescent homes, rehabilitation services, and facilities for the handicapped. In 1967 there were 22,635 beds in sixty-three Jewish-sponsored hospitals.[31] With the exception of Washington, D.C., Jewish hospitals have been established in all cities with a Jewish population of over

40,000. But smaller communities also have such facilities: half of the cities with a Jewish population of 15,000 to 40,000 maintain a Jewish hospital.

Most Jewish hospitals have not been content to be obscure, sectarian-sponsored institutions confined to the backwaters of American medicine. A surprisingly large number are recognized among the leading medical institutions of their community. Some Jewish hospitals have sought more than local recognition; indeed several have achieved national reputations. In an effort to retain its preeminence the most ambitious Jewish hospital in the country, The Mount Sinai Hospital of New York City, has gone so far as to establish its own medical school.

The progress of Jewish hospitals is remarkable considering that some of the original needs that were reputed to have led to their establishment have disappeared: they are no longer needed to provide an affiliation for Jewish doctors who are excluded from other facilities, or in order to service unacculturated Jewish patients who would feel out of place in a general facility. In fact, Jews exhibit relatively little loyalty to Jewish hospitals in terms of their own medical needs. When asked how they would feel about using a Jewish facility should they require hospitalization, only 17 percent of Boston Jews said that they would prefer a Jewish hospital.[32] The vast majority—75 percent—said that they were indifferent to the sponsorship of the hospital, while 5 percent said that they would prefer not to use a Jewish facility.

These responses reveal that Jews are now patronizing hospitals sponsored by a variety of groups. Thus only 25 percent of Boston Jews who had been in a hospital during the past year utilized a Jewish hospital, while some 56 percent utilized a non-Jewish voluntary institution.[33] Accordingly, the Jewish hospital is making an ever-decreasing contribution to meeting the health needs of Jews. Nevertheless, there is still an abiding interest in the hospitals. While their contribution to serving the health needs of the subcommunity may be minor, their contribution to satisfying identity needs is substantial: for a significant segment of the Jewish population the hospitals demonstrate a Jewish presence in the larger community and perform a vital and esteemed civic service. Eminence is also important: the high reputation of the Jewish hospital enhances the reputation of the group.

While considerable loyalty for supporting the hospitals if not for patronizing them remains, they have recently become the subject of controversy. The controversy is rooted in two considerations of the role of the Jewish hospital: on the one hand the hospitals serve the general community, and on the other hand Jews no longer need them in order to meet their health needs. A further complication is that many hospitals do not adhere to traditional Jewish culture. Thus a substantial number of institutions—of which Mount Sinai Hospital in New York City is the model—have been heavily influenced by highly acculturated German Jews and are difficult to distinguish from comparable institutions in the general community. To be sure, there are hospitals like Maimonides in Brooklyn that have been sponsored by East European Jews and retain a noticeable degree of traditionalism. They serve kosher food exclusively and facilitate the observance of Jewish rituals and holidays.

Jewish students and others who are interested in a radical reconstruction of the Jewish community have been highly critical of the support extended to the hospitals. When the Concerned Jewish Students demonstrated at the 1969 General Assembly of the Council of Jewish Federations and Welfare Funds they distributed a leaflet that read: "While hospitals are certainly necessary humanitarian organizations, the funds used to support 'Jewish' hospitals could be easily replaced by grants from the Federal government." In effect they were suggesting that Jewish sponsorship of hospitals be discontinued; they believed that hospitals were expendable as Jewish communal institutions. They reasoned that if the hospitals were abandoned funds could then be shifted from meeting medical needs to meeting Jewish identity needs, specifically to supporting Jewish educational and cultural services. Ironically, the very identity needs that moved the Concerned Jewish Students to stress the need to support Jewish education and culture has motivated highly acculturated communal leaders to remain loyal to the idea that there should be a

Jewish hospital in every Jewish community. Consequently despite the students' demonstration, allocations for Jewish hospitals were voted by local federations at their subsequent budget meetings.

FAMILY AND CHILD CARE. Jewish family and child care agencies are not as widely known as Jewish hospitals. Yet all large- and middle-size communities have specialized agencies that render these services. Sometimes a single agency handles both family and child care needs while in other instances there are two separate agencies. In smaller communities the services are frequently rendered by a multifunctional Jewish agency. The prevalence of these agencies and the support accorded to them originates in traditional Jewish attitudes toward the essential importance of marriage and family life.

During an earlier period in Jewish history the main function of the family agencies was to extend relief. Not only was such relief necessitated by the lack of public assistance but it was also dictated by Jewish religious law, as well as by the age-old Jewish practice of "taking care of one's own." Another motivating factor was the fear that anti-Semitism would grow if the economic problems of indigent Jews should become a matter of public concern.

The beginning of public assistance together with the principle that such assistance was a matter of right not privilege, plus the establishment of the social security system and most recently of Medicare, have made it possible for the agencies to disengage themselves from the costly responsibility of extending financial assistance. Financial assistance, when it is presently extended, is generally on a short-term basis. It is concentrated in certain groups that do not qualify for public assistance or social security, such as refugees.

With minimal economic maintenance assured by government, Jewish family agencies changed their emphasis by shifting to assisting individuals who were suffering from psychological disabilities. They began to stress the creation of counseling services and therapy programs for individuals and families suffering from varying degrees of malfunction. Jewish agencies soon became noted for their psychological sophistication and they provided a model for those Gentile-sponsored agencies interested in moving in a similar direction. The Jewish agencies also began to attract a new type of client, because psychological problems were to be found among all social classes. Because free care for the middle and upper classes was inappropriate, payments for service were introduced. Such payments served both to attract members of the middle class as well as to justify taking them on as cases, and to help meet the high costs of employing the staffs of highly skilled case workers, psychiatric social workers, and psychiatrists that the agencies required.

Unlike the hospitals the clientele of most of the agencies is largely Jewish. But like the hospitals the agencies render only a minor proportion of the psychological services utilized by Jews. The most important single source of help is the therapist practicing privately—the psychoanalyst, psychiatrist, psychologist, or psychiatric social worker. In Boston some 39 percent of those who indicated that they had obtained help with a personal problem said that they had consulted a psychiatrist or psychologist.[34] An additional 15 percent consulted a medical doctor. While it would be safe to infer that in both instances the majority of respondents consulted a practitioner who was Jewish, the fact is that only 9 percent of the respondents said that they had utilized the services of a Jewish agency. This is in contrast to 21 percent who said that they had utilized the services of a non-Jewish sponsored agency. Thus even when help is sought from an agency there is no strong tendency to limit oneself to a Jewish setting.

Child care services have followed somewhat the same course as family services. At an earlier period these services concentrated on caring for orphans and homeless children. The setting was the orphan home where the physical needs of hundreds of youngsters could be met with maximum efficiency. As the social disorganization attendant upon the immigrant period waned, and as the increased longevity of adults resulted in a diminution of the orphan population, the need for such homes lessened. Practices also began to change: widowed mothers were encouraged to keep their families together rather than to place their children in an institution. Greater understanding of the psychological needs of children dictated that large and impersonal institutional settings be abolished. Accordingly, the agencies began to utilize foster homes instead of orphanages; they also established residential facilities to simulate family settings. Sometimes these were cottage-type arrangements located outside the city but more recently the model has become the urban apartment setting.

The typical child under care today is not an orphan but rather a youngster who is suffering from a psychological disability. As a result, the emphasis of child care agencies largely parallels that of family agencies, and if anything more stress is placed upon intensive psychological treatment.

Many family and child care agencies accept a limited number of Gentile clients. Some members of the professional staffs of the agencies, as well as some of the lay leadership, believe that the agencies must move further in this direction: that they should serve the total community, make their contribution to solving the urban crisis, and in essence follow the path that the Jewish hospitals have taken. But there is strong resistance to this view: some maintain that the primary responsibility of the agencies should continue to be to serve Jews, that a Jewish component in their services will be diluted if the agencies become more nonsectarian, and, finally, that the problems found within the Jewish community are sufficiently serious and challenging to justify a continuing sectarian emphasis. Those who hold this view are deeply troubled by Jewish family disorganization, by the alienation of Jewish youth, and by the use of drugs among younger Jews.

Hospitals have become increasingly nonsectarian in emphasis; family and child care services are at the crossroads. We now examine an area of Jewish social service that has retained a highly sectarian role in the Jewish community.

AGED CARE. In theory there should be no need for aged care: according to Jewish tradition all adults should marry, all marriages should produce children, children should outlive their parents, and most importantly of all, when children grow to adulthood they should assume the obligation of caring for their aged parents. But such responsibility has meant something different in the United States than it did in Europe. There it was related to the existence of the three-generational household. We have already suggested that the three-generational household of grandparents, parents, and children is more exceptional than typical in the United States (see Chapter 3). While this practice does not account for the establishment of Jewish old-age homes in the United States—they would be required in any case because not all adults marry, not all marriages result in children, and not all children outlive their parents—it does help to explain the strong demand that exists for the care of aged persons.

The *moshav z'kanim,* or old-age home, is a venerable Jewish institution once regarded as an agency serving unfortunates. But it is in the midst of acquiring a new respectability, both as adult children seek to free themselves from guilt feelings about their responsibility to care for aged parents unable to manage their own households, and as aged parents hesitate to enter households headed by their children—households where they would necessarily assume subordinate roles. The new respectability of the old-age home is also connected with the changing class level of its clientele. The homes have ever-fewer lower class residents, particularly residents whose children are also lower class. Increasingly residents are members of the middle class; their children are frequently prosperous and well-educated.

While at one time the communally sponsored old-age home maintained a near monopoly, in recent years private entrepreneurs have entered the field in large numbers. Their facilities vary widely in quality and in cultural content: some uphold a rigorous interpretation of Jewish tradition while others are Jewish merely by virtue of the clientele they attract and the Jewish delicacies that they include in their menus. In any case there is no real competition between the communal and the private sector; there are long waiting lists at most of the communally sponsored old-age homes. The constantly expanding ranks of the Jewish aged are large enough to accommodate all who seek to serve them.

The traditionalism of communally connected old-age homes varies widely, depending to some extent on whether they were established by German or East European Jews. But even the less traditional homes generally accept only Jews, although administrators have become sensitive on this score because of the increasing use of government funds. The easy acceptance of sectarianism is related to the fact that residents of the homes are less acculturated than younger Jews, and they live in a setting where social distance is necessarily minimal. But it also suggests a kind of reverence for the aged—an attitude that is very much a part of traditional Jewish culture. It implies that the aged will be more comfortable if their declining years are spent in the company of their fellow Jews; it would be unreasonable to expect them to live with members of the outgroup in order to prove the abstract principle that the Jewish community not only serves its own but renders help to the general community. After all, how many more years of life do they have? Are they not ultimately to be buried in a Jewish cemetery, an institution that demonstrates the final solidarity of the subcommunity?

Thus far the American Jewish community has managed to achieve a measure of solidarity in life as well as death. It has made a transition from the belongingness of European communities with their roots in a closed society to the voluntarism of the subcommunity in the open society of America. However, there is concern among Jewish leaders that this achievement may be short-lived. The fear is frequently expressed that the present communal structure is endangered by indifference or by an even more serious threat: the possible attachment of Jews to other subcommunities.

What then should be done to insure group continuity? True to the thrust of Jewish culture there is a widespread belief that education—Jewish education, that is—constitutes the solution to the problem. Thus we turn in the next chapter to an analysis of that enterprise known as Jewish education. The enterprise is a *terra incognita* to most students of American social structure, for the Protestant Sunday school and the Catholic parochial school have preempted both the popular and the scholarly imagination. Nevertheless the system of Jewish schools established in the United States represents a large and multifaceted effort to continue cultural transmission in the "first new nation."

Notes

1 Milton M. Gordon, *Assimilation in American Life* (New York: Oxford University Press, 1964), p. 247.

2 All of the Jewish communal histories contain material on the range of Jewish organizations and on the problem of communal coordination and control. See, for example, Selig Adler and Thomas Connolly, *From Ararat to Suburbia: the History of the Jewish Community of Buffalo* (Philadelphia: Jewish Publication Society of America, 1960); and Louis J. Swichkow and Lloyd P. Gartner, *The History of the Jews of Milwaukee* (Philadelphia: Jewish Publication Society of America, 1963). Arthur A. Goren's *New York Jews and the Quest for Community* (New York: Columbia University Press, 1970) is a sophisticated analysis of an abortive attempt to organize the Jews of that community for purposes other than philanthropy. For an excellent analysis of European communal structure in the period just before Emancipation, see Jacob Katz, *Tradition and Crisis: Jewish Society at the End of the Middle Ages* (New York: The Free Press, 1961).

3 On the usage of the term "sacramental" see Marshall Sklare and Joseph Greenblum, *Jewish Identity on the Suburban Frontier: A Study of Group Survival in the Open Society* (New York: Basic Books, 1967), p. 46. Some of the paragraphs that follow are adapted from Chapter III of this work.

4 Morris Axelrod, Floyd J. Fowler, and Arnold Gurin, *A Community for Long Range Planning—A Study of the Jewish Population of Greater Boston* (Boston: Combined Jewish Philanthropies of Greater Boston, 1967), p. 119. Most of the balance of 15 percent have no preference, or consider themselves nonreligious.

5 The low status occupied by Orthodoxy until recent years is an additional consideration. This factor has apparently operated only among Ashkenazim.

6 It is apparent that individuals who were reared in observant households are seldom prepared to neglect the dietary laws altogether. And when they do violate them they are aware of their violation, sometimes acutely so. Frequently they are prepared to concede to the demands of Orthodox Jews who maintain that the laws should be observed on public occasions.

[7] Sidney Goldstein and Calvin Goldscheider, *Jewish Americans: Three Generations in a Jewish Community* (Englewood Cliffs, N.J.: Prentice-Hall, 1968), p. 201. The true figure may be somewhat lower. Given the nature of community, the sponsorship of the study, and the affect surrounding *kashrut*, it seems likely that respondents would overstate their religiosity.

[8] *Dreydl:* a spinning top on the four sides of which are engraved the Hebrew initials of the phrase "a great miracle happened there."

[9] Note that in Boston this category is defined as more than once a month.

[10] In evaluating cross-religious comparisons (particularly in the case of New York City) it should be noted that Orthodox Judaism does not require regular synagogue attendance on the part of women.

[11] Note the case of Park Forest, Ill. See Herbert J. Gans, "The Origin and Growth of a Jewish Community," in Marshall Sklare (ed.), *The Jews: Social Patterns of An American Group* (New York: The Free Press, 1958).

[12] So great is the stress on the building of synagogues that it has drawn the attention of students of art and architecture. See, for example, Avram Kampf, *Contemporary Synagogue Art: Developments in the United States 1945–1965* (New York: Union of American Hebrew Congregations, 1966).

[13] Albert J. Mayer, *Flint Jewish Population Study: 1967* (Processed, Flint, Mich.: Flint Jewish Community Council, 1969), p. 45.

[14] See Sidney Goldstein, *A Population Survey of the Greater Springfield Jewish Community* (Springfield, Mass.: Springfield Jewish Community Council, 1968), p. 93.

[15] Albert J. Mayer, *Jewish Population Study-Series II* (Detroit: Jewish Welfare Federation of Detroit, 1964–1966), p. 24; and Axelrod et al., *op. cit.*, p. 136.

[16] In Springfield where inquiry was made into reasons for nonaffiliation, the most frequent response was the cost of synagogue membership. Only about one out of ten went so far as to say their reason for nonaffiliation was a lack of interest.

[17] In recent years the congregational unions such as the Union of American Hebrew Congregations (Reform), the United Synagogue (Conservative) and the Union of Orthodox Jewish Congregations of America (Orthodox) have taken greater initiative in forming new congregations.

The most notable exception to the freedom of the local congregation to determine its own affairs are synagogues affiliated with Young Israel (Orthodox). Title to the property of a Young Israel synagogue is vested in the national movement. The purpose of the arrangement is to prevent a congregation from instituting religious practices that violate Orthodox norms.

[18] Sidney Goldstein, *The Greater Providence Jewish Community: A Population Survey* (Providence: General Jewish Committee of Providence, 1964), p. 141.

[19] One important aspect of the synagogue center (very much emphasized in the writings of Mordecai M. Kaplan, for example) is the conception that nothing Jewish should be alien to the synagogue—that the synagogue should offer its facilities to all Jewish organizations that make a contribution to Jewish survival and that it should seek to facilitate the work of such organizations. But inasmuch as there are inherent strains in the relationship of the congregation to the community, this is more easily said than done.

[20] Eugene B. Borowitz, *A New Jewish Theology in the Making* (Philadelphia: The Westminster Press, 1968), pp. 45–46.

[21] *Ibid.*, pp. 53–54.

[22] Jacob Neusner and Ira Eisenstein, *The Havurah Idea* (New York: The Reconstructionist Press, n.d.).

[23] See Sklare and Greenblum, *op. cit.*, pp. 97–178.

[24] Michael Kaufman, "Far Rockaway–Torah-Suburb By-the-Sea," *Jewish Life,* 27, No. 6 (August 1960), 25–28.

[25] *JWB Year Book*, 18 (1969), 6.

[26] New York, with its extremely low rate of synagogue affiliation, has a similarly low rate of community-center affiliation.

[27] Norman Bentwich, *Solomon Schechter* (Philadelphia: Jewish Publication Society of America, 1938), pp. 215–219.

[28] See Oscar I. Janowsky, *The JWB Survey* (New York: Dial Press, 1948).

[29] As a result of the urban crisis and the pressure upon social agencies (some of it internally generated) to make a contribution to solving social ills, a new nonsectarian emphasis has recently emerged in the Jewish center field.

[30] See "Symposium on the Relationship Between the Synagogue and the Center," *Conservative Judaism* (Winter-Spring 1962), pp. 1–50.

31 S. P. Goldberg, *Jewish Communal Services: Programs and Finances* (New York: Council of Jewish Federations and Welfare Funds, fourteenth edition, 1969), p. 39.

32 Axelrod et al., *op. cit.*, p. 106.

33 *Ibid.*, p. 81.

34 *Ibid.*, p. 91.

Chapter 5 ◉ Jewish Education and Identity

Of all the institutional arrangements developed in the American Jewish community none involves as many fateful implications for Jewish identity as the Jewish educational system. Since Jewish education is that enterprise concerned with formal training in the cultural heritage of the Jewish people, it is both an index to the type of Jewish identity practiced and desired, as well as a force contributing to the shaping of identity.

Jewish tradition is special in the stress that it places upon acquiring mastery of the Jewish cultural heritage. It denigrates the ignorant man and it casts doubt upon his religious piety. The system assumes universal education for males; its ideal prescribes that each male Jew will be educated to the maximum of his ability. And regardless of at what point he is compelled to drop out of the system of formal instruction, the Jew is to continue learning. As a consequence there evolved the tradition of adult study groups, meeting regularly for the study of one or another classical Jewish text. As an alternative, individuals with high religious aspirations and strong preparation might continue their education by self-study, perhaps occasionally consulting an authority upon encountering a particularly knotty text. So strong was the cultural ideal of learning that some continued to be full-time students throughout their mature years. They did not pursue the ideals of monasticism, however, for they were husbands and fathers as well as students—their spouses took over responsibility for the earning of the family livelihood. While exact statistics on the proportion receiving an elementary or advanced Jewish education in past eras is lacking, and while we also do not know how many continued their studies either on a part- or full-time basis, the singularity of the Jewish tradition of learning in the Western world is at once apparent.

What, then, is the place of secular education in this system? Because Jewish learning is not restricted to narrow limits, the conventional distinction between sacred and secular studies is not made. Nevertheless, there is recognition of an area of learning that is general and therefore not Jewish. The stance of traditional Jewish culture is to confer primacy on Jewish learning, placing such learning in the area of the sacred. Jewish learning is therefore mandatory while secular learning is distinctly optional. Depending upon the time and place, Jews have viewed secular learning with varying degrees of suspicion. According to traditional norms, if secular learning is to be pursued the individual should first have a thorough grounding in Jewish learning. Caution must be exercised that secular learning does not undermine religious faith. And even while he is pursuing secular learning the individual is admonished to continue his Jewish studies.

Maimonides, the great sage of the twelfth century, is sometimes adduced as an example of the happy mating of Jewish and secular learning. Actually his predecessor of the eleventh century, Rashi, is a more representative figure, certainly for Ashkanezic Jewry. Maimonides' occupational problem was the necessity of striking a balance between his commitments as an important physician and as a famed rabbinical authority; his intellectual problem was that of balancing the demands of Jewish faith and the philosophical challenges of his era. But these were not Rashi's concerns. Rashi had no obligations to the general community and no acquaintance with the intellectual currents of his time. Devoting his life to the explication of Jewish texts, he became the commentator *par excellence* on the great Jewish books. His work achieved such wide recognition that even today, after mastering the rudiments of learning, the student who follows the traditional curriculum proceeds to the study of Jewish texts accompanied by Rashi's commentaries.

The Hasidic movement, established in the eighteenth century, strongly opposed the preeminence of learning and its close relationship to religious piety. However, Hasidism was eventually to be strongly influenced by traditional norms. It was secularism not Hasidism that provided the real challenge to the traditional system. Secularism undercut Jewish learning because it insisted that the world could no longer be understood through the mastery of Jewish culture; it held that the questions to which Jewish learning were addressed were no longer of significance. In effect it maintained that Jewish culture had been superseded, that Jewish culture was worthy of attention only by a few specialists who would study it out of scientific curiosity rather than religious obligation.

Problems of American-Jewish Education

What then of the American Jew? We have noted that a significant percentage of those who came to the United States during the period of mass immigration were at best nominally Orthodox. There were many who had been touched by the secularization process in eastern Europe. For them the encounter with America greatly speeded their secularization. But the effect of the American experience was so overwhelming that it even influenced those who arrived with a traditional orientation and desired to follow established models.

The net result was that very few immigrants sought to educate their children in conformity with Jewish tradition. They did not provide a setting in which the primary learning experience would be Jewish culture. Rather, they looked to the public school system to provide the basic educational framework for their offspring. The choice of the public schools was a fateful decision, because granting primacy to secular learning undermined the assumptions on which the traditional system rested.

The favor that the public school system found in the eyes of the immigrant is a highly significant index of his secularization and desire to accommodate to America (see Chapter 1). And the public school in turn served to speed the process of integrating both parent as well as child into American culture. Given the attitudes of those who came to America during the period of the mass migration, together with the challenges and opportunities of American life (and particularly the way such challenges and opportunities were interpreted by the immigrant), the traditional orientation to Jewish learning was abandoned and a new orientation to secular education came into being. It is possible to contend that the shift was so extreme that values actually became transposed: secular education assumed the place that Jewish education had occupied, while Jewish education was shifted to the position formerly assigned to secular education.

There is evidence to buttress this contention. In our analysis of the level of secular education we noticed the overwhelmingly strong attraction that such education exercised (see Chapter 2). Jewish immigrants—in most cases possessing only the most rudimentary training in secular studies if any at all—encouraged their children to attend grammar school. While in many states school attendance was already required by law, parents among other immigrant groups encouraged evasion rather than conformity. Furthermore, Jewish immigrants frequently stimulated their offspring, particularly their sons, to continue on to high school. The desire for higher education is even encountered in the immigrant family. So strong was this desire that half a century ago private institutions of higher learning that were located in the major centers of Jewish population began to fear that they would be confronted with more Jewish candidates than they were prepared to accept. Remarkably, desire for higher education among the second generation represented conformity to parental aspirations rather than rebellion against family values.

In our discussion of the level of secular education we made the point that the desire to attend college cannot simply be explained by the wish to achieve economic advancement. We suggested that it is also connected with the Jewish attitude toward learning. We see now that this attitude has deep roots in traditional society, and that in the process of acculturation secular learning came to be substituted for the old sacred learning. Thus for some the American college became a kind of secularized *yeshivah*. The institution most perfectly exemplifying this trend is the College of the City of New York

(CCNY) which has afforded the opportunity for higher education to the largest number of immigrant children. One of its most famous graduates and faculty members, Morris Raphael Cohen, is an excellent example of the secularized version of the *yeshivah bochur* (student).[1] True to traditional norms he achieved his position by strength of mind rather than body, by mental rather than physical courage, by manipulating the abstract rather than the concrete. Climbing from obscurity to fame, in his later years he became a secularized counterpart of a *rosh yeshivah* (head of a *yeshivah*). By virtue of his brilliance he established an international reputation among scholars; by his dedication to the life of the mind he came to serve as a model for his students.

If many immigrant Jewish parents were not only enthusiastic about enrolling their children in the public schools but even found the secularism of the American college acceptable, they also wanted to maintain their opinion of themselves as good Jews—that is, as conforming to Jewish norms. They wished to retain Jewish culture, or at least as much Jewish culture as they could without being disloyal to what they considered their commitments as Americans. They wished to pass something on to their children that would make *them* Jewish. All of this meant that despite their acceptance of the school system of the general society the immigrants felt compelled to establish some type of Jewish educational system.

This desire by the parent for Jewish education for his child has not been easily fulfilled, whether in the first, second, third, or subsequent generations. Developing an educational system that would be both "American" in that it conformed to the limitations (and was capable of meeting the challenges) of the environment, and simultaneously "Jewish" in that it would have continuity with the past, has constituted an almost insurmountable problem. For example, the adaptation of the traditional curriculum has proven to be difficult because it concentrates so heavily on textual study. In order for the student in the traditional curriculum to make progress he must pursue his studies intensively. He must achieve linguistic mastery to conquer the Hebrew texts, as well as acquire some knowledge of cognate languages for his advanced studies.

In addition to such formidable technical problems there are cultural obstacles. First and foremost is the fact that the child's primary learning experience is in American culture. The secularism, pragmatism, and modernism of this culture serves to alienate him from the Biblical and Talmudic worlds. Consequently the texts do not "speak" to him. Whether the question being discussed is the purity of the high priest or that of the construction of the Temple where he officiates, the problems are far from his suburban milieu. And not only is the traditional curriculum profoundly at odds with the life that the student is leading but his parents provide little reinforcement: they like to think of themselves as good Jews but their loyalty to tradition tends to be more of a sentimental gesture than a hard commitment.

While all of these factors place considerable pressure on the school perhaps the greatest problem is the introduction of a new objective into Jewish education: Jewish identity. In traditional society identity is assumed; it is the job of the school to prepare the child scholastically. Accordingly, the emphasis is on a very long school day, under the assumption that the longer the child is in class the more he will learn. And since the pupil should always pay attention there is even tolerance for the teacher who believes that it is necessary to use the rod in order not to spoil the child. To be sure, rabbinical authorities sought to curb excesses, stressing that teachers should treat their pupils kindly, should avoid punishment, and should seek to inspire rather than to compel. But because identity was taken for granted and inasmuch as the Jewish school was not competing with any other form of education, the attitude of the pupil was not deemed crucial. The new emphasis on identity, on the other hand, means that the response of the child to the school is of first importance.

The identity-emphasis has been escalated by the parent's fastening upon the Jewish school to assure group survival. The parent thereby places a great burden upon Jewish education—one that it has been ill-prepared to assume. And the emphasis on identity-formation means that there is yet another reason why the traditional curriculum creates difficulties: it was not developed with an eye toward furthering identification.

While the need for identity apparently requires a new curriculum it is by no means obvious what type of curriculum will succeed in producing identity. Indeed it is dubious whether identity can be manufactured, as it were, in a classroom. Furthermore, while parents want something new from Jewish education, such as identity, they simultaneously want something old—or what is considered as old. The most clear-cut example is the ceremony of Bar Mitzvah. Several years of intensive linguistic and textual study arc required if a boy is to be well-prepared for Bar Mitzvah in the sense that he has the ability to comprehend the portion from the Prophets that he chants in Hebrew. But there is no assurance that painstaking preparation will produce better identity; there is in fact the possibility that the mixture of an apathetic student, an uninspiring teacher, and a demanding curriculum may produce a negative reaction to the educational process, and by extension to Jewishness itself. Furthermore, if his objective is identity the parent may resist the idea of putting his child through an intensive program. He may question whether identity formation requires that the child be subjected to an intensive educational experience. As some American Jews have put it: "Is my child going to be a rabbi?"

The teacher shortage has further compounded the educational situation. The shortage has its roots in the fact that the teacher of Jewish subjects—*melamid*—on the primary level was never highly esteemed in the Jewish community, if only because in theory every male Jew was capable of performing such duties. American economic opportunity, together with the attraction of other occupations, meant that immigrants who might have practiced the profession did not do so. Furthermore, many native-born individuals—especially men —possessing the required preparation have not been interested in entering the profession. And even when the teacher is both qualified and prepared to make a commitment there has been the difficulty of bridging the culture gap between teacher and student. In an earlier period it was the European-trained teacher who was the problem; in the present era it is the Israeli-trained teacher, on whom many schools rely to fill out their faculty roster. And now even the American-trained teacher can create difficulties if he is incapable of making contact with the values of the youth culture that his older students increasingly share.

The Afternoon School: Talmud Torah and Hebrew School

If these are the essential problems of Jewish education in American society what type of system did the immigrants and succeeding generations establish in the United States? During the early period of the East European immigration one impulse was to look to the homeland for established models of elementary education. In eastern Europe the *mela-mid* might live in the household if it was a prosperous one and act as a private tutor. Or, much more typically, he would teach a group of children in his home, charging each family a fee. While these models were not copied in their entirety, for a time many children received their Jewish education from *melamdim*, who generally went from house to house giving Hebrew lessons. As a rule such tutors covered only the most rudimentary material—their instruction being geared to minimal preparation for the ceremony of Bar Mitzvah. It was generally conceded that the system was unsatisfactory. Private instruction by *melamdim* was geared to the size, social organization, and culture of the *shtetl;* it was not efficient or effective in the American metropolis.

Another solution was the supplementary or "afternoon" school. Initially the institution was called the "Talmud Torah"; today it is more frequently referred to as the "Hebrew School." In the period from 1890 to 1930 many of the larger schools of this type were independent entities housed either in their own quarters or in synagogue buildings, though the smaller schools tended to be congregationally sponsored. Generally speaking the largest schools presented a viewpoint that can be characterized as "moderate Orthodox." Some of the schools also had a strong Zionist emphasis; they stressed mastery of the Hebrew language qua language, not only as it was required for the comprehension of the classical texts.

The modernism of the Talmud Torah is further attested by the fact that its student body generally included girls, though they were in a decided minority. The public school had familiarized parents with the idea of educating their daughters as well as their sons. However, the real impetus to sending girls to a Jewish school was the new conception that one of the purposes of Jewish education was to build Jewish identity. Because girls were as much in need of identity as boys, they became candidates for Jewish schooling.

The Talmud Torah showed very mixed results. The best schools succeeded in attracting idealistic teachers who combined a strong feeling for Zionism, a love for the Hebrew language, and a measure of traditionalism. Following an intensive five-day-a-week schedule, each class met after public school on Monday through Thursday, and on Sunday for several hours of instruction per day. Parents accustomed to the routine of the traditional *cheder* (school) had no qualms about the schedule: although their children attended two schools, they were spending fewer hours in the classroom than was customary in the *cheder*.

The better Talmud Torahs succeeded in producing a graduate with some capability in the Hebrew language and a familiarity with simple texts. But as was to become apparent later, the success of such schools was based as much on factors extrinsic to the school situation as upon anything else. The students tended to come from homes where traditional culture could still be experienced and they resided in neighborhoods where it still had vitality. And there was a selective factor in operation: students who lacked linguistic ability, motivation, and acquaintanceship with traditional culture either dropped out of the better schools or were never enrolled there.

The average Talmud Torah showed the grave defects of the system. Teachers had difficulty creating interest and attention in children who had spent their day in public school. Some children had limited talent for linguistic study. The problem of what to teach and how to teach it was chronic.

The morale of the teaching staff was low. Teachers were inadequately paid and had no tenure or security. Classes were limited to the elementary level because the school did not succeed in retaining boys after Bar Mitzvah. The ceremony of Bat Mitzvah was not widely known and there was always the danger that girls would drop out. The typical student attended for relatively few years: many were not enrolled until age eight, nine, or ten and left on their thirteenth birthday.

The present-day Hebrew School is the successor to the Talmud Torah. The Hebrew School is typically a congregational school: it is not an independent entity but an integral part of a larger institution. The defenders of the congregational Hebrew School feel that Jewish education benefits from sponsorship by the agency that has emerged as the strongest in the subcommunity. Furthermore, the school has the advantage of rearing the child in the "natural" setting of the congregation. The critics of the congregational school point to the less-intensive program of the Hebrew School as compared to the old Talmud Torah: classes generally meet only three or four times a week and for shorter periods. They also point to the danger of indoctrinating the child with narrow "denominational" loyalties.

The survivalist emphasis in the Jewish community that emerged after World War II, in combination with the influence of the State of Israel, resulted in strong efforts to improve the Hebrew School. One approach has been to stimulate enrollment of the child at an earlier age by requiring pupils to attend for a given number of years in order to qualify for Bar Mitzvah. The ceremony of Bat Mitzvah has been stressed in order to improve the enrollment of girls. Another effort has been to arrest the decline in the number of hours of instruction. Efforts have also been made to raise teacher's salaries and to improve benefits. Finally, revisions in curriculum have been attempted. One area of change has stressed the utilization of new developments in language teaching, while another has emphasized the use of conceptual thinking in relationship to the study of classical texts. But in spite of these improvements a leading educator who is identified with the Conservative movement maintains that·

. . . even when pupils complete the requirements established by the curriculum, they have no recognizable fluency in Hebrew and cannot understand more than carefully edited texts based on a limited vocabulary. Caught in the crossfire of Bible study as an independent subject and the use of the biblical text, and an abridged one at that, as a Hebrew language workbook, the pupils learn neither. Despite the fact that close to 50 per cent of the instructional time is devoted to the study of Hebrew and *Chumash* [Pentateuch] the pupil leaves the school upon graduation with only the most infantile notions of biblical thought and ideas, and a capability in Hebrew which hardly goes beyond monosyllabic responses to carefully worded questions. The study of history is a pious wish, restricted as it usually is to less than one hour a week. Understanding and generalization fall prey to the hurried accumulation of disconnected fact.[2]

The Sunday School

The one-day-a-week school ("Sunday School") constitutes another significant form of American-Jewish education. Modeled on Protestant prototypes the Sunday School was developed in the nineteenth century by the Reform movement. It represents a radical solution to the problem of Jewish education since instruction is in English and students are not provided with any real knowledge of the Hebrew language. Although classical texts may be utilized they are consulted in English translation. In sum, the Sunday School does not hesitate to concede the primacy of the general culture in a direct way, a way that the Hebrew School is able to avoid.

The original thrust of the Sunday School curriculum emphasized Bible stories, the study of the Jewish religion, and especially the ethical teachings of the prophets—teachings that were conceived by the early Reformers as the essence of Judaism. In recent decades there has been an attempt to upgrade the Sunday School and develop a more variegated and "Jewish" curriculum. The contemporary Sunday School teaches much more than Bible tales and prophetic ethics: Jewish history is emphasized, courses on Israel are offered, and comparative religion is taught. There is an attempt to familiarize the student with some Hebrew words, phrases, and prayers. Arts and crafts, music, dramatics, as well as the project method, have been introduced. Considerable emphasis is placed on the celebration of Jewish holidays and festivals; such celebrations include occasions that were once avoided inasmuch as they commemorate particular happenings in the history of the Jewish people rather than events of universal religious significance. In sum, the contemporary Sunday School is symptomatic of the shift away from Classical Reform and shows the influence that East Europeans have brought to bear upon American Reform Judaism. But in spite of many changes the one-day-a-week school is capable of providing only a superficial Jewish education. As a consequence those who are seriously concerned with upholding standards of Jewish knowledge view it disdainfully:

> When judged by even the least demanding standard of what it means to be an educated Jew, it is hard to avoid the feeling that the academic aspirations of the one-day-a-week school are either a colossal joke or an act of cynical pretentiousness.[3]

Reform Judaism established Confirmation as the ceremony marking the transition from childhood to adulthood. In keeping with Reform's acculturation to Western norms Confirmation includes girls as well as boys. Because it is a *rite de passage* without traditional standing there is no set age at which it must be performed. The tendency in American Reform has been to delay Confirmation until age fifteen. Thus the student is required to remain in school longer, and his teachers and rabbi are able to present a more mature interpretation of Judaism than would be the case if the ceremony were performed at age thirteen.

The emergence in Reform of a more traditional orientation (generally termed "Neo-Reform") has meant a change in the attitude toward the Hebrew language. The shift is also traceable to the impact of Israel upon Jewish life in the United

States. The attitude to Hebrew has also been influenced by a very specific factor: the pressure that East Europeans exerted upon Reform to shift its attitude toward Bar Mitzvah. An influential segment of the East European group wished to continue the practice of Bar Mitzvah despite their affiliation with Reform—and Bar Mitzvah without Hebrew was hardly conceivable.

In recent decades the majority of larger Reform congregations have opened two-day-a-week Hebrew Schools. While Hebrew classes are now an integral part of Reform's educational system, the original conception of a one-day-a-week school has been preserved: Sunday School students are not required to attend mid-week Hebrew classes. Furthermore, although Bar Mitzvah has been introduced in the majority of congregations and is a strong attraction for enrollment in the Hebrew School, it is viewed by some as an unfortunate compromise rather than as a desirable change. Nearly all congregations uphold the superior sanctity of Confirmation; they make it clear to boys scheduled to have a Bar Mitzvah that they are expected to continue their Sunday School training and to be confirmed.

The Day School

In addition to the Sunday and Hebrew schools there is an additional type of Jewish education that is significant.[4] This is the day school, sometimes referred to as a *yeshivah,* or more properly *yeshivah k'tanah.* The day school is a direct descendant of Jewish education in its traditional dimensions—by the very structure of its curriculum the day school affirms the crucial role of Jewish culture. The day school also follows the traditional model insofar as the child is enrolled in a school under Jewish rather than state control.

While the day school affirms traditional norms, even those schools sponsored by right-wing Orthodox groups are deviant by past standards: they offer a curriculum of secular subjects. Furthermore, this curriculum begins in the first grade; it is not delayed until the child has achieved some mastery of

Jewish culture and some conviction about its superiority. There is of course no alternative to the teaching of secular subjects: although the day school is under Jewish control it is chartered by the state and must fulfill certain curricular requirements. But in many schools the secular curriculum (usually referred to as "general studies") is taught more out of choice than compulsion, for there is recognition that however crucial Jewish culture may be other cultures have significance as well. The right-wing schools justify inclusion of the secular curriculum pragmatically: the child needs a mastery of the secular culture if he is to earn a livelihood. The left-wing schools view the matter ideologically: the child requires a mastery of the secular culture if he is to be a complete human being.

Whatever approach to the general culture the individual school takes, the typical day school has a two-track system, one devoted to Jewish subjects and the other to secular studies. There is considerable variation from one school to another in the character of each curriculum and the "mix" between them. Some schools only offer a minimal secular curriculum that barely meets the requirements of state law, while others place considerable emphasis on secular studies and claim that their course of study is equal to the best that the public school has to offer. With regard to Jewish studies some schools follow the traditional model very closely. Others stress Bible and Hebrew language and literature, and deemphasize the study of Talmud and Jewish legal literature. The spectrum is wide, ranging from schools under Hasidic and ultra-Orthodox sponsorship to the Solomon Schechter schools that are under Conservative sponsorship. However, the great majority of children are enrolled in Orthodox schools.[5]

Despite the wide differences among day schools sophisticated observers claim that all of them suffer from a similar defect: the two-track approach. The result of such compartmentalization is that the secular curriculum never receives the benefit of cross-fertilization by Jewish culture, and vice versa. To its detriment Jewish culture is doomed to exist in splendid isolation from general culture. Furthermore, the student may be taught one thing in the secular curriculum and its precise opposite in the Jewish curriculum. Sensitive educators concede the danger of curricular separatism and the consequent desirability of integrating secular and Jewish studies, but little progress has been made.

However serious this defect the miracle is that the day school exists at all. During the latter half of the nineteenth century—by which time the public school system had become firmly established—an earlier acceptance of parochial education had withered away. Public opinion favored the establishment of a Jewish educational system that would be completely integrated with the public system and give it primacy, thus avoiding any hint of separatism. So pervasive was this sentiment, and so fully was it shared by the new East Europeans, that during the period of mass immigration almost no day schools were established. It was as if parochial education constituted a heretical idea, and as if obedience to the American system of public education was a religious commandment.[6] Thus in 1917, when the Jewish population of the United States had reached almost three and one half million, there were only five day schools in the entire country enrolling a total of 1,000 students.[7]

The day schools made some progress in the period from 1917 to 1940: thirty new schools were established, twenty-six of them in New York City, and enrollment climbed to 7,700 students. While the increase was significant, prior to World War II the day school was a miniscule institution concentrated in a single city and enrolling only a tiny fraction of all children under age eighteen receiving a Jewish education. In the past three decades, however, the day school has made enormous strides. During the period from 1962 to 1966 alone, for example, while overall Jewish school enrollment decreased by 6 percent, day school enrollment increased by 19 percent and the student body reached a total of 60,000.[8] Several hundred day schools are now in operation and they are to be found in all of the large and middle size communities. Furthermore, the progress of day school education has had wide ramifications: it has cast doubt on the efficacy of the Hebrew School at the same time that it has stimulated such schools to raise their standards. The day school movement has even provoked debate in Reform circles where the assumption had long been held that the Sunday School represented the optimal type of Jewish schooling for the American-Jewish child.[9]

How can the rise of the day school be explained? One significant influence is the character of the Jewish immigration during World War II and thereafter. We are familiar with the fact that the Orthodox Jews who arrived in America during this period were refugees rather than settlers: they came out of necessity rather than choice. They were firmly committed to giving primacy to Jewish culture. Unlike their Orthodox predecessors in the United States they disdained conformity to American culture, and even took pride in their refusal to conform to the prevailing culture in such externals as dress and hair style. In fact, their version of the American dream was that they should have the freedom to reestablish the way of life they had enjoyed before the Holocaust. Thus without hesitation they proceeded to organize their own schools—schools that would give primacy to Jewish culture and shield their children and others from the influence of the secularism of the public schools.

While the influence of the ultra-Orthodox was of great importance in sparking the development of day schools, it would not have sufficed without widespread disillusionment with the results of Hebrew School education on the part of moderate and centrist Orthodox elements, as well as some traditionally minded adherents of Conservative Judaism. These groups witnessed the passing of the better Talmud Torahs and were appalled by the limited results of the Hebrew Schools. Concerned with the ever more powerful impress that the general culture was having on the Jewish community in general and the Jewish child in particular, they began to doubt that the Hebrew Schools could stem the tide of acculturation; they feared that if they did not implement a more intensive program of Jewish learning assimilation would be the eventual result. Thus the day school, which had been rejected previously, now came to be viewed as a desirable alternative to combat the threat to the continuity of Jewish culture and ultimately to survival itself. But the shift is only understandable if we remember that by the post-World War II era there had emerged a sufficient group of first, second, and third generation Jews who felt secure enough in their identity as Americans to reject public education. Unlike their predecessors they did not require the common school in order to validate their American identity.

Is the day school the solution to the problem of the formal socialization of the Jewish child? Proponents of the movement feel that while most of the schools are still rather new their alumni have already demonstrated that they are more observant of Jewish rituals, more knowledgeable about Jewish traditions, and more involved in Jewish concerns than those educated in supplementary schools. Proponents concede that for the foreseeable future day school education will be limited to a minority, but they conceive of graduates of the system as an elitist group which will be prepared to make sacrifices in order to maintain Jewish survival, and which will provide leadership for the mass of American Jewry.

Those who are less sanguine stress that the day school has been unsuccessful in integrating Jewish and secular culture. They also suggest that the pull of the general environment may be so strong that even an improved Jewish education may not suffice. Finally, they point out that the graduates of elementary schools do not always continue on to high schools and colleges that are conducted along similar lines. However satisfactory a Jewish education might be provided at the primary or even secondary level, it may not be sufficient to meet the more sophisticated challenges to Jewish faith and culture that are encountered at the university level.

These are the strictures of friendly critics. Unfriendly critics attack the schools by minimizing the Jewish convictions that lie behind their growth. They suggest that enrollment has risen because parents are interested in avoiding the public schools, especially the necessity of sending children to racially integrated schools. Others say that the day schools have succeeded because they are private schools rather than Jewish schools—that prosperous parents like to send their children to an institution that has the privilege of selecting its student body. While enrollment has undoubtedly been helped by these factors they do not explain why day schools can be found in better city neighborhoods and in wealthy suburban areas, why parents who desire private school education should turn to Jewish schools, or why day schools have emerged at this moment in American-Jewish history.

What unfriendly critics are really concerned about is that the day school is necessarily in opposition to the pattern of adjustment that was so characteristic of the community until World War II: the primacy of secular learning and the limiting of Jewishness to the private arena. At least in theory the day school rejects such primacy; it also invades the public domain. Thus to some it appears to be a violation of the American-Jewish social contract. It seems retrogressive—a "return to the ghetto." Opponents have become all the more embittered because the day school emerged at a time of lessened anti-Jewish discrimination—just at the moment when the general society seemed to be more accepting of Jewish participation.

Confrontation between proponents and opponents of the day schools has taken place over the issue of financial subsidy. The growing financial needs of the schools has meant that tuition payments and donations of supporters do not cover their budgets. In lieu of governmental support the natural place to look for financial aid is the Jewish community—specifically the federations. But those who oppose day schools (and who are also antagonistic to the Orthodoxy for which most of the schools stand) have taken the position that the schools should not be a charge on the entire Jewish community, as is the case with hospitals, family agencies, old-age homes, and other facilities. They maintain that the schools should be privately supported by those who are sympathetic to their aims.[10]

The educational system that we have analyzed—including Sunday Schools, Hebrew Schools, day schools, and others—enrolled an estimated 554,000 children at last count. The current annual cost of the system is estimated at $100 million, exclusive of capital expenditures. In spite of enrollment campaigns the ideal of every Jewish child in a Jewish classroom has not been realized: as with synagogual and center membership, size of community is an important influence on enrollment. Thus the larger the city the less chance there is of a child attending a Jewish school. Nevertheless, approximately 80 percent of elementary-school-age children spend some time in a Jewish classroom.

Additional facts about the educational system include the following:

1. Some seven out of every ten Jewish children (69.8 percent) who are between the ages of eight and twelve are enrolled in a Jewish school. On the other hand, only one-sixth (15.8 percent) of the youngsters aged thirteen to seventeen are enrolled. Slightly more than one-fifth (21.4 percent) of the six to seven years olds and one-tenth (11.6 percent) of the three to five year olds are enrolled.

2. An almost identical proportion of students attend Sunday Schools (42.2 percent) as Hebrew Schools (44.4 percent). About one-seventh (13.4 percent) of all students attend day schools.

3. More boys than girls are enrolled in Jewish schools (57 percent versus 43 percent). On the whole boys attend more intensive types of schools than girls.

4. Most of the schools are under congregational auspices; almost all schools are religiously oriented. Some 35.7 percent of the students attend schools under Reform auspices, 34.3 percent under Conservative auspices, and 21.5 percent under Orthodox auspices.[11]

Adult Study

A notable characteristic of the American-Jewish educational system is that it is so heavily centered around the child and adolescent. We recall that according to traditional norms Jewish learning is a lifetime avocation. And as we discovered, some adult males even felt obliged to devote themselves to Jewish learning on a full-time basis. The character of American society, as well as the proclivities of the immigrants themselves, made modification of these norms necessary. Even the emphasis on identity-formation worked against continuity of the norms, for such an emphasis means that Jewish learning is necessarily geared to the requirements of the young—their needs for identity-formation must take priority. Nevertheless, the tradition of adult study has remained alive, if not well.[12]

Among the Orthodox the traditional adult study circle devoted to the learning of classical texts is still encountered. In the larger cities, and especially in New York, such circles can be found in many Orthodox synagogues. In addition, the *yeshivah*—the institution devoted to the advanced study of Talmud and ancillary subjects—has been transplanted to the United States. The first such school was opened in New York City in the late nineteenth century and in the decades following a few others were established. During and after World War II many new *yeshivot* were founded, both in New York as well as in other major cities. Many present-day *yeshivah* students pursue their studies as an avocational interest. They do not intend to utilize Jewish learning in order to earn a livelihood—whether as a rabbi, a Jewish teacher, or in some related field. Whatever the professional interests of such students, there is adequate warrant in Jewish tradition for their choice of Jewish studies as an avocation. In any case, one of the most significant aspects of the *yeshivah* is its very existence on American soil, for at the beginning of the century there was little expectation that the native-born generation would be attracted to Talmudic learning.

The *yeshivah* world and the traditional study circles are only a portion of the total enterprise of Jewish learning in the United States for those age eighteen and older. Another significant effort is generally known as "adult Jewish education." The phrase is significant because it indicates that Jewish education *per se* has come to stand for the education of the young. But the phrase "adult Jewish education" also shows the hardy persistence of the idea that Jewish learning is a lifetime interest.

The synagogues have been the prime movers in the adult Jewish education field: most of the larger Reform and Conservative congregations, as well as some of the Orthodox, sponsor adult classes. Certain community centers, as well as several Jewish organizations, have also been active in this endeavor. While descended from the traditional study circles, adult education classes are not limited to the study of classical texts—they cover a wide gamut of subjects of Jewish interest. Furthermore, even when a course is based on a classical text it is not studied in traditional fashion. Women attend these courses, and frequently they comprise the majority of those who come. In recent years the study of Hebrew has become an important part of the course offerings, although the majority of those who attend do not progress beyond an elementary level.

The scientific study of Jewish culture in an academic environment constitutes the final part of the Jewish educational effort. Such study must be distinguished from the efforts of the synagogues, for even the most ambitious adult Jewish education programs are not academic in orientation. Before World War II opportunities for the scientific study of Jewish culture were available only in the less traditional rabbinical seminaries and in the network of Hebrew teachers' colleges located in some of the largest cities. In the 1950s and 1960s a new trend emerged. Courses on Jewish culture (or "Jewish studies" as they are generally known) began to be offered at institutions of higher learning. So rapidly have these courses proliferated that the Association for Jewish Studies was established in 1969. Membership is composed primarily of full-time academicians teaching Jewish studies; the purpose of the organization is to ". . . promote, maintain, and improve the teaching of Jewish studies in American colleges and universities." There had always been some limited opportunities for Jewish study at American universities, but these were generally in the form of study groups or courses organized under the auspices of the Hillel Foundation. They had no academic standing or permanency, and were in fact the university counterpart of the adult Jewish education courses. These courses still continue in many places, and on some campuses there are now study groups sponsored by Yavneh, the organization of Orthodox university students.

Diverse forces have stimulated the development of Jewish studies as an integral part of the university curriculum: in-

creased acculturation and feelings of security among surviv-
alist-oriented Jewish leaders who have taken the initiative and
requested universities to establish courses (sometimes such
leaders have raised funds within the Jewish community for
chairs of Jewish studies); the impact of the example of black
studies upon both Jewish students and Jewish leaders; the
interest in non-Christian religions; and the desire of the university to extend its humanities curriculum beyond the traditional emphasis on Western civilization. The hope in the
Jewish community is that these new programs will remedy
some of the defects of primary and secondary Jewish education, that those who did not study in a Jewish school as children will take Jewish studies in college, that those who were
enrolled in Sunday and Hebrew schools and received only a
superficial knowledge of Jewish culture will supplement their
learning at the university, and that those who received a sound
Jewish education as youngsters will avail themselves of the
opportunity to further their studies at a more advanced level.

In the Jewish community the development of Jewish studies
at the universities is generally viewed from the perspective of
strengthening Jewish identification. However, there is little
desire for an overtly propagandistic approach—the assumption is that an increase in knowledge of Jewish culture will
bring an increase in commitment to Jewish values. This attitude has deep roots in traditional Jewish culture.

While there has been considerable difficulty in fitting Jewish
studies into the framework of existing departments, there has
been little if any controversy about the introduction of Jewish
studies into the American university. In nineteenth century
Germany the discipline of *Wissenschaft des Judenthums*, the
scientific study of Jewish culture emerged. While an adaptation of the ago-old tradition of sacred learning, this new discipline conformed in all essentials to the spirit of the secular
university. In fact, the field of Jewish studies is so much a
part of the present academic milieu that it betrays the same
tension existing in other fields: the division of opinion between professors who believe that their discipline should be
above the battle of men and affairs, and those who maintain

that there can be no responsible scholarship without commitment—in this case, Jewish commitment.[13] A very recent development—the emergence of the underground or free Jewish
university—further underlines the relationship between Jewish
studies and the present academic milieu.

Granted that the spirit of Jewish studies is congruous with
that of the secular university, there remains for some the
problem of aspirations for programs that far exceed present
resources. While Jewish culture is one field of study it consists
of many special topics. Included are such diverse areas as
Bible, Midrash, Talmud, Codes, liturgy, philosophy, languages
(especially Hebrew but including four or five additional
tongues), literature (including modern Hebrew literature), history (covering many centuries and many continents), contemporary Jewish studies, and Israel and the Near East. Since
many of the leading universities have no more than one or
two faculty members specializing in Jewish studies, offerings
are necessarily limited. Furthermore, while registration has
grown rapidly in recent years, only a minor proportion of the
Jewish student body is enrolled. Registration is not exclusively
Jewish; some Gentile students are also attracted to courses
in Jewish studies, particularly in the fields of Bible and
Hebrew.

While it is still too early to predict what the ultimate effect
will be, it is doubtful whether the new thrust of Jewish studies
will be able to remedy the defects of elementary and secondary
level Jewish education. But whatever the ultimate impact there
is a kind of poetic justice to the emergence of Jewish studies
on the American campus. The university helped to move Jews
away from their age-old interest in sacred learning; for many
intellectually minded Jewish students the university became
a surrogate *yeshivah* where new truths could be discovered—
truths that would replace a fossilized Jewish culture. The same
university, now less confident about the Western culture that
has formed the basis of its humanistic learning, is presently
including Jewish studies. This development has wide implications, for Judaism is a historical antagonist of Christianity,
and is, therefore, necessarily critical of Western culture itself.

Notes

[1] See Morris Raphael Cohen, *A Dreamer's Journey* (Boston: Beacon Press, 1949). See also Leonore Cohen Rosenfield, *Portrait of a Philosopher: Morris R. Cohen in Life and Letters* (New York: Harcourt, Brace & World, 1962).

[2] Walter I. Ackerman, "Jewish Education—For What?" *AJYB*, 70 (1969), 22.

[3] *Ibid.*, p. 21.

[4] In addition to the three major types there is a network of Yiddish schools. Only some 4,364 children were enrolled in such schools in 1966 according to the *National Census of Jewish Schools* (New York: American Association for Jewish Education, Information Bulletin No. 28, December 1967).

[5] The first day school under Reform sponsorship opened recently in New York City. For a classification of the different types of schools see Alvin I. Schiff, *The Jewish Day School in America* (New York: Jewish Education Committee Press, 1966), pp. 87–105. Almost without exception day schools are under religious sponsorship. According to Schiff there is only one elementary school in the nation, and no high school, that can be classified "national-cultural" (i.e., a school whose dominant impulse is either Yiddish-secularist or Zionist). The implication is that only the religious groups (i.e., those who are guided by a suprasocial value system) are capable of establishing educational institutions that give parity to Jewish culture. Thus, only under a suprasocial value system can the integrationist impulse be resisted.

In places where—until recently—the integrationist impulse has been much weaker, as for example in Mexico and in the South American countries, day schools are predominantly Yiddish-secularist or Zionist in orientation. Thus the situation in these countries is almost precisely the opposite of that in the United States.

[6] The situation is highlighted by the fact that while a notable defense of the principle of parochial education was made by the greatest Jewish leader of his time—Louis Marshall—he submitted an amicus curiae brief on behalf of the American Jewish Committee in a case that involved Catholic parochial education. See Charles Reznikoff (ed.), *Louis Marshall, Champion of Liberty: Selected Papers and Addresses* (2 vols., Philadelphia: Jewish Publication Society of America, 1957), pp. 957–967.

7 See Schiff, *op. cit.*, p. 67.

8 *National Census of Jewish Schools, op. cit.*, pp. 9–11.

9 See Sylvan Schwartzman, "Who Wants Reform All Day Schools?" *CCAR Journal*, April 1965, pp. 3–10, 13. Cf. Jay Kaufman, "Day Schools: Not Whether, But How?" *CCAR Journal*, October 1964, pp. 3–9, 17.

10 Until very recently Federation support for Jewish education went almost entirely to the coordinating and servicing agencies which exist in most communities of substantial size. These agencies are collectively referred to as "bureaus of Jewish education."

11 The statistical material in this section is drawn from the *National Census of Jewish Schools*. Data for this study were gathered in 1966.

12 It is impossible to present statistics comparable to those contained in the *National Census of Jewish Schools* for the educational situation of those eighteen years of age and over. Although there has been some attempt to gather data on the growing area of Jewish studies at American universities, surveys of Jewish education have basically been concerned with children and youth rather than with adults.

13 See Leon A. Jick (ed.), *The Teaching of Judaica in American Universities: The Proceedings of a Colloquium* (New York: Ktav Publishing House, 1970), especially the contributions of Irving Greenberg and Gerson D. Cohen.

Chapter 6 ◉ The Interaction of Jew and Gentile: The Case of Intermarriage

If the Jews are the classic case of a minority then their relationship to the non-Jewish world is a crucial aspect of their existence. The relationship between Jewish minority and Gentile majority can be studied from many different vantage points. Indeed the fascination of the subject has been so great that the bibliography on Jewish-Gentile relations is enormous —spanning the centuries and including items in a wide variety of languages.

The conventional social science approach is to view Jewish-Gentile relations from the perspective of anti-Semitism—namely to stress the factor of anti-Jewish hostility, whether expressed in verbal prejudice or implemented in the form of discrimination. For many liberal social scientists—whether Jewish or Gentile—part of the attraction of this approach is that studying anti-Semitism constitutes an act of protest against bigotry. By revealing the pathology, unfairness, and self-defeating quality of anti-Semitism the social scientist "acts." And for the Jew the analysis of anti-Semitism serves an even deeper function. It inevitably results in the elaboration of a theory to account for the social reality which the minority group member confronts. Every member of a minority group, whether scholar or layman, requires an explanation of why the majority treats his group as it does.

The highly developed sophistication of Jewish "community relations" agencies has made them responsive to the interest of scholars in the phenomenon of anti-Semitism. The most widely known work that eventuated from this collaboration is

The Authoritarian Personality.[1] The title of this work indicates the theory of anti-Semitism that the investigators sought to validate. *The Authoritarian Personality* grew out of the World War II era and the experience of Nazi anti-Semitism; it was part of a series of researches on anti-Semitism sponsored by the American Jewish Committee under the overall title "Studies in Prejudice." The volumes presented different facets of anti-Semitism such as the historical background of Jew-hatred in Germany, a study of American anti-Semitic agitators, the effect of social mobility on anti-Semitism, and the psychoanalytic understanding of the prejudiced individual.[2] The most recent investigations have been supported by the Anti-Defamation League and have appeared under the series title "Patterns of American Prejudice." They cover such diverse topics as the connection between religious belief and anti-Semitism, reactions to the Eichmann trial, and the extent of Negro anti-Semitism.[3]

While these are important investigations both with respect to content as well as the functions that they serve—they cover only a small portion of the diverse interaction of Jew and Gentile in American society. Some of this interaction is direct, such as the contact that occurs in the office, faculty club, Parent-Teacher Association, or over the back fence. An even more significant aspect of the interaction is indirect, as for example the effect of the mass media on Jews and, conversely, the effect of the Jews on the mass media. Finally there is the area of intergroup relations that has to do with the images that members of one group hold of another group (the more common social science term is "stereotype"). Images may exist with or without interaction, but it is always a two-way street: there is the image of the Gentile held by the Jew as well as the image of the Jew held by the Gentile.

The most significant aspect of contemporary Jewish-Gentile relations is not the traditional concern with anti-Semitism or authoritarianism. Rather it is contained in the interactions that occur between the two groups in present-day American society. Because the diversity of these interactions is enormous, we may select one for detailed attention. The area that we have chosen represents the most intimate of human relationships: marriage. The reason for our choice is that of all the areas in contemporary Jewish-Gentile relations marriage (or "intermarriage") is the most crucial for the study of Jewish identity and survival.

Intermarriage is an issue that all minorities face. If the minority is assimilationist in orientation, intermarriage is experienced as an opportunity; if the group is survivalist intermarriage is experienced as a threat. For survivalist groups the threat exists both on a collective as well as on an individual basis. In its collective aspects intermarriage menaces the continuity of the group. In its individual aspects it menaces the continuity of generations within the family, the ability of family members to identify with one another, and the satisfaction of such members with their family roles.

How, then, is intermarriage experienced in the Jewish community? American Jews experience intermarriage more as a threat than an opportunity. To be sure, attitudes are not uniform throughout the Jewish community. For example, Jewish members of college faculties tend to be much more positive toward intermarriage than other Jews. Nevertheless, the Jewish group is noted for its desire to resist intermarriage. It is this desire that makes the study of this aspect of the relationship between American Jews and Gentiles so significant, and in some respects so poignant.

Statistical Aspects

Given the survivalist aspirations of American Jewry the group must seek to control the rate of intermarriage and keep it at a minimum level. The control of intermarriage presents some special problems for Jews. The most obvious one relates to group size. Intermarriage is a formidable threat because the Jews are such a small group. If Jews married at random on a nationwide basis over 98 percent of their spouses would be Gentile. The potential danger of this randomization process means that the threat of intermarriage is ever-present. Unless Jews seek each other out, or are brought together by special arrangements that allow the factor of propinquity to operate, very few marriages would occur between two Jewish individuals.[4]

Each new case of intermarriage is capable of further reducing the size of the group. Thus the threat of randomization is increased and hence the probability of additional intermarriage. Furthermore, if the intermarried Jew is not lost to the group his children may be. Such losses cannot be absorbed—there is no surplus of population to cushion the impact of intermarriage. The loss of the children of the intermarried constitutes a grave threat to group continuity. In sum, the Jewish group depends heavily on each individual to remain Jewish and to pass on his identity to his children. In theory any decrease in Jewish population means an increase in the probability of intermarriage.

Potentially, each instance of intermarriage may also have a multiplier effect. Children of intermarried Jews may create additional intermarriages by themselves marrying Jews. This process may be facilitated by the fact that the offspring of an intermarriage already has some contacts with Jews through his relatives. Unless the non-Jewish partner in an intermarriage is detached from family he may serve as a change agent, initiating and cementing relationships between members of his Gentile family and his spouse's Jewish family. Such relationships might otherwise not come to be established.

Perhaps the most important aspect of the multiplier effect is that when intermarriage reaches a certain frequency it creates a measure of approval for itself. It becomes fashionable. It confers some degree of status. While it still may be somewhat unconventional the impression is fostered that intermarriage is the wave of the future. From whatever vantage point, then, the desire for group survival makes it imperative that the frequency with which intermarriage takes place be contained. Furthermore, when intermarriage does occur it is necessary that its impact—that is, its effect on group survival —be minimized.

Intermarriage is a new-old problem, inasmuch as it has occurred before in Jewish history. Its current phase became evident soon after modernism touched the Jews of western

Europe. Thus the old forms of arranged marriage not only became unacceptable (as we discovered in Chapter 3), but some of the most liberated members of the generation that followed Moses Mendelssohn took Gentile spouses as well. The frequency of such occurrences varied from country to country. One factor that held the rate of intermarriage in check for a time was that until church-state separation took place there was no civil marriage. Hence, intermarriage involved conversion to Christianity. While such conversion was not always regarded seriously, it complicated the situation of persons who might otherwise find an intermarriage acceptable.

Intermarriage has long been a problem in American-Jewish life. While civil marriage did not exist everywhere in colonial times it has been an option during most of American Jewish history. It was to be expected that some intermarriage would occur in the United States prior to the heavy immigration of German and East European Jews, for in the colonial period and immediately thereafter the Jewish population was sparse and the sex ratio was unbalanced. Intermarriage did indeed take place: it is estimated that 28.7 percent of the marriages involving a Jew that took place in the United States during the period from 1776 to 1840 were intermarriages.[5]

The intermarriage rate dropped with the immigration of the German Jews. It declined still further with the arrival of the East Europeans. The Jews soon won a reputation for endogamy. For example, on the basis of an examination of approximately 100,000 marriage licenses issued in New York City between 1908 and 1912, Julius Drachsler found that of all white groups the Jews were least prone to marry members of the outgroup. The intermarriage rate between Jews and non-Jews was only 1.17 percent, a figure scarcely higher than that between Negroes and whites. Drachsler bracketed Jews and Negroes together as "low-ratio" groups, in contrast to "middle-ratio" groups (Italians and Irish) and to "high-ratio" groups (English, Germans, Swedes, and others).[6]

This pioneering study gave no assurances, however, that the rate would remain at a low 1.17 percent. As was clear from the data, the reason for such a minimal figure was that a substantial proportion of those marrying were East European immigrants, whose intermarriage rate was under one percent. The rate for second generation East Europeans was appreciably higher: some 4 percent for men and 3 percent for women. And, according to Drachsler, the intermarriage rate of German Jews was well above these levels. For the first generation it was 5 percent for men and 3 percent for women, while in the second generation the rate jumped to 9 percent for men although it remained the same for women.

These generational differences during the period from 1908 to 1912—as well as the contrasts between the German Jews and their less socially mobile East European cousins—suggested that the Jewish reputation for endogamy was less firm than it appeared at first glance. Furthermore, Drachsler's data pointed out other problems. The unbalanced sex ratio suggested that some Jewish women would either have to marry Gentiles or remain single. To be sure, spinsterhood would not affect the intermarriage rate but it would influence another significant demographic factor: the birth rate. Finally, the rate for New York City from 1908 to 1912 must have been considerably lower than for the nation at large. Since the rate of intermarriage should vary inversely with the absolute size of the Jewish population and with its ratio to the general population, the Jews of New York ran the smallest risk of intermarriage.

If this is the background against which to measure the present we are then led to inquire into the current rate of intermarriage. Accurate data on a nationwide basis is not readily available. The best way to accumulate the required statistics would be to have bride and groom supply information about their religious backgrounds to an official agency. Only two states, Iowa and Indiana, require such a procedure. While the statistics for these two states are of considerable interest they do not lend themselves to extrapolation—the Jewish population of the two totals a mere 31,000 persons.

It is to be expected that the intermarriage rate in Iowa and Indiana would far exceed that of more heavily Jewish areas. During 1953 to 1959 the average rate in Iowa was 42.2 percent while during 1960 to 1963 the rate in Indiana averaged 48.8 percent.[7] These rates are very high. They suggest that if

the offspring of the intermarried assimilate and are not replaced by new "immigrants" to these states, Jewish communities in Iowa and Indiana cannot long endure. Nevertheless we
must not lose sight of the fact that religion still plays a highly
significant role in Jewish marital choice in Iowa and Indiana.
The Jewish population in each state is less than 1 percent. If
individuals who reside there married at random the probability of their marrying another Jew would be infinitesimal;
at present there is approximately a fifty-fifty chance that they
will marry within the group.

With a single exception other statistics on Jewish-Gentile
intermarriage emanate from private rather than public sources.
Such statistics are of widely varying quality but they all share
one characteristic: unlike the Indiana and Iowa data they tell
us how many people have intermarried rather than how many
are currently intermarrying. That is, they represent the ratio
of intermarried to inmarried. These statistics, then, are cumulative—they include people who have taken their vows in
Czarist Russia where civil marriage did not exist, as well as
people who have married in the United States; people belonging to the comparatively closed community of the immigrant
generation as well as people living in the wide world of the
fourth generation. Cumulative figures, it should be understood,
must not be extrapolated or confused with current figures, for
present-day research highlights what Drachsler pointed out
some decades ago—that intermarriage rises in each generation. As a consequence a cumulative rate is always considerably lower than a current rate.

The most widely quoted cumulative intermarriage statistic
is reported by the Bureau of the Census and is based on its
Current Population Survey of March 1957. This is the only
survey in the recent history of the Bureau to include a question on religion.[8] In its sample of 35,000 households the
Bureau found that 7.2 percent of the husbands or wives of
Jews were of a different faith. But the figure must be regarded
as minimal, for the Bureau noted that its statistics on intermarriage were probably subject to a larger margin of error
than would result from normal sampling variation. In an
unusual aside the Bureau stated that while it had told its

personnel not to assume the same religion for all members of a given family and directed them to ask about each adult member of a household separately, some interviewers might have overlooked this instruction.

The bulk of Jewish intermarriage statistics comes from surveys conducted by local Jewish communal agencies. These surveys seek to gather a wide range of demographic, attitudinal, and behavioral data. While we have employed such surveys to good effect in our analysis of social characteristics, they have serious limitations when used as a source of intermarriage statistics. Some surveys utilize lists of names supplied by Jewish organizations, and intermarried persons are less likely than others to appear on such lists. The better surveys seek to overcome this and other biases of the list approach by utilizing area sampling. Although the underrepresentation of the intermarried may be overcome by the area-sampling technique, should their response rate be abnormally low a bias against the inclusion of intermarried families would persist.

Reviewing the Jewish communal surveys we encounter wide variations in intermarriage rates. Some are well below the 1957 Census Bureau figure of 7.2, some are about the same, and some are considerably higher.

Camden, N. J.	4.0%
(1964)	
Springfield, Mass.	4.4%
(1966)	
Providence, R. I.	4.5%
(1963)	
Boston, Mass.	7.0%
(1965)	
Washington, D. C.	13.1%
(1956)	
San Francisco, Calif.	18.5%
(1958)	

While one or another of these surveys may understate the extent of intermarriage, there is no question that wide variations between communities actually exist. But such variations cannot be explained by relative and absolute size of the Jewish population. For example, the proportion of Jews to the total population in Providence is actually smaller than it is in Washington: 3.3 percent for Providence vs. 4.7 percent for Washington. Furthermore, Providence had only 19,457 Jews in 1963 as contrasted with Washington, whose Jewish population at the time of the survey was 80,900—making it the seventh largest Jewish community in the nation.

The sociological character of the cities with the highest rates—Washington and San Francisco—supply us with significant clues as to why so many intermarriages occur. Historically, Washington has attracted many single young Jews. These individuals are probably unusually independent of their families. They work in settings where their peers are from diverse backgrounds; they lead a mixed social life. Intermarriage results. In addition, Washington has probably attracted a higher than average proportion of couples who are already intermarried. Washington has an extremely high percentage of intermarried persons who were born in the community itself. Added to the possible multiplier effects of an already large intermarried group, the high educational level in Washington and the relatively small percentage of individuals who are self-employed appears to have worked against endogamy.

Turning to San Francisco we find that it too has a special history and reputation. Jews were among its earliest and most prominent citizens, and extensive intermarriage has taken place among the descendants of its older families. San Francisco has long prided itself on its urbanity and sophistication. Intermarriage there has probably been regarded with less disapproval than elsewhere. In addition to intermarriage among its native population San Francisco has apparently attracted a disproportionate number of intermarried families. It is also a city of high immigration that has attracted many single Jews with weak family ties.

These two cities demonstrate that cumulative rates of well over 10 percent can be found in populous Jewish communities. However, because of their special character Washington and San Francisco are not adequate indicators of the national picture. But neither is Providence, Springfield, nor Camden where cumulative rates are under 5 percent. Having such a low rate they seem to be exeremely endogamous communities. Apparently they attract very few intermarried families. It is a reasonable supposition that a significant percentage of those from these communities who do intermarry choose to settle elsewhere.

Which of these six communities, then, can best serve as an index of the national picture? Clearly, Boston has the most to recommend it. With 185,000 Jewish residents Boston has a larger Jewish population than Washington or San Francisco. And the temper of its Jewish life is much closer to that of the giant communities where the majority of the Jews of the nation reside. Its occupational pattern is more typical. It has a balance of new and old families. Individuals of diverse educational attainment and differing levels of sophistication reside there. While the city attracts intermarried couples, at the same time its well-organized Jewish community draws those who are interested in an intensive Jewish experience.

The Boston study, which indicates a cumulative rate of 7 percent, unfortunately does not present a current rate. However, a tabulation of the religious composition of married couples by age of the husband allows us to make an approximation. We find that the intermarriage rate varies from a low of 3 percent for husbands 51 years of age and over to a high of 20 percent for husbands age 30 and younger (see Table 15).

Because this last group is predominant in marriage formation the figure of 20 percent should be approximately the current rate. (If Boston is typical the figure of 20 percent also suggests that a multiple of at least 2.5 may be justified when converting a cumulative rate into a current rate.) Of course if one wished to take a conservative position on the current rate it could be emphasized that recently wed husbands who are in older age brackets have a lower rate of intermarriage than younger husbands. But the significance of the marital choices of such older husbands is less than that of younger husbands. The younger the husband at the time of marriage the greater the likelihood of his having children, and the greater the likelihood of his having a larger than average family. Thus it is the marital pattern of the young that is crucial: they contribute substantially to the newly married group, they

Table 15. *Religious Composition of Married Couples in Greater Boston Jewish Population by Age of Husband*

| RELIGIOUS COMPOSITION | AGE OF HUSBAND | | | |
OF MARRIED COUPLES	30 and under	31 to 40	41 to 50	51 and over
One partner is not Jewish	20%	7%	7%	3%
Both partners are Jewish	80	93	93	97
Total	100%	100%	100%	100%

SOURCE: Axelrod et al., *Boston*, p. 169.

have the greatest impact on the demographic future of the Jewish community, and finally, they are a potential influence on those younger than themselves. Perhaps their marital style even exercises a subtle pull on their elders as well.

The Jewish Response

It was not until the 1960s that intermarriage became an important topic of discussion in the Jewish community. The first book on the subject sponsored by a Jewish organization made its appearance in 1963.[9] And it was in the same year that the *American Jewish Year Book* published its first article on the subject.[10] In the sixty-three previous volumes of this standard reference work the topic had been discussed only once—in a brief two pages. But perhaps the editors of *Look* magazine had most to do with stimulating discussion on intermarriage; in 1964 they published an article boldly entitled "The Vanishing American Jew."[11]

There is good reason why the problem should have been evaded for so long. Intermarriage presents the American Jew with a bitter series of dilemmas. Its control involves taking steps that conflict with many of the values that the American Jew upholds.

In the chapter on the Jewish family we analyzed how arranged marriage was replaced by the notion of romantic love. Thus the contemporary Jewish parent affirms a belief in the idea that love is the basis of marriage, that marriage is a union between two individuals rather than two families, and that the final determination of a mate is the prerogative of the child rather than the parent. These ideas—which constitute a radical departure from the norms of traditional Jewish society—were endorsed by some of the more advanced immigrants from eastern Europe as well as by a substantial majority of the American-born generation. Of course an overwhelming proportion of the third generation give enthusiastic assent to the romantic-love syndrome.

When a young Jewish person becomes romantically involved with someone from the ingroup the belief in romantic love need not be called into question. But when a Gentile is involved romantic love is cast in a new light: it now conflicts with the values of endogamy and Jewish survival. If the parent should seek to discourage the match he must in effect ask his child to fall *out* of love—to disbelieve in the idea that love is its own justification. He must ask his child to renounce values that he himself has been affirming for so long.

While belief in the romantic-love syndrome makes parental opposition to intermarriage difficult, such opposition is undercut by even more basic considerations. The American Jew has generally assumed a strongly liberal stance toward social issues, particularly with respect to aspects of the American Creed that concern the equality of all people regardless of race or religion. We need not concern ourselves with whether the Jew has been stimulated in this direction by Jewish values or by Jewish self-interest. The central issue is that the result of such an equalitarian perspective has been to call Jewish ethnocentrism into question. If it is an article of faith that all men are created equal, and that the differences that distinguish them are environmental and hence transitory in nature, the Jew is under pressure to abandon the notion that his group is more equal than others. Again, no problem arises when the child becomes romantically involved with a member of the ingroup. Under these conditions one may continue to affirm equalitarianism without any strain. But when the romance is with a Gentile the scenario is different: objection can only be advanced on ethnocentric grounds. In effect, the parent must ask his child to renounce the American Creed. He is maneuvered into the uncomfortable position of affirming what he has sought to deny or repress: that one people— the Jews—are more equal than others, that they are superior to others, and that the Gentile is less worthy of the Jew than the Jew is of the Gentile. The irony is that objections that would not be on such an obvious collision course with the American Creed are foreclosed. Thus parental objections to intermarriage might be based on religious grounds, but many Jews lack the firm spiritual commitment that such an affirmation would necessitate.

Here we approach another and even more bitter dilemma:

as much as the Jew may be opposed to intermarriage, never-theless it is the logical culmination of his quest for full equality. Intermarriage in fact symbolizes the end of all those discriminations that preserve social distance between the minority group and the dominant group, that restrict Jewish opportunity, and that underline Jewish subordination. While it may be recognized that intermarriage has its unfortunate effects, intermarriage can also appear to the Jew as a harbinger of a better future, signaling the final end of an age-old story of bitter persecution and demeaning discrimination.

We see, then, that many of the value commitments of the Jew make it difficult for him to confront the issue of inter-marriage head on and to affirm unyielding opposition to it. Indeed, if we reflect further upon the matter it becomes clear that intermarriage is the quintessential dilemma for the American Jew. It calls into question the very basis on which American-Jewish life has proceeded—that Jewish survival is possible in an open society. With the exception of certain Orthodox groups, American Jewry has held that it is possible to simultaneously achieve a meaningful Jewish identity to-gether with full societal participation. Once it is conceded, however, that the intermarriage rate is already substantial and gives every indication of increasing, a contradiction in the basic strategy of American-Jewish adjustment appears. It no longer seems so obvious that the twin goals of Jewish identity and of Jewish participation in the general society can be simultaneously fulfilled and equally achieved.

Despite the fact that the intermarriage question was not widely discussed in public until very recently, there is ample evidence that Jews have had a covert awareness of the prob-lem as well as an inclination to take protective measures. For example, the residential pattern that developed after World War II appears to be related to the desire to prevent inter-marriage. The erosion of inner-city neighborhoods, the strong demand for housing, and the social mobility of Jews—to-gether with their increased acculturation—all combined to motivate a significant number of families to move to the outer edges of the city. Jewish pioneers on the suburban frontier had a degree of choice with respect to area of residence. Their religious stance did not place them under pressure to live in a "Jewish" area—they did not require a synagogue within walking distance or a kosher butcher shop within easy reach. Neatly supplementing their religious flexibility was the fact that residential discrimination in older suburbs was declining, while in new post-World War II suburbs it hardly existed. However, instead of taking advantage of this new freedom of choice and distributing themselves widely, these settlers concentrated in a relatively few places. Indeed in the largest cities many suburbs and new areas became as heavily Jewish as the old neighborhoods. And some came to have an even higher proportion of Jews, because the old neighborhoods always contained a preexistent Gentile population. Also, some of the old neighborhoods had a wider choice of housing and thus a more heterogeneous population. In sum, the tendency for Jews to live together resulted in some new areas quickly becoming 80 percent or more Jewish. As Jews began to bid against one another the cost of housing rose. But families were willing to pay a premium to live in a "Jewish" area.

The desire to protect oneself against intermarriage is not the entire explanation for the development of new Jewish suburban and semi-suburban areas. But choice of residence among acculturated Jews cannot be understood without consideration of the intermarriage factor. For most Jews a desirable area is one that has, in addition to the usual amenities, a sufficient number of Jewish families so that one's children will have an opportunity to play with other Jewish youngsters, a significant proportion of classmates in elementary school who are Jewish, and a high school where there are enough Jews so that a reasonably homogeneous dating pattern is feasible and natural. Only when children are adult (and presumably married), or away at college, does the factor of the ethnic composition of the neighborhood loom less important. At that point in the life cycle an apartment in an ethnically heterogeneous neighborhood—perhaps one close to the center of the city—may be considered.

Jewish education is another aspect of the same process.

As we discovered in Chapter 5, in spite of considerable acculturation and secularization the demand for Jewish education for the young has been very strong. Such demand is indicative of the parents' desire to give their children a Jewish identity, and, more specifically, of the desire to take protective measures against intermarriage.[12] Jewish education as a prophylactic against intermarriage is clearly observable in the emphasis that is placed upon Bar Mitzvah, Bat Mitzvah, and Confirmation. Astute observers have noticed the latent function of these ceremonies—that in acculturated families the Bar Mitzvah, for example, has come to have a significance out of all proportion to its traditional importance. Such escalation is not simply a result of status consciousness, the desire to keep up with ones Jewish peers, or even to outdo them. Rather, the ceremony has come to signify the commitments of parents to Jewish survival despite their wide acculturation; it publicly affirms their desire to have their child follow in their ethnic footsteps. Specifically the Bar Mitzvah serves to indicate the importance that the parent attaches to what should follow: an endogamous marriage. Thus in its new elaborateness the Bar Mitzvah party has taken on elements of a Jewish wedding celebration; it has come to constitute a rehearsal for such a celebration. Understandably then, rabbinical attempts to discourage elaborate Bar Mitzvah celebrations have been met with firm objection by parents.

Nevertheless, parents who wish to discourage intermarriage must convey more explicit clues to their offspring than those provided by the preference for a Jewish neighborhood, the provision for a Jewish education, or the arrangement of an elaborate Bar Mitzvah party. In short, the parent must confront the subject of marriage head-on. However, because of the cross pressures we have already delineated many feel constrained to present their endogamous sentiments indirectly. Thus the Jewish parent may speak about the essentiality of exercising wisdom in the selection of a mate so that the child will find happiness in his new relationship. An important aspect of such wisdom is that of finding someone with whom there is compatibility. Compatibility is best assured by confining marital selection to the Jewish group. The marital relationship is such a fragile one and the sources of incompatibility are so numerous that one is well advised not to run the risk of introducing yet another source of discord. Thus the Gentile is not to be shunned because he is a Gentile but because he is not a Jew. The stern words of the late Albert I. Gordon, a well-known Conservative rabbi, illustrate the approach of the modern Jewish parent:

> Insurance companies set their rates on the basis of mortality rates. In the same manner persons considering intermarriage should recognize that the odds are three-to-one against their marital success. . . . We know that not all intermarriages fail. But we also know that they are three times more likely to fail than to succeed. . . . Interfaith marriage is a great gamble.[13]

In phrasing his objection to intermarriage in terms of a desire to assure his child's happiness, the parent need not reject his commitment to the American Creed or his loyalty to the value of romantic love. He need only maintain that the experts have concurred that exogamy is a greater risk than endogamy. Romantic love is fine but it can be destroyed by incompatibilities that never before had occasion to rise to the surface, or by ethnic prejudices that partners were unaware of.

In sum, the parent phrases his objections in terms of his commitment to his child's happiness. He is spared the embarrassment of asking his child to reject the thought of marrying a Gentile out of the necessity of continuing a culture that he himself has half-rejected or a religion that he has imperfectly practiced. Thus the need to confront the painful contradictions in his own position is evaded:

> Respondents [in Lakeville] who focus on the discord theme generally have at least one case history at hand to buttress their argument that the wages of intermarriage are unhappiness. Yet even as they recite their story and seek to advance their image of sweet reasonableness . . . it does not require much insight to realize that they are far from being unbiased students of marital

problems; they have not judiciously weighed the evidence and reluctantly come to the conclusion that an interfaith difference intrudes such a strong disharmonious element in marriage as to place an otherwise sound relationship in jeopardy. Rather, their advocacy of the view that interfaith marriage is a pathological relationship seems to be a safe way of expressing the desire to continue the chain of tradition while at the same time avoiding the appearance of ethnocentrism. Widely approving of the integration of the Jew into the general community, our respondents are under pressure to formulate a respectable alternative for their disinclination to sanction what is the ultimate in interfaith acceptance. Furthermore, they are apparently seeking to harmonize their desire for Jewish continuity with their belief that enlightened people have the right to freedom of marital choice. The notion that a Jewish-Gentile marriage is inherently unstable represents a resolution of this conflict; there is freedom to choose, but wisdom dictates that the choice be a fellow Jew.[14]

The recent reconnaissance in Lakeville suggests that some residents have a growing sense of unreality about the discord approach.[15] We encountered individuals who acknowledged that successful cases of intermarriage were to be found among their relatives, friends, or acquaintances. It is apparent that while parents in Lakeville and elsewhere may still attempt to convince children that intermarriage is a trap, the discord approach cannot long endure. The intermarriage rate is so substantial that most extended families will soon have multiple cases of intermarriage. It is inevitable that one or more of these marriages will constitute a successful match, even as it is inevitable that an extended family will have one or more intrafaith marriages that turn out unsuccessfully. In sum, the prevalence of successful intermarriage will increase the parent's difficulty in rationalizing the discord approach both to himself and to his child.

This is not the only aspect of the intermarriage problem that is changing in Lakeville. In revisiting the community one senses that people feel more strongly than before that intermarriage is (as one person phrased it) "in the air." They feel that intermarriage is the law of life, that it cannot be resisted, that it may occur at any time. Under these conditions the parent seems to be more concerned with himself than with his child. He wonders how he will act should an intermarriage become inevitable. He wonders whether he is capable of responding to the situation, as he terms it, "intelligently." Thus we find the parent speaking of the necessity of placing reason before emotion, of accepting that which cannot be changed. The parent who is concerned with responding intelligently hopes that when put to the test he will act fairly—measure the intended Gentile partner by the same criteria he would use if the partner were Jewish.

What does it mean to respond "unintelligently"? The parent defines this as reacting in such a way as to alienate his child and his child's future spouse. The bonds of family, carefully cultivated by the parent for so many years, would be severed. Responding unintelligently also means being a bad parent by bringing marital disharmony into the life of the young couple. An unintelligent response may also have an additional consequence: imperiling one's psychological adjustment. One woman related how a relative had worked herself into such a state over a daughter's intermarriage that she required psychiatric treatment. The respondent went on to say that when confronted with the same situation in her own household she succeeded in keeping herself under control. All of these reactions, then, suggest a declining certainty that intermarriage is wrong and a lack of confidence that the battle against intermarriage can be won. But above all they represent the attempt by the highly acculturated Jew to adjust to a social reality that he cannot quite bring himself to condemn.

The essence of the intermarriage question is the threat it poses to Jewish survival. However, to the parent who is confronted with the problem, or fears that he may be so confronted, the issue is experienced in much more personal terms. He may interpret it to mean that he has failed as a parent. After all, the parent has not succeeded in forging a close enough psychic identification between himself and his child so that when the child chooses a mate that mate will have the same background as his own and that of his spouse. In short, the child who intermarries does not reproduce the parental marriage.

How does the parent attempt to handle this challenge to his self-esteem? The response of some Lakeville parents whose offspring had intermarried, or whose child was romantically involved with a Gentile boy (or with a "little Gentile girl" as she was invariably referred to), is suggestive. These parents stress that their child had been given a Jewish education. Among Reform Jews the name of the temple where the child was confirmed was generally volunteered and frequently the name of the rabbi was mentioned as well. What the parent appeared to be saying was that he provided his child with every opportunity to become immune to intermarriage. If the serum was not effective it is because the doctor failed. If the rabbi or the temple had been more competent ("inspiring") the result might have been different. In any case the parent did his duty; he employed the best talent available to immunize his child against the disease of intermarriage. In sum, responsibility for the intermarriage is placed at the door of the rabbi and/or the Jewish institution.

There is an additional aspect to the handling of the self-esteem problem in Lakeville. It appears that many parents of an intermarried child (particularly parents of Reform background or affiliation) made one last request of their offspring: that consent be given to have a rabbi officiate at the wedding ceremony. However, such parents frequently experienced more difficulties with their rabbi than with their child: the rabbis of all four of the local Reform temples refuse to officiate at intermarriages. Parents who had approached them on this score were bitter, as were some other respondents who identified with such parents. Several respondents went so far as to state that Lakeville's rabbis were immoral. Do the rabbis have any hesitancy, they asked, about officiating at a marriage between a Jewish boy and Jewish girl in which the boy may be of the lowest character, or the girl a tramp? What right then do they have to refuse to officiate at a marriage where the Gentile partner fulfills the highest aspirations of the Jewish moral code?

Some respondents went even further, maintaining that the rabbis were not only immoral but anti-Jewish. If the rabbis were really interested in preserving the Jewish religion why do they hesitate to marry mixed couples? By rebuffing these couples the rabbis close the door to their eventual conversion, or to raising their children as Jews. The rabbis, it was maintained, know that the right thing to do is to perform intermarriages. However they cannot be reasoned with. They are afraid of getting into trouble with their fellow rabbis, with the rabbinical association, with what one respondent bitterly termed the "rabbis' union."[16]

If there are "bad" rabbis there are also "good" ones. The good rabbi in this case serves a Reform congregation in an adjoining suburb. He is agreeable to officiating at intermarriages and according to one of our respondents he does a "land-office business." This particular rabbi seems so widely known that referrals appear unnecessary. A respondent who had been rebuffed by two Lakeville rabbis when her daughter was about to be married to a Gentile found this rabbi not only agreeable to officiating but felt that he performed as impressive a ceremony as his Lakeville colleagues. She believes that he is fearlessly devoted to doing the "right" thing and is thereby accomplishing more for Jewish survival than any of the local rabbis.

Lakeville Jews—certainly those who are highly acculturated —give no evidence that they question the validity of a civil ceremony. Denunciations of Lakeville's Reform rabbis—and the refusal of parents to be impressed with the rabbis' argument that by performing a religious ceremony they would be committing a fraud since the ceremony would not constitute a valid marriage under Jewish law—indicates that parental reactions are as much connected with the fulfillment of their own needs as with the advancement of Jewish survival. The function of the rabbinical presence at the nuptials (in place of an official representing the secular order) is that the appearance of a rabbi apparently supplies the parent with the possibility of fantasizing that a "normal" marriage is taking place. If the official spokesman for Jewish identity officiates at the wedding then it must not be such a bad wedding after all. If the rabbi appears then the child is not leaving the fold and the marriage is not so dissimilar to the parent's. In sum, the parent has not failed.

Intermarriage and Jewish Identity

Although intermarriage is frequently experienced as a personal and family issue it is preeminently a social problem. This is true because of the connection between intermarriage and the assimilation process. However, the relationship between intermarriage and assimilation is less than perfect, for Jews who intermarry do not always assimilate.

Part of the reason for the failure to assimilate lies in the motivation for intermarriage. In recent decades in particular assimilation has rarely been the motive for Jewish-Gentile marriage. Thus it is the exceptional case where the Jewish young person makes a careful calculation and comes to the conclusion that it would be the better part of wisdom to become romantically involved with a Gentile in preference to a Jew. The Jew who intermarries, then, generally does so because he wishes to *marry* rather than because he wishes to intermarry.

The absence of a compelling assimilationist motivation on the part of the intermarrying person is complemented by the attitudes of his parents. Rather than acting in a traditional manner and severing relationships with an errant child, they are prepared—however reluctantly—to accept the marriage. They are willing to pay the price of accepting an exogamous union in return for the retention of their relationship with their child. Finally, the continuation of this relationship may have a side-effect: a relationship with the group may be retained as well.

In sum, no compelling motivation to transform personal identity originates either from the direction of the parent or from that of the child. We find, consequently, that community studies of such diverse cities as Providence, Springfield, Camden, Boston, Washington, and San Francisco all contain intermarried persons who identify themselves as being Jewish.[17] The connection between intermarriage and assimilation, then, is more ambiguous than appears at first glance.

While the Jewish partner in an intermarriage who retains his identity is by no means rare, there is still the crucial issue of whether he will pass it on to his children. Thus our perspective must extend beyond the first intermarried generation —the couple themselves—into the second generation. The obstacles to the transmission of Jewish identity in the intermarried family are substantial. For example, the creation of a Jewish religious identity for the child may be considered provocative behavior by the Gentile partner, whose cooperation would be required in any such enterprise. But even a less affect-laden form of identity, such as one based upon Jewish culture rather than religion, is fraught with problems. Thus, Jews who intermarry are generally highly acculturated and do not follow a distinctively Jewish way of life: in order to transmit an identity based on cultural differences they would be obliged to make noticeable changes in their way of life. Such changes are difficult to effect even in homogeneous households where both partners are convinced that the home should be more Jewish, and where the question of the ethnocentrism of one of the partners is irrelevant.[18]

Unless the distribution of power in the intermarried household is entirely one-sided the presumption of the partners is that neither one will press his identity upon the child. Many intermarried parents declare, therefore, that upon maturity their child will have the right to choose his own identity. This generally means that his identity will be with the majority group. Only if the child has formed a particularly strong identification with the parent who is Jewish will he be motivated to integrate into the minority community.

The majority of the children of intermarried Jews, then, will be Gentile—at best they will have a kind of latent Jewish identity. We do find many cases where the Jewish parent considers that his offspring is being reared as a Jew. In Providence, for example, where the intermarried are few and where they tend to have a stronger Jewish identity than elsewhere, it is reported that 58 percent of the children living in inter-married households are being reared as Jews.[19] It might well be that this is a response which tells us more about the aspirations of parents than the identification of children. In any case, it is reasonable to suppose that a Jewish respondent living in a smaller city who is responding to a survey conducted by a Jewish organization may be motivated to give a more ethnocentric reply than the facts warrant. In contrast to Providence only 18 percent of the intermarried families of Washington report that their children are being reared as Jews.[20]

Even if we make the dubious assumption that all children who are presumably being reared as Jews do in fact consider themselves to be Jewish, we cannot assume that they will so consider themselves in later life. In most cases they are being reared in a Jewish environment that is marginal at best; their identification may lack the kind of reinforcement necessary if it is to persist much beyond the present stage in their life-cycle. And it should be remembered that the group we have been considering is encountered in a Jewish communal study. Such studies undoubtedly overrepresent the more positively Jewish among the intermarried.

Intermarriage and Conversion to Judaism

In theory at least intermarriage is as much an opportunity for Jews as it is a threat to their group survival. Assuming that an equal number of Jewish men and Jewish women intermarry and that they succeed in maintaining their own Jewishness *and* in inducing their spouses to identify with their group, the Jewish community would be magnified rather than diminished by intermarriage. And with these conditions fulfilled there should be no ambiguity about the group identification of the offspring of such marriages.

These conditions do not accord with Jewish historical experience. Except during the earliest phases of Jewish history exogamy has involved the shedding of group identity. Furthermore, the conversion of the Gentile spouse to Judaism was well-nigh impossible. For centuries such conversion—or indeed any effort to interest a Gentile in Judaism—was a criminal act fraught with dire penalties. In the United States, however, not only is the intermarried Jew free to continue with his identity but the State does not place any barrier to the conversion of his spouse to Judaism.

How is conversion to be evaluated? Conversions to Judaism which occur prior to—or following upon—marriage to a Jew may be discounted as a mere gesture to placate the Jewish partner or his parents. But why the need to placate? Observation suggests that conversions to Judaism are seldom an act of pure expediency. To be sure, a wide spectrum of readiness to change group-belongingness is undoubtedly represented among any group of converts. Granted that conversion is rarely a guarantee of long-range identity, by definition it represents a formal acceptance of a new identity. Thus it must be regarded seriously. Further, in the United States conversion is the accepted way to enter the Jewish group and to validate one's claim to a Jewish identity. The requirements of *halachah* (or in the case of Reform Judaism, an interpretation of Jewish tradition), the religious structure of the general society, and the psychological needs of the prospective spouse all conspire to give conversion a significant importance.

Since the phenomenon of conversion to Judaism in connection with marriage is so new to modern Jewish experience it upsets many of the traditional notions about the motivation for—and the expected result of—a Jewish-Gentile romance. Its novelty is apparent from the Providence study where we discover that conversion occurs more frequently among the spouses of third-generation Jews than it does among those of the first or second generation.[21]

In what percentage of intermarriages, then, does a conversion to Judaism take place? Since there is no central registry of conversions it is difficult to determine the exact proportion. It is clear that conversion does *not* take place in the majority of intermarriages. Yet it is also apparent that the number of conversions to Judaism is on the rise. While this is undoubtedly related to the increase in frequency of intermarriage, the phenomenon cannot thereby be discounted. Because of the increase in conversion a new phenomenon is encountered in Jewish life: classes for converts. Such classes now meet regularly in a number of large cities. Most were initially organized under Reform auspices. This contrasts sharply with the situation before World War II when prospective converts were scarce and hence were instructed on an individual basis.

One investigation has estimated that in a twelve month period during 1952 and 1953 some 2,250 Gentiles were converted to Judaism, over 90 percent of them in connection with marriage to a Jew. Largely because Jewish men marry out of the group more frequently than do Jewish women, over 80 percent of these proselytes were female.[22] Due in part to the fact that there are now more intermarriages, the number of Gentiles presently converting to Judaism is undoubtedly substantially higher than it was in the early 1950s. Also the ratio between male and female conversions appears to be more balanced now than in the past.

What is the Jewish identification of the convert? Because there has been very little research on this question, opinion in the Jewish community—both among rabbis and laymen—has been free to seek its own level. Some rabbis, for example, maintain that conversion has a negative effect—they believe that it helps to encourage intermarriage in the Jewish community by making it more acceptable. Those holding this opinion generally look upon conversion as a compromise at best—one that only serves to delay assimilation. On the other hand there are many rabbis who feel that conversion is a boon to Jewish survival, that it is a way out of the intermarriage dilemma, and that it will have many beneficial side effects on the Jewish community.[23]

The question of the Jewish identification of the convert is more complicated than it appears at first glance. Should a proselyte be held to a standard that many born-Jews do not uphold, or to which their Jewish spouses do not assent or aspire? One approach is to inquire whether the proselyte is a member of a synagogue, active in Jewish life, or in some other easily observable way is part of the Jewish community. But perhaps the most strategic approach is to look at the issue from the vantage point of the identity of the children. Are they being provided with a Jewish environment? With a Jewish education? No study has yet answered such questions authoritatively. We do know that in Providence and Springfield—admittedly more intensively Jewish than other communities—all children of mixed marriages that were sampled are being reared as Jews.[24] While this result may be traceable in part to the fact that respondents were aware of the Jewish auspices of the study and reacted accordingly, there is no doubt that some converts have shifted to a Jewish identification.

It is a sociological truth that although an individual may be converted to a faith he may remain outside of the group. The task of assimilating proselytes is relatively new for the Jewish community: Jewish experience has almost entirely been directed toward assimilating into other groups rather than in integrating outsiders into their own. The born-Jew has a clear advantage over the convert: through instrumentalities such as the nuclear family, the extended family, and the all-Jewish clique group, he is provided with resources that help him to establish a Jewish identity and a feeling of belongingness to the Jewish community. The proselyte does not have such avenues—if his identity is to grow it is strongly dependent upon his own desires as well as those of his spouse. But it cannot flourish in a vacuum—it must be supported by a community that desires to include him.

In the next several decades we will know whether conversion is a mere sociological curiosity of the American-Jewish experience or a significant factor modifying the impact of intermarriage upon the Jew who lives in the open society.

Notes

[1] T. W. Adorno et al., *The Authoritarian Personality* (New York: Harper, 1950).

[2] See Bruno Bettelheim and Morris Janowitz, *Dynamics of Prejudice* (New York: Harper, 1950); Nathan W. Ackerman and Marie Jahoda, *Anti-Semitism and Emotional Disorder* (New York: Harper, 1950); Paul W. Massing, *Rehearsal for Destruction: A Study of Political Anti-Semitism in Imperial Germany* (New

York: Harper, 1949); Leo Lowenthal and Norbert Guterman, *Prophets of Deceit: A Study of the Techniques of the American Agitator* (New York: Harper, 1949).

3 See Charles Y. Glock and Rodney Stark, *Christian Beliefs and Anti-Semitism* (New York: Harper & Row, 1966); Charles Y. Glock, Gertrude J. Selznick, and Joe L. Spaeth, *The Apathetic Majority: A Study Based on Public Responses to the Eichmann Trial* (New York: Harper & Row, 1966); Gary T. Marx, *Protest and Prejudice: A Study of Belief in the Black Community* (New York: Harper & Row, 1967); Gertrude J. Selznick and Stephen Steinberg, *The Tenacity of Prejudice; Anti-Semitism in Contemporary America* (New York: Harper & Row, 1969).

4 The randomization process as well as certain other aspects of the intermarriage problem are discussed in Marshall Sklare, "Intermarriage and the Jewish Future," *Commentary*, April 1964, pp. 45–52. For some comparative material see also Moshe Davis, "Mixed Marriage in Western Jewry: Historical Background to the Jewish Response," *Jewish Journal of Sociology*, 10, No. 2 (December 1968), 177–220.

5 Malcolm H. Stern, "Jewish Marriage and Intermarriage in the Federal Period (1776–1840)," *American Jewish Archives*, 19 (November 1967), 142–143.

6 Julius Drachsler, *Democracy and Assimilation* (New York: Macmillan, 1920), pp. 120–132.

7 Erich Rosenthal, "Studies of Jewish Intermarriage in the United States," *AJYB*, 64 (1963), 37, and "Jewish Intermarriage in Indiana," *AJYB*, 68 (1967), 245. These rates do not reflect marriages of Iowa or Indiana residents that take place out of state. There is also the question of out-of-state marriages of the children of Iowa or Indiana residents who reside elsewhere. There is some evidence that if such persons were included the rate would drop somewhat.

8 See U.S. Bureau of the Census, "Religion Reported by the Civilian Population of the United States: March 1957," *Current Population Reports*, Series P–20, No. 79.

9 Werner J. Cahnman (ed.), *Intermarriage and Jewish Life* (New York: The Herzl Press and the Jewish Reconstructionist Press, 1963).

10 Rosenthal, "Studies of Jewish Intermarriage," *op. cit.*, pp. 3–53.

11 Thomas B. Morgan, "The Vanishing American Jew," *Look*, May 5, 1964, pp. 42–46, and "A Threat to Survival," *Time*, January 17, 1964, p. 41

[12] See Erich Rosenthal, "Acculturation Without Assimilation? The Jewish Community of Chicago, Illinois," *American Journal of Sociology*, 66, No. 3 (November 1960), 285–287.

[13] Albert I. Gordon, "Intermarriage: A Mixed Blessing?" *Unitarian-Universalist Register-Leader*, June 1963, p. 11.

[14] Marshall Sklare and Joseph Greenblum, *Jewish Identity on the Suburban Frontier: A Study of Group Survival in the Open Society* (New York: Basic Books, 1967), p. 313.

[15] See Marshall Sklare, "Intermarriage and Jewish Survival," *Commentary*, March 1970, pp. 51–58.

[16] The *Yearbook* of the Central Conference of American Rabbis includes numerous discussions of the issue of performing marriages between Jews and Gentiles. For a pointed analysis of the dangers involved see Jacob J. Petuchowski, "Realism about Mixed Marriages," *CCAR Journal*, October 1966, pp. 34–39.

[17] See, for example, Stanley K. Bigman, *The Jewish Population of Greater Washington* (Washington, D.C.: Jewish Community Council of Greater Washington, 1957), p. 135.

[18] For a glimpse into some of the difficulties experienced in homogeneous households see Sklare and Greenblum, *op. cit.*, pp. 297–301.

[19] This figure, based on responses of Jewish spouses in intermarried households, includes a total of 144 children. See Sidney Goldstein and Calvin Goldscheider, *Jewish Americans: Three Generations in a Jewish Community* (Englewood Cliffs, N.J.: Prentice-Hall, 1968), pp. 168–169. The Springfield survey yields an even higher proportion of children being raised as Jews. See Sidney Goldstein, *A Population Survey of the Greater Springfield Jewish Community* (Springfield, Mass.: Springfield Jewish Community Council, 1968), p. 147.

[20] In an additional 10 percent of the households—probably because they include the offspring of prior marriages—some children are being reared as Jewish and others as non-Jewish (see Rosenthal, "Studies of Jewish Intermarriage," *op. cit.*, pp. 30–31). Note that the Providence and Washington surveys calculate these statistics differently.

[21] See Goldstein and Goldscheider, *op. cit.*, pp. 159–161, especially Table 8–2. Note that while in this instance Goldstein and Goldscheider distinguish between intermarriages where conversion has taken place and those where it has not, they do not uniformly make this distinction.

[22] See David M. Eichhorn, "Conversions to Judaism by Reform and

Conservative Rabbis," *Jewish Social Studies*, 16, No. 4 (October 1954), 299–318.

23 The prevalence of conversion in the United States has introduced a new complication into Jewish life. A sizeable proportion of the conversions are conducted by Reform rabbis. Presumably they are not performed in accordance with *halachic* standards and as a result can be subject to challenge.

The possibility of a sundering in American Jewry—potentially more serious than the familiar German-East European split explored in Chapter 1—has not escaped the attention of some members of the Reform rabbinate and of the faculty of the Reform seminary. See, for example, Jacob J. Petuchowski, "The Ramifications of Realism," *CCAR Journal*, June 1967, pp. 81–88.

24 Goldstein and Goldscheider, *op. cit.*, p. 168, and Goldstein, *op. cit.*, p. 147. The term "mixed marriage" is frequently used by students of the subject to denote a marriage between a born-Jew and a convert to Judaism. In this usage the term "intermarriage" denotes a marriage between Jew and Gentile where there has not been a conversion to Judaism.

Chapter 7 ◉ The Homeland: American Jewry and Israel

In principle, all ethnic minorities have the problem of resolving their relationship with their homeland. Shall they sever their ties and consider the place of their origin to be a dim remembrance of things past? Or shall they think of themselves as countrymen who have been compelled to settle abroad by circumstances beyond their control and who look forward to the day when they will return to the homeland?

In nations where the emphasis is on assimilation, and where national unity is the preeminent value, the ethnic group member does not have a choice of alternatives. He is under pressure to cut his ties with his homeland. Furthermore, the government of his homeland is under pressure to keep him at arm's length; any effort to continue the old link would be regarded as an unfriendly act by officials of his adopted nation. In the United States, however, the relationship between the ethnic group member and his homeland is a matter of indifference. As a consequence the ethnic may decide for himself what the strength of the bond with his homeland shall be. And the freedom that is given to the individual is extended to his former nation as well. Only when the policy of a foreign nation is clearly hostile to American interests will there be an attempt to control the interaction between the ethnic and his former government.

Jews from eastern Europe did not seek to take advantage of the permissive approach characteristic of America. Their estrangement from the eastern European homeland has its source in their experience overseas, and in the contrast between such experience and life in America. However senti-mentally Jews from eastern Europe might remember life in the *shtetl,* they viewed the government of the old country as oppressive and anti-Semitic. And it was clear to them that anti-Semitism was not only imposed from above but to some extent reflected popular sentiment as well. Even if the regime should be replaced, then, Jews might still be treated badly. For example, while most Jews who came to America from Poland ardently hoped for the end of Czarist autocracy, they suspected that even if Poland should be freed from Russian domination it would still be deeply influenced by its long tradition of Catholic hegemony and anti-Jewish hostility. The most that one could reasonably expect was that a new regime would repress the most blatant and harmful forms of anti-Semitism. In sum, while Polish Jews might discover that life in America had its disappointments and difficulties, they saw no possibility that a new Poland was prepared to offer them comparable dignity and freedom.

The difference between Catholic Poles and Jewish Poles is readily apparent when the extent of emigration is considered. Both before the establishment of the Polish state as well as afterward Catholic Poles returned to their homeland in signifi-cant numbers. Jewish Poles did not. And the relatively few Jews who returned were not attracted by the call of Polish soil, by the love of the Polish language, or by the desire to be part of a new national experiment. Rather, they emigrated from the United States because they feared that the American environment would wean their children away from traditional Jewish values.

The reluctance to return is quite clear even in the case of those who should have been most eager to emigrate: the radical Jews. Faithful to the idea of revolution, they were convinced that the uprooting of traditional society would usher in a great new day in the territories of the Czar. How-ever, most politically active radicals preferred to redirect their energies toward social change in the relatively uncongenial environment of the United States. Radicals might continue to talk about revolution in eastern Europe but they did so from American shores. The handful who felt compelled to return to the homeland were more Russian than Jewish; with the exception of the Socialist-Zionists they had lost all connection with their ethnic past.

At least until the rise of Hitler, German Jews had a warmer attitude toward their homeland than did the East European Jews. Nevertheless they too had a low rate of emigration. The German example is instructive. It demonstrates that even when Jews were given equal rights—as occurred in Imperial Germany—they were not motivated to emigrate in large numbers. To return would be to exchange greater freedom for lesser freedom. To the Jew America was the first new nation; it constituted an unparalleled opportunity to make a fresh beginning. It offered the possibility of disassociating oneself from lands where Jews had been degraded and dishonored for centuries.

While American Jews have not maintained a close relationship with homeland they have not thereby lacked a homeland relationship. Such a relationship has been provided for them in their linkage to Israel. Indeed, the linkage to Israel substitutes for any connection that Jews might have had to their countries of origin. The linkage is long-standing, for the contact between Diaspora communities and *Eretz Yisrael* (the Land of Israel) has been characteristic of Jewish experience for millennia.

The contact between American Jewry and the Jews of Palestine took place as early as the colonial period. It increased during the nineteenth century when officials of Jewish agencies in Palestine began to travel with regularity to America to enlist support for their institutions. The linkage took on a new significance after the establishment of the Zionist movement and became much stronger in the years immediately prior to the establishment of the State of Israel. After the establishment of the State in 1948, it began to play a decisive role in the American Jewish community.

To place the relationship in perspective we must remember that American Jewry was not responsible for transforming the historic connection of the Jewish people with Palestine into the present State of Israel. It is true that many Israeli leaders have had close connections with America: David

Ben Gurion lived for a time in New York City and Golda Meir spent much of her childhood and adolescence in Milwaukee. Furthermore, American Jews helped in the efforts that led to the securing of the Balfour Declaration in 1917. They were also involved in mustering support for the establishment and the recognition of the State of Israel. Both political and financial activity on behalf of a Jewish homeland attracted a wide spectrum of American Jews, ranging from East European immigrants on the margins of American society to highly acculturated German Jews who had achieved positions of great eminence in the general community. But whether he was a pushcart peddler or a justice of the Supreme Court, the role of the American Jew in the Zionist movement was not decisive. The impetus for the establishment of a new Jewish commonwealth derived from the position that Jews occupied in nineteenth and twentieth century European society rather than in the American nation.

While the majority of American Jewry favored the Balfour Declaration, as well as the later establishment of the State of Israel, emigration from the United States to Israel has generally remained at a low level. It is difficult to obtain an accurate statistical picture of the ebb and flow of emigration, particularly because some of those who moved to Palestine (or later to Israel) eventually returned to the United States. Furthermore, in the days of the British Mandate there were restrictions on Jewish immigration; not everyone who wished to go was able to enter the country. But even when the establishment of Israel brought an end to such restrictions, the number of American *olim* (immigrants to Israel) was small. It is estimated that in the period from 1948 to 1967 the annual number of *olim* from America varied from 600 to 1200, of whom an appreciable number returned to the United States. Up to 1967 the total number of *olim* from the United States has been estimated at 15,000.[1]

American *olim* were of several types. There were traditionalists who were responsive to the theme of the return to Zion; secularists who were either political Zionists or ardent Hebraists, but in either case had retained a close connection with their European origins; and senior citizens, whether secular or traditionally minded, who preferred Israel as a place for retirement. However, the group that attracted the most attention consisted of young people belonging to various Zionist youth movements. Not only were they Jewish nationalists but most of them espoused the twin ideals of collective living and pioneering (*halutziut*). Thus they were motivated to go on *hachsharah* (preparation) to make themselves fit, both psychologically and occupationally, for living on a *kibbutz*. Before 1948 *hachsharah* took the form of residence on a training farm in the United States. On such farms agricultural skills were emphasized and the routines of physical labor were learned. After *hachsharah* came *aliyah*—the return to the Land of Israel.[2]

While the rate of emigration has been small this has not detracted from the importance of the relationship of American Jewry to Palestine, and more recently to the State of Israel, as a major factor in Jewish life. That is to say, the relationship of American Jews to Israel is much more significant than the small numbers of emigrants suggest. Or to put it another way, whatever the impact of the American Jew on Israel (the impact is more profound than the modest numbers of American *olim* would suggest), the impact of Israel on the American Jew is enormous.

The most significant aspect of the impact of Israel concerns its effect on the Jewish self-image, on the psychological make-up of the American Jew, on the feeling of the American Jew toward his Jewishness. In this connection we must understand the psychological import upon the Jew of his history and experience. Jewish history and group experience teaches that to be Jewish is to be a member of the "martyr race." Although America might offer the Jew freedom, the import of Jewish history and experience is not thereby changed. In fact the old lessons· have even been reinforced, because to be Jewish in the twentieth century has meant to be in even greater danger than in earlier eras. It has taken no great imagination on the part of the American Jew to realize that he owed his life to his foresight—or to that of his parents or ancestors—in making the decision to leave western or eastern Europe. Only thus was he spared.

The special significance of the State of Israel derives, then, from the unique historical experience of the Jewish people. The establishment of the State of Israel is not just another happening. Rather, it can be seen by the Jew as a wondrous event, a kind of recompense for ages of persecution, as assurance that to be Jewish brings triumph as well as suffering. The establishment of Israel means that the Jewish people are no longer weak and defenseless. Because of the existence of a national state being Jewish makes more sense—more psychological sense—than before. The establishment of Israel can also be interpreted to mean that the Jewish people has not been deserted by God or man. While the establishment of Israel is of great significance to orthodox religionists, it can also hold great appeal to secularists who lack a firm commitment to the idea that the Jews are a people by virtue of Divine covenant.

If this analysis of the psychological import of a Jewish state is correct we should be able to observe significant changes in American-Jewish life. Such changes are indeed present. For example, in Chapter 1 we described the emergence in the nineteenth century of a set of understandings designated as the American-Jewish "social contract." The contract meant that Jewishness was to be a private matter—its display was limited to the home, the synagogue, the Jewish school, and similar islands of privacy. Jews would not routinely appear in public as Jews. When such appearances were made they would be forced upon the group, as in the case of rallies protesting anti-Semitic outrages. We noted that the only group of Jews not prepared to abide by the social contract were the ultra-Orthodox who arrived in the United States during and after World War II.

At the present time the social contract is regularly disregarded by diverse segments in the Jewish community. The clearest evidence of this change is the parade that takes place annually on Fifth Avenue in New York City—the "Salute to Israel" parade. The parade was first held in 1965. At the beginning it was a small-scale and hesitant event but it has grown into a mammoth spectacle involving hundreds of thousands of participants and spectators. The idea is now widely imitated in other major centers of Jewish population. The occasion of the parade is a new holiday in the ancient Jewish calendar: *Yom haatzmaut* (Israel Independence Day). To the community at large the deviation of Jews from their traditional reticence to appear in public as Jews is little realized: the parade appears to be just another ethnic event comparable to what Irishmen have been doing for decades on St. Patrick's Day, Italians on Columbus Day, or Germans on Steuben Day. Even Jews are generally unaware of the novelty of their behavior, as well as the fact that it is Israel that has given them the psychological freedom to appear in public as Jews.

The reaction to the crisis that occurred in the spring of 1967, and to the Six-Day War that followed, supplies even more impressive evidence of the impact of Israel on the American Jew.[3] The incessant Arab threats that the Israelis would be thrown into the sea, together with the efforts to isolate Israel, suggested the possibility that the state might be destroyed. As a consequence there was an outpouring of young American Jews who volunteered to go to Israel and serve in whatever capacity they were needed. The crisis also produced the greatest flood of financial contributions in American Jewish history, and this from a group that had already displayed an extremely high level of generosity by general standards.

The intent of contributors in 1967 went beyond traditional philanthropic purposes. The objective was to indicate solidarity with Israel as well as to help provide the financial means to defend the state against annihilation. Accordingly, rather than following the usual ritual of signing pledge cards donors insisted on giving cash. Among such donors were individuals who lacked ready cash, but who had arranged bank loans so that they might participate. The resulting flood of checks produced a jam in the offices of the local federations. Donors complained when they found that there was a delay in cashing their checks, for they wished their money to reach Israel immediately. A significant number of the checks were from individuals who had never contributed to Israel before. Large sums were also forthcoming from donors who had previously given only modest amounts.

Solidarity with Israel was expressed by highly marginal Jews.⁴ In Lakeville, for example, the Unitarian Church indicated its support for Israel and solicited donations from its membership, although no other church in the community took similar action. The universalist-oriented Unitarians should have been the last to concern themselves with the welfare of yet another new national state. But the explanation for their startling action is clear: the church is the only one in Lakeville where a significant segment of the membership is of Jewish origin. As someone in the community commented, the members wanted to show that "we Jewish Unitarians are doing our part."

The reaction of American Jewry took the Israelis by surprise. It even amazed American-Jewish leaders. Why was the response so extreme? The obvious explanation is that American Jews wanted to protect Israel. True enough. But the response becomes more understandable if we proceed on the assumption that the desire on the part of American Jews to protect Israel was also a desire to protect themselves— that is, to protect their sense of meaning, their feeling of the worthwhileness of life, and of the rightness of being Jewish. And in the case of "Jewish" Unitarians, their response can be seen as a desire to protect their sense of confidence in their ancestors and in the community from which they stem. In sum, if Israel were to be destroyed the American Jew would fall prey to *anomie*— the breakdown of social norms and values. By acting as he did the American Jew was not only assisting his fellow Jews abroad; he was also protecting himself from the bottomless pit of *anomie*.

The reaction to the crisis of 1967 highlighted a trend that had been growing for two decades: the interdependence between Israel and American Jewry. While such interdependence had been apparent for some time it had always appeared to be one-sided—Israel being more dependent upon American Jewry than American Jewry upon Israel. The reasons were clear. Since Israel was in constant peril of being isolated politically it needed whatever influence American Jews could bring to bear upon United States foreign policy. In addition there was the constant necessity for funds, and American

Jewry was the natural source for such support. And even numerically American Jewry overshadowed Israel, whose Jewish population was only half as large as its own. But the events of 1967 demonstrated that in actuality American Jewry was highly dependent upon Israel. Unless Israel's viability was assured the future of American Jewry would be in doubt. While Israel's destruction might not endanger the physical security of the American Jew, the psychological effect could be devastating.

American Jewry responded with immense relief and gratification to the decisive Israeli victory of the Six-Day War. The reaction was more than a simple identification with a military triumph. The results of the war seemed to indicate that although the Jewish people had been forced to endure the agony of the death camps just a few brief years before, it was nevertheless fated to triumph over those who would destroy the one ray of hope in its recent tragic history. Furthermore, to both secular as well as religious Jews the results seemed to suggest a suprasocial dimension: in addition to the lightning victory there was the reunification of Jerusalem, and especially the new access to the Western Wall.

The relationship between American Jewry and Israel has intensified in the years since 1967. The most notable aspect of this process is the phenomenon of immigration to Israel from the United States. American *olim* numbered 4,617 in 1968, 6,020 in 1969, and an additional 6,129 by the end of September, 1970.[5] Thus not only is the number of immigrants from the United States on the rise but it is many times larger than in earlier years. Furthermore, the rate has increased despite the growing threat to Israel's security. There is also the expectation that a higher proportion of American *olim* will remain in the country than previously. For the first time Americans constitute a significant segment of the immigration to Israel.

The practice of residency on a training farm in the United States has long been discontinued—the newer emphasis is on bringing technological skills to Israel rather than on training American Jews to be agricultural laborers. Whatever orientation to the country is required is conveyed in Israel rather than in America. Only a very small proportion of those who emigrate from America do so via the Zionist youth movements. Accordingly, present-day *olim* from the United States represent a wider spectrum of American Jewry than before. And in terms of life cycle a significant percentage of the *olim* are between the ages of thirty and fifty-five. This group includes individuals who have occupied responsible positions in business and in the professions.

It is still too early to give a definitive explanation for this sharp rise in *aliyah*. One hypothesis is the impact of the Six-Day War itself. Another is a growing pessimism about the future of American-Jewish life—a pessimism sometimes expressed in terms of the difficulties posed by the non-Jewish environment, especially with respect to rearing children whose Jewish commitments will be both strong and "natural." However, a third factor must be reckoned with: pessimism about America itself. Such pessimism has two aspects: the attitude on the part of some that America is on the decline as a nation, and the attitude on the part of some that America is on the decline as a place where Jews will have a secure future.

Although an increased sense of frustration about the ability of America to solve its social ills is encountered in many other segments of the American population, Jews have certain special concerns. As members of a minority group that has achieved considerable social mobility and notable status gains in the United States, they notice that such gains are being challenged by other minorities. They fear that dominant elements in American society may consider Jews to be expendable. But even if the Jews are defended there is the suspicion that group status will decline. Thus, pessimistic Jews vary in orientation: some react to questions of Jewish status and security while others respond mainly to shifts in societal attitudes.

We have emphasized the profound feeling that Jews have had about the possibilities of life in America, as well as the fact that America meant more to Jews than it did to most other ethnic groups. Nevertheless, it would be unrealistic to expect Jews to be immune to the new pessimism, if only because they are concentrated in just the educational and occupational levels where such pessimism has taken deepest root. The new pessimism helps to stimulate the attitude that life in the United States lacks certain vital and attractive features that are present in Israel. Thus it is frequently said—even by those who do not entertain the thought of *aliyah*—that Israel has a sense of purpose and cohesion which is absent in America. Once the new pessimism makes older Jewish attitudes toward America seem less compelling—and once the cult of gratitude toward America has run its course—the appeal of Israel is much stronger than before. In sum, the ground is prepared for a rise in Jewish emigration from the United States. Such emigration involves a shift in the relationship of American Jewry to Israel: the relationship no longer occurs outside the framework of *aliyah*.

These changes are quite evident in the shifting attitude toward American *olim*. The older sentiment in the United States was that the *olim* were sacrificing themselves upon the altar of Zionism. *Olim* were viewed as idealists who were prepared to renounce the comforts of America in the service of the cause. And if the *olim* were youngsters interested in *halutziut* the feeling was that their idealism was costing them dearly, inasmuch as they were foregoing brilliant careers in the United States. Although those interested in *halutziut,* as well as other *olim,* might take pains to deny their idealism and stress instead the motivation of self-realization (*hagshama atzmit*), they could not help but think of themselves as a cut above their fellow American Jews.

The newer sentiment of American Jews toward *olim* from the United States tends to be as follows: "While I would not consider *aliyah* for myself there is no denying that life in Israel has much to recommend it." Or: "I've been to Israel and I can understand how someone could be very happy there." *Olim,* then, are seen as realists as well as idealists. If the matter is probed further one discovers among some American Jews the revolutionary sentiment that life in America is more difficult than life in Israel. America may have more material abundance than Israel but hazards abound: anti-Semitism, drugs, the New Left, urban crime. The current formulation in the Jewish community contends that in America the borders are safe but the cities are dangerous; in Israel the borders are dangerous but the cities are safe. In summary, the new attractiveness of *aliyah* is related to—although it is not a function of—the new pessimism about America. And the new pessimism is all the more singular because it is evinced by members of a group that has had such complete faith in America—in its unlimited possibilities, its infinite capacity for good. If any group believed that America was the first new nation—and as such represented a decisive turning point in human history—it has been the Jews.

It would be incorrect to infer that pro-Israel attitudes— much less sympathy toward *aliyah*—characterize all segments of American Jewry. There has never been unanimous approval of the idea of a Jewish homeland. Jews on the left were always apathetic, if not critical, of Zionism. However, the center of anti-Zionism in the Jewish community was located in upper class, extremely acculturated, German-Jewish circles. The American Council for Judaism, which was established in 1943, gave the clearest expression to these hostile sentiments. The Council saw the idea of a Jewish state as a threat to the American Jews' sense of belonging. But they feared even more that a Jewish state would lead the public at large to infer that Jews were not loyal citizens of the United States.

These fears have receded into the background. The newer phenomenon is the hostility of the New Left toward Israel. In the extreme New Left version of the Middle East conflict Israel is regarded as an imperialist nation bent on subverting progressive Arab regimes. In a more mild interpretation Israel is regarded as an ally and tool of American imperialism. Consequently American Jews who support Israel are guilty of supporting American foreign policy. Thus in contrast to the old fear that Jews who support Israel would be regarded as disloyal to America, Jews who support Israel are now being charged with loyalty to America.

Relatively few Jewish students and young people support the position of the New Left on Israel. However, the impact of such New Leftists on the Jewish community is considerable. These individuals are not old-line German Jews who are peripheral to the subcommunity; rather in most cases they are Jews of East European origin. Accordingly, stories circulate in the Jewish community that some New Leftists come from "fine" Jewish homes. That an American Christian might support the Arab cause is understandable to many Jews; that a Jew of East European origin could do so is inexplicable. That those who share one's own identity can make common cause with the enemies of the homeland is bitter medicine indeed.

The creation of the State of Israel has had a profound effect on the American Jew, particularly on his psychological make-up. It has given him a heightened sense of morale—morale that enables him to abide newer challenges on the American scene to Jewish status and security. Most recently there has emerged a small, but nevertheless significant, emigration movement to Israel. The great majority of American Jews are as yet untouched by this development. Nevertheless, American Jews have not been able to turn their attention to other concerns, secure in the knowledge that the young state will make steady progress to maturity. The homeland is surrounded by enemies and the Jew feels that he is obliged to rise to its support. Paradoxically, the effort by Israel's enemies to destroy the young state has resulted in a reinforcement of the linkage between America's Jews and their old-new homeland.

Notes

[1] See *New York Times*, October 18, 1970. See also Gerald Engel, "North American Settlers in Israel," *AJYB*, 71 (1970), 185.

[2] On motivations for *aliyah* during the post-1948 period, and the problems of adjustment of the American *oleh*, see Engel, *op. cit.*, pp. 161–187.

[3] On the reaction see Lucy S. Dawidowicz, "The Arab-Israel War of 1967—American Public Opinion," *AJYB*, 69 (1968), especially pp. 203–218; Marshall Sklare, "Lakeville and Israel: The Six-Day War and Its Aftermath," *Midstream*, October 1968, pp. 3–21; Arthur Hertzberg, "Israel and American Jewry," *Commentary*,

August 1967, pp. 69–73; Milton Himmelfarb, "In the Light of Israel's Victory," *Commentary*, October 1967, pp. 53–61; and Robert Alter, "Israel and the Intellectuals," *Commentary*, October 1967, pp. 46–52.

4 For an example see David Bronsen, "A Conversation with Henry Roth," *Partisan Review*, 36 (1969), especially 278–280.

5 *New York Times*, October 18, 1970.

◉ Appendix

DEMOGRAPHIC STUDIES CITED IN *AMERICA'S JEWS*

Axelrod, Morris, Floyd J. Fowler, and Arnold Gurin. *A Community Survey for Long Range Planning—A Study of the Jewish Population of Greater Boston.* Boston: Combined Jewish Philanthropies of Greater Boston, 1967.

Bigman, Stanley K. *The Jewish Population of Greater Washington.* Washington, D.C.: Jewish Community Council of Greater Washington, 1957.

Elinson, Jack, Paul W. Haberman, and Cyrille Gell. *Ethnic and Educational Data on Adults in New York City 1963–1964.* New York: School of Public Health and Administrative Medicine, Columbia University, 1967.

Goldstein, Sidney. *The Greater Providence Jewish Community: A Population Survey.* Providence: General Jewish Committee of Providence, 1964.
    A Population Survey of the Greater Springfield Jewish Community. Springfield, Mass.: Springfield Jewish Community Council, 1968.

Massarik, Fred. *The Jewish Population of San Francisco, Marin County and the Peninsula, 1959.* San Francisco: Jewish Welfare Federation, 1959.

Mayer, Albert J. *Jewish Population Study-Series II.* Detroit: Jewish Welfare Federation of Detroit, 1964–1966.
    Milwaukee Jewish Population Study 1964–1965. Milwaukee: Milwaukee Jewish Welfare Fund, 1967.

Westoff, Charles F. *Population and Social Characteristics of the Jewish Community of the Camden Area.* Cherry Hill, N.J.: Jewish Federation of Camden County, 1966.

◎ Index

ABOUT THE AUTHOR

Marshall Sklare, Appleman Professor of American Jewish Studies at Brandeis University, received his M.A. from the University of Chicago and his Ph.D. from Columbia University in 1953. He was formerly professor of sociology at Yeshiva University, and director of the Division of Scientific Research of the American Jewish Committee. Professor Sklare has been Fulbright lecturer at the Hebrew University of Jerusalem, and has also taught at Clark University and the Princeton Theological Seminary. Professor Sklare's published works include *Conservative Judaism: An American Religious Movement* (1955), *The Jews: Social Patterns of an American Group* (1958), and with Joseph Greenblum, *Jewish Identity on the Suburban Frontier: A Study of Group Survival in the Open Society* (1967).